A CASUAL KNACK OF LIVING

A Casual Knack of Living

COLLECTED POEMS

HERBERT LOMAS

Love —
Bertie

Arc
PUBLICATIONS
2009

Published by Arc Publications,
Nanholme Mill, Shaw Wood Road
Todmorden OL14 6DA, UK

Copyright © Herbert Lomas 2009

Design by Tony Ward
Printed in Great Britain by the MPG Books Group,
Bodmin and King's Lynn

978 1906570-52-1 (pbk)
978 1906570-41-5 (hbk)

ACKNOWLEDGEMENTS
The poems in this volume are taken from
the following publications:

Chimpanzees are Blameless Creatures (Mandarin Books, 1969)
Private and Confidential (London Magazine Editions, 1974)
Public Footpath (Anvil Press, 1981)
Fire in the Garden (Oxford University Press, 1984)
Letters in the Dark (Oxford University Press, 1986)
Trouble (Sinclair and Stephenson, 1992)
Selected Poems (Sinclair and Stephenson, 1995)
A Useless Passion (London Magazine Editions, 1998)
The Vale of Todmorden (1981, Arc Publications, 2003)
Nightlights (unpublished, 2007)

Cover picture:
Mary Potter, 'Crag Path, Aldeburgh, *circa* 1953'.
Reproduced by permission of Julian Potter.

Supported by
ARTS COUNCIL
ENGLAND

**Arc Publications
Poetry from the UK & Ireland**

*for Peter Dickinson and
Murray Bodo –
true artists
and true friends
and i.m. Alan Ross*

A WORD

I hope it's true that 'men may rise on stepping stones / of their dead selves', as Tennyson once thought. Some artists, like Giacometti, have a product, others, like Picasso, develop. I don't intend to compare myself with these geniuses, of course, but it's obvious I'm a developer; and also that my poems reflect the times and the lives I've lived through – not fashionably, I hate fashion – but because of my way of enduring them.

I like lightness of touch. Lightness of touch doesn't imply unawareness of the depths. Sometimes depths may be best approached obliquely. Boldness can be foolhardy.

Humour, as Shakespeare showed, is not incompatible with even the worst horrors. We've lived through an incredibly cruel and mismanaged world, and the horrors and the mismanagement are still going on. There is very little you or I can do except try to sort ourselves out personally – our only way of influencing 'society', the relationship between you and me. 'We can do no great things but only small things with great love', as Mother Teresa said.

I hope the poems reflect my own struggles to understand myself and the world. In a way the poems are strategies – strategies given to me, which I try to pick up from wherever they come from. But I'd like the poems to bring some cheer to the reader too and some recognition.

Herbert Lomas
September 2009

CONTENTS

CHIMPANZEES ARE BLAMELESS CREATURES (1969)
Chimpanzees are Blameless Creatures / 25
Vampires / 26
Venus's Flytraps / 27
Judas speaks / 28
Lazarus / 30
You see What I mean / 30
Hell / 32
True Love / 33
Two Old Ladies, A Scientist and Deadly Nightshade / 33
Something, Nothing and Everything / 34
Anyway, It isn't Somatic / 34
A Visitation from Brother Rico / 37

PRIVATE AND CONFIDENTIAL (1974)
Notes on Wittgenstein / 41
Ezra Pound in Old Age / 41
A + B = ? / 42
Short Story / 42
The Byways of Desire / 43
Suddenly / 44
Clear Night / 45
Blue Aegean / 45
The Sins Never Committed are Worst / 45
Through the Needles / 46
Peepshow Cabinet / 46
On the Way to the Post Office / 47
Venus is married to Industry and commits Adultery with War / 48
Love Story / 48
Who? / 49
At Midnight on the Astral / 49
Precambrian Rock / 50
Birds in Finland / 50
Walnut / 51
The Struggle for the Soul of Man / 51
Musk / 52
The History of Love / 53
Haunting / 54
Epitaph / 54
At the Camden Arts / 55
Imagination / 56
Don't be Nervous, Chloe / 56

A Survior speaks / 57
A Spring called Bandusia / 58
Advice / 58
Two Poems about Art / 59
'Inside the Thimbles were the Purple Elephants' Helicopters' / 60
Afterwards / 60
Lord suspends Law of Karma for Lucky Luciano / 61
The Papers are not An Instrument of the Ruling Class / 63
In Spite of Everything Most of the Middle Classes
Never get Hurt / 64
'Avarice & usury & precaution must be our gods for a
little longer still' / 65
Death Valley / 65
'Ye shall be as Gods, knowing Good and Evil' / 66
In the Cave of the Skull / 67
Private and Confidential / 67
Sought / 68
Message / 68
Being Elsewhere / 69
Olives / 69
Prodigal / 70

PUBLIC FOOTPATH (1981)
Blackbirds in London / 75
Groves of Academe / 78
Razmak / 79
The Paper Gates of Jerusalem / 80
Sent / 83
New Sources of Sex / 83
A Present in the Park / 84
A Child of the Sun / 85
Perseus and Andromeda / 85
The Size of the Sea / 86
Hamlet / 87
A History of English Music from Byrd to Cage / 88
Services –
1. At the Maltings, December 1976 / 90
2. Aldeburgh Beach / 91
3. February / 91
Elegy for John Ridgewell / 92
Water into Wine / 97
Well, So That is That / 98

Imitations of Horace –
1. Palms Upwards / 100
2. Not Yet / 101
3. Concentrate on Loving / 102
Auden at His Villa on Ischia / 103
Minor Victorians –
1. Nude Study / 103
2. A Tramp / 104
3. Trippers Caught by a Wave / 105
Retreat to the Sheets / 106
Lucidity / 106
Persephone Again / 107
Clock Stop / 108

FIRE IN THE GARDEN (1984)
St. Martin-in-the-Fields / 111
A Way of Life / 111
Down the Hill / 113
In the Vale / 114
Change of Address / 115
At the Funeral of Lilian Wilson / 115
The Great Church, Helsinki / 116
Elegy for Robin Lee / 118
Nunhead Cemetery / 119
How I love My Sister / 120
The Chapel Perilous / 121
The Graveyard by the Sea / 122
With the Pike behind Her / 126
Round and Round / 127
Strassenbahnen / 127
Sad Cows / 128
The Ghost of a Rose / 128
The Dew Drop Inn / 129
Two Notes on the Literary Life / 130
The Bridges that Matter / 130
Failed Ancestors / 131
Expert beyond Experience / 132
Mother Skin / 132
I Am What I am – YHVH / 133
Why is there Something rather than Nothing? / 133
After the Seminar / 134
Greece 1950 / 135

Sunday Joint / 136
Emma Lavinia Hardy / 136
Murder in the Public Sector / 137
Roses are blooming in Picardy / 138
Jesus as a Proponent of *Realpolitik* / 139
Hawks Stones, Kebs / 140
Wealth / 140
Dead Reckoning / 141
The Baptist Choir / 142
What She Finally said / 142
Fire in the Garden / 144

LETTERS IN THE DARK (1986)
1. I lay awake writing letters to you / 149
2. So here I am in my usual pew, between / 149
3. Outside the competers: competent and virtuous / 150
4. Insight is sousing in: grizzly mist on the horizon / 150
5. A week ago, what should I see but two young swans / 151
6. Shakespeare buried his actor brother / 151
7. If the brain's the mind's rind / 152
8. *Yes*, you will smile, *but does the mind exist* / 153
9. The hoisted leg and waddle of crows / 153
10. I've forgotten the scruffy intellectual I once was / 154
11. The pelican hacks her breast and suckles with blood / 154
12. Innate science / 155
13. Lionel Lockyer claimed his pills / 155
14. There's something we're always missing among / 155
15. Ave verum corpus: we're here – and halt – / 156
16. The lake crazes into splinters, jaggings, chips / 157
17. Hagar's in prayer – but breaks when the angel comes / 157
18. Oaks: nervous systems / 158
19. This fly was born in this attic / 158
20. So here's the alarming silly tale again / 159
21. Brown in the autumn time, the grass is blown / 159
22. St. Cuthbert's hopping – a cassock on the shore – / 160
23. All my most intimate talkers – they've been / 160
24. Now here's a cosy photo / 161
25. William Austin looked on his mother's face / 161
26. All thoughts are parrots, pretty mocking birds / 162
27. To be sponged on / 162
28. *O God*, prayed Andrewes in secret every night / 163
29. By the standards of Parliament / 165

30. On the cover of *Honest to God* there's a depressed / 166
31. Elizabeth Newcomen once sold milk / 166
32. The shark survives / 167
33. You who have bitten to the core / 167
34. We look for chocolate wrapped in silver paper / 168
35. At the summit of St. Thomas's Hospital / 168
36. We meet again at the kneeling place / 169
37. Midnight Mass: Mervyn tells us / 169
38. Listening's dissolving. After I go / 170
39. Dear God, though I'm sweating round the park for death / 170
40. Whisky's a risky aspect of the Body / 170
41. Imbecile to the wise and sane, our baby divination / 171
42. I hardly ever meet my brothers and sisters / 171
43. *Bore men if you must* / 172
44. Of hem, that writen us to-fore / 173
45. My chest crackles with bronchitis / 174
46. When I was thirty-two I got cancer / 175
47. Somewhere there's a man who took me fishing / 176
48. Perhaps those childish ecstasies of terror / 177
49. Some day I'm going to have to meet my mother / 177
50. There's no abiding city here / 179
51. People that swim clambered / 180
52. Invisible reader, impossible God / 182

TROUBLE (1992)
I: Feux d'Esprit
Trouble / 187
Greenwich Park / 187
Chanson triste / 188
Remembering Adlestrop / 189
Other Life / 189
Shingle Street / 190
First Kisses / 191
Assisi and Back / 191
Two-hundred-mile-an-hour Winds / 192
Refractions / 193
In Spite of Everything / 193
Unaccompanied Voices / 194
II: Esprit du Soir
Solvitur Acris Hiems / 202
The Wild Swans at Aldeburgh / 202
Sea Lady / 204

Suffolk Evenings / 205
Heron / 208
Ashes / 209
Ignorance / 210
Night Fears / 211
Keith Vaughan's Last Journal / 212
Meeting / 213
Growing Up in the Thirties / 214
The Long Retreat / 217
III: Jeux d'Esprit
Economics in Aldeburgh / 217
Ancient Walls / 218
The Slow Motion of Trees / 219
The Opera Lovers / 219
Mathematics / 220
Holy Leisure / 220
The Longest Sentences / 221
At the Seminar / 222
Egg on a Mantelpiece / 222
Hard / 223
Waiting in Wet / 223
By the Lake / 224
Holes / 224
Notes on Lao Tzu / 225
The Santa Sophia of Air / 228

from SELECTED POEMS (1995)
– UNPUBLISHED POEMS
Visitations –
1. The Child / 231
2. The Face / 231
3. The Man / 232
Despatches 233
Faustus speaks –
1. Purple Heron / 235
2. Faustus Today / 236
3. Fly / 237
4. Passionate Friendship / 238
5. Sunflowers / 238
6. The Purple Heron Again / 239
7. Earthly Paradise / 240
8. Why He Wants to go to Bed with Her / 240

9. The Healer / 241
10. Bells / 242
11. Redemption / 243
12. Skin / 243
13. Sehnsucht / 244
14. The End / 244

A USELESS PASSION (1998)
Called to the Colours / 249
Lincoln, Autumn 1943 –
1. Pissoles / 251
2. Students / 251
3. Lincoln Cathedral / 252
Maidstone, Winter 1943 –
1. The Regimental Sergeant-major / 253
2. First Booze-up / 253
3. Defenders of Freedom / 253
4. Vera Lynn / 254
5. The War Office Selection Board / 254
6. The Lance-corporal's Cadre / 255
7. Lance-corporal / 256
8. Corporal Cosgrove / 256
Dover, Spring 1944 –
1. Dover Beach / 257
2. Arris / 257
3. Triplane / 258
4. Thought in the Ranks / 258
5. Roll Me Over in the Clover / 259
6. Shells / 259
7. War Literature / 260
8. June 6 / 261
9. A Red Light in the Night / 261
Transit, Winter 1944 –
1. Pre-octu, Wrotham / 262
2. Dancing to Victor Sylvester / 263
3. Escaping Curfew / 263
4. Unidentified / 264
Troopship, December 1944 –
1. Inside the Whale / 264
2. Sea-gale Mathematics / 264
3. The Mediterranean / 265
4. Port Said / 265

5. Wild Life / 265
OTS, Dehra Dun, January 1945 –
1. Bombay / 266
2. Dehra Dun. Watch Your Saluting / 266
3. Poetry / 267
4. Learning Urdu / 267
5. Infantile Paralysis / 268
6. McCulloch / 268
7. Religion / 269
Leave in Tehri-Garhwal, Spring 1945 –
1. Guests of the Rajah of Tehri-Garhwal / 270
2. Killing / 270
3. Bordering Tibet / 271
Jungle Training, Summer 1945 –
1. Saharanpur: Our First Mess / 272
2. Ringworm / 272
3. Albert / 273
4. Military Exercises / 273
5. Horses / 274
6. Ralph / 275
7. September 1945 / 275
The North-West Frontier, Autumn 1945 –
1. Razmak / 276
2. Second-lieutenant Pettit / 276
3. Out of the Body / 276
4. Intoxication / 277
5. Nights in the Sixth Battalion Mess / 277
6. In the Sick Bay / 278
7. Dum-dam / 279
8. Dashera / 279
Kohat, Spring 1946 –
1. Holi / 280
2. Mrs. Eaton / 281
Lansdowne, Summer 1946 –
1. The Regimental Centre, 9,000 Feet Up / 282
2. Straw Huts in Kumaon and Albert's There Again / 282
Demobbed, September 1946 –
Liverpool University / 283
Death of a Horsewoman –
Cortège / 284
Je reviens / 284
Sleeping / 285

Anniversary / 285
Broken Contract / 286
Shades / 286
Distracted / 287
Voices / 287
Ghost at the Gateway 288
Bored / 288
Waiting / 289
Heart / 289
Dancing / 289
Dream Dog / 290
Red Shoes / 290
Glass Darkly / 291
Mary Moon / 292
Secret Agent / 292
Dream Chocolates / 293
Premonition / 293
At Sea / 294
Note / 294
Horses / 294
Burdens / 295
Dream Shoes / 296
Under Another Sky / 296
Martha / 297
Pansies / 297
How to die / 298
Evening Gown / 298
Manhattan / 299
A Visit from the Hill –
Beach / 300
Bedroom / 300
Cat / 301
Cold February / 301
Witch Goddess / 302
Hands / 302
Breath / 302
Hydrophone / 303
Moon / 303
Fire / 304
Ice / 304
Furnace / 304
Tree / 305

Head / 305
Heart / 306
Murderer / 306
Distance / 307
Labyrinth / 307
Bridge / 308
Pilgrim / 308
Angel / 308
Black One / 309
Kali / 309
Hare / 310
The Accuser / 311
Pearl / 311
The Sign of the Ram / 311
Blue Rose / 312

THE VALE OF TODMORDEN (1981 & 2003)
The Pennine Way / 315
The Black Swan / 316
Water / 316
Buckley Wood / 317
Grandfather Garner / 318
Granma Garner / 318
Millstone Grit / 319
In the Old Black Swan / 320
Swag / 321
Carter / 321
Miles Weatherill at the Vicarage / 322
Miles Weatherill at the Black Swan / 322
Freedom / 323
Performing for Granma Lomas / 323
Grandfather Lomas / 324
The Town Hall / 325
Princes and Toads / 325
Cornets and Trumpets / 326
Soldiers / 327
Dad / 328
Rochdale Road / 329
Mr. Hyde / 330
Tram and Bert / 330
Brass / 331
Rebuilding / 331

The Rochdale Canal / 332
Fly / 333
Darkness / 334
Gulliver / 334
Chemistry / 335
Science / 336
Lifeboat Day / 336
Mad Mouse / 337
Keith / 337
Rabbit / 338
Kiss / 339
Dobroyd Castle / 339
Drink / 340
Love / 342
Billy Holt / 343
Father, Sons and Daughters / 343
Where are You Now? / 344
Roomfield School / 345
Urine / 346
Books at School / 347
Our Headmistress / 348
All the Animals of Empire / 348
Knickers / 349
Teachers / 350
Aquariums / 350
Olga / 351
Marjorie Green / 352
Mary Pristley / 353
The Rechabite Concert Party / 355
Sin / 356
Stoodley Pike / 357
Listening / 358
Rupert / 358
Dog Show / 358
Albion Barker / 359
Gramophone / 360
Christ Church / 360
The Choirmaster / 361
Choirboys / 362
Seeing Stars / 362
Funeral March / 363
Ridge-foot House / 364

Leaving the Choir / 364
Slump / 364
The Golden Lion / 365
Depression / 366
The Sentence / 366
Auntie Edith / 367
Uncle Herbert Rexstrew / 368
Tommy Dodd the Daisher / 369
Goodbye to the Vale / 370
Writer's Workshop at Lumb Bank / 371
Cross Stone Church / 371
Haworth / 372
'Artemidorus Farewell' / 373

NIGHLIGHTS (unpublished, 2007)
Pastorals –
Essence of Lavender / 377
A Youth of Beauty / 377
Le petit pont de pierre / 378
Widowed Roses / 378
Mother and Daughter / 379
Eclipsed by the Moon / 381
Daylight comes and Night goes / 382
The Fly's Poem about Emily / 383
The Edge of Everything / 384
Three Prayers for Children / 385
Boy, Ape and Fool / 387
Christ the Tiger / 387
Intimations of Mortality / 388
Quaker Meeting / 388
Samadhi / 389
Goshawk / 389
All That's Transitory is Only a Trope / 390
Swan / 392
Elegies –
The Month of Holy Souls / 393
The Matter of Eternity / 393
Restaurant on the Sumeda River / 394
At Night Outside / 394
But the Jewel You lost was Blue / 395
A Casual Knack of Living / 396
Hawthornden Castle / 397

Epistles –
An Die Ferne Geliebte / 399
Aegir / 400
Eau de vie / 400
A Very Odd One / 401
Deyá, Mallorca / 402
The Wink of a Fly's Wing / 403
Gryphon / 403
Light and Angels / 404
Kentucky / 405
John XXIII / 406
A Fountain in Helsinki / 407
Seventh Seal / 407
Glass / 408
Satires –
Night Fishing / 409
Sappho and He / 410
The Institution of the Family in Antarctica / 410
The Vegetable Will / 411
Sam Agonistes / 412
Streaky Bacon / 413
The Artist seen as a Camel / 414
Anyway / 415
The Alternative War / 416
Rondo on the Turd / 417
The Skin is Greater than the Banana / 418

Notes / 421
Biographical Note / 423
List of Subscribers / 425

*... But soon they joke, easy and warm,
As men will who have died once
Yet somehow were able to find their way –
Muttering this was not included in their pay.*

*Later, sleepless at night, the brain spinning
With cracked images, they won't forget
The confusion and the oily dead,
Nor yet the casual knack of living.*

                                    Alan Ross 'Survivors'

CHIMPANZEES ARE BLAMELESS CREATURES
(1969)

CHIMPANZEES ARE BLAMELESS CREATURES

They spend most of their time eating
or looking for food: i.e. working.

Or if they aren't messing about in trees
or absent-mindedly pushing off their children
they groom each other with great
concentration, eating the salt: i.e. loving.

They're a bit promiscuous.
They share mates comfortably
without getting angry
and if a row breaks out
it's for no apparent reason
and suddenly stops
without anyone being hurt.

They cuddle and touch each other
a lot and there's much
curiosity in their sex.

Sometimes a mother will want to
join another group:
there's a fair amount of shifting around.
She feels very shy about it
and the new males look her over
without tension.

Then she kisses someone's hand
and someone shakes hers.
She goes round shaking and kissing hands
and she's part of the group.
No one makes much fuss.

Chimpanzees are blameless creatures,
and it's only if they're frightened
that they'll tear your cheek off.

VAMPIRES

Vampires hung behind the curtains in my childhood:
those who'd killed themselves, practised black arts,
fallen under a curse, bloodsucking ghosts,
bloodeating bats, restless souls of dead men,
sucking the living.

Sometimes when a vampire awakes in his grave he begins to
gnaw his own hands and feet or to chew his shroud,
making his kindred die.

Sharp incisor teeth pierce the skin, lap up blood with the
tongue, without waking the victim, hairy-legged vampire
feeding on practically any quiet warm-blooded animal.

They carry diseases – disease in the bite –
even the bats can die of their own diseases.

They stake hearts, devour them,
or expose a stolen heart over a fire,
roasting it magically,
and the breast that lost it
roasts with unholy longings.

It seems a natural and rational explanation of how a patient
becomes thin, weak pale, bloodless, a shadow,
and dies.

The incisors and canines are specialised for cutting,
sickle or shearlike, cutting edges with a V.
They prefer retreats of almost complete darkness,
caves, old wells, mineshafts, tunnels, graves, hollow trees,
old buildings: shy and agile, crawling like spiders,
walking rapidly on feet and thumbs,
or horizontal on vertical surfaces.

Most active before midnight.

Flying fairly straight courses
they forage low over the ground.
The face is immediately recognisable:
seen in Bosch's Hell:
flat eager faces, intelligent about blood

and nothing else, sharp ears.
Their method is to alight near their victim
and walk or climb on him.
They attack the anus or genitals,
a quick bite shears away skin painlessly,
and they lap up the blood with their long tongues.
Sometimes they consume so much blood
they can hardly lift themselves and fly.

Vampires have faces that are neither young nor old.
As you lie in your cot they have old faces.
As you lie on your deathbed
their faces are young.

VENUS'S FLYTRAPS

Victoria couldn't abide
a vegetable insecticide.
It certainly wouldn't be right
to encourage a plant with an appetite.

Victoria's daughter, christened Hope,
dreamed of Venus's Flytraps and Scope.
She had visions of them growing,
especially when they set her sewing.

Felicity followed, an optimist,
who put them on her shopping list.
She planted them, to her husband's surprise,
and fed them daily with slaughtered flies.

The plants soon learned to need their
benefactress and feeder.
They gave her fingers affectionate nips,
and one day they kissed her on the lips.

JUDAS SPEAKS

Someone had to take a cool look at him.
Would-be martyr and messianic publicist,
he's got everything to make you love him
and everything to make you distrust him.

He stumps the country, lecturing to misfits,
undeniably curing hysterics, staging so-called
miraculous enactments of his message,
leading his starry-eyed followers
into a nebulous mysticism, and they're believing,
everyone's dropping into the delusion
that far-out truths are being revealed.

I love him, but someone's got to stop him,
someone's got to take a cool look.

He doesn't want to compete, spurns
the profit motive, despises what he considers
the rat-race, thinks we're being dehumanised
by a greedy society. He's no faith in
politics and politicians, says they're merely
promoters of self-interest groups,
distrusts all authority and social rules,
accuses the priests of being rotted by dogma,
legalism, literalism and state allegiance.
Well, maybe some are, but someone,
something's got to cohere. You can't
turn all values upside down at once.

                      He adores
spontaneity, but finds work tedious,
lives parasitically off the crumbs
of the Affluent Society. He wants a world
where everyone's happy and loving.
He styles himself the Son of God
and proclaims the reign of Love Alone.
These born-again fanatics offer
no formulated theory or blueprint
for the future. He merely urges you
to live for the day and swallow prayer
as the ultimate panacea. In so far as
he's got any political aims, these are,

quite simply, to opt out of 'the world',
meant pejoratively. He's excessively permissive,
and his idea of redemption for the world
is to change consciousness through love and such,
and thus change everything. New heaven, new earth!

So far his followers are still a minority
among the quiet conforming majority
creating the Affluent Society,
but he does twitch a contemporary nerve.
His philosophy may be full of holes
but his followers aren't philosophers.
He doesn't know what he's stirring up.
Their bizarre ideas and behaviour
are gaining currency and his sayings are
slipping into the prevailing trendy jargon.
His followers don't work: they stand for
anarchy and nihilism. They're
good-hearted wrong-headed
non-productive self-indulgent layabouts.
His version of Utopia may be
naive and foolish but that doesn't
disillusion his horny-handed fans:
they lap it up of course, like the booze
he conjures up at his love feasts.
And the health-hazard's patent. He can produce
disastrous panics, toppling the neurotic
over the edge into madness, rendering
the unwary so helplessly confused
they physically do harm to themselves.
Deaths occur.

                    That being said,
It'd be unwise to underestimate
his long-term effects on Crime.
Toleration would be a disaster.
I've a responsibility to my conscience,
my family, and my loved ones. I don't deny
he fooled me too for a while,
and in a way it's my duty to atone.

Of course some people will call this
a betrayal. But let them. I can't help that.

LAZARUS

Even then he didn't believe. He simply thought he'd been
asleep. We had to tell him he'd been dead. Naturally
we were all feeling out of this world, terrific. But gradually
well, his disbelief was too strong for us. You see,
it could all be a conjuring trick, couldn't it? Who could prove
he'd been dead? The heart can stop, the blood can stop,
and a man may not be dead. That's what the doctors say.
And we don't want to deceive ourselves, do we?

Pretty soon, of course, both of them were dead.
Catalepsy, you know, is fairly common:
people have often been buried alive. They're found
upright on the shelf of a tomb, constricted in a coffin,
or collapsed after hammering on a charnel door.
There is a sort of moral in this story, though.

YOU SEE WHAT I MEAN

And after all time may not be a dimension.
Could be it's only a miscalculation
       of a physicist who was, anyway,
       not very good at mathematics.

Not for a minute would I say we
in our unrealistic unwillingness
       to swallow the bitter pills
       had really been right all the time –

as though life were a fairy story where
the wise men were wicked magicians,
       who could somehow
       hypnotise us

into only believing our eyes –
falling back on the most invisible things
        to do so. Oh no,
           I'm not so naive,

only... after all, Newton was wrong,
and think of all the poor sods
        who went to their no doubt
        uncomfortable graves

bravely believing the Royal Society had
somehow proved something they didn't
        want to believe. And now...
        supposing Einstein's wrong?

After all time may not be a dimension.
Perhaps it's only the equation
        makes it look that way.
        I measure the room with bottles, say,

and it's thirteen bottles long. So I think:
looked at from another point of view
        the thirteen bottles
        are a room long:

the two items are reducible to the same law.
Therefore it's truer to speak of
        bottles-room
        or room-bottles

than make any artificial conceptual distinctions.
Not for a moment would I say this was true,
        of course, but
        you see what I mean:

people are dying without knowing whether $E=mc^2$ or not.

HELL

Hell was a place where people
dressed in the paraphernalia of totemistic
    pre-Christian cults,
horns, tails and hooves, grilled others
with the typical apparatus
    of medieval torture technology.

Hell, though instituted BC in the interests of
    Property and Caste,
seemed reasonable to the Christian
for frightening men of faith out of
    fornication, theft and masturbation.

In those days, if you went down to Hell,
you'd be unlikely to find God there personally
    supervising the torture,
or even Satan. What you'd find would be
    other Christians, under inquisitorial cowls.

And now, if you went there, you wouldn't even find
the medieval machinery, the thumbscrews. You'd find
    people in stiff white
clinical collars and no dangly ties,
explaining persuasively that Hell
    isn't a place, it's a State.

They'd be giving homely illustrations:
they'd be showing that Hell was the State
    of your choice:
that Hell wasn't Hell at all
in the old superstitious sense, but actually
    God's unbearable love for the damned.

If you went to Hell at any time
You'd find the full fashion range
    from dog collar
back to cowled Spanish Inquisitor
and forward again to cowled Ku Klux Klan
but never God. If you walked round Hell
    at any time

you'd find no trace of God, only Man.
You'd find Man had landed on, conquered,
    colonised,
and impregnated with his peculiar smell
most of the places in eternity, from Heaven,
       down through Purgatory to Hell.

TRUE LOVE

In the dark scented air
of coal dust and cat piss
two infant lovers stare
and shyly kiss.

No denser human bliss
can ever come to birth
on the dung and primrose earth
than this.

Later brutal kisses
and adult sweaty heats
will cheat them out of this
in laundered sheets.

**TWO OLD LADIES, A SCIENTIST AND
DEADLY NIGHTSHADE**

Some years ago our most eminent botanist
found two old ladies
uprooting deadly nightshade in a lane.

Beyond the grey trees a sour moon
watched itself wickedly in the silver ditch.

It's dangerous, you see, they said.
A queer wind walked down the lane
and some bird chuckled in the bushes.

Our most eminent botanist said, *Maybe.*
But it's a rare plant
and besides England is overpopulated.

And all day long the frantic ants
had hustled their eggs across a yard of earth.

SOMETHING, NOTHING AND EVERYTHING

There was nothing between us
then something took off her dress
something took off my shirt
something took off her brassiere
and something took off my trousers
then something took off her knickers
something took off my pants
there was nothing between us
we touched each other
everything was touching between us
we kissed each other
there was something between us
then everything entered her body
there was everything between us
there was nothing between us

ANYWAY, IT ISN'T SOMATIC

It's impossible to be a conformist
unless I stupefy myself with smoke.
        As soon as I give up smoking
        I get notions:

like, why not try some new ideas?
But liberty, of course, means
        a rather frightening
           polymorphous kind of freedom.

Byron, for example, why did he escape to Greece
instead of creating a society
	for the protection
	of good ideas?

And what about the long overdue Leisure Party?
Even with planned obsolescence, meat mountains,
	wine lakes, and
	subsidised idle acres,

can we make buying and selling money
the main business till the big bang
	reverses and contracts
	towards the crunch?

Must we admit we're snuffing production
to buck up the rationing system?
	Can we really go on generating money
	as our main product?

The fear rises that Bingo would be
more harmless than banking, insurance
	and the bourse, even though
	computer games are fun.

As the smoke clears from my cortex,
I start to visualise a new
	eighteenth-century aristocracy,
	for us all.

The cabinet appears on the media
and tells everyone that toil
	and money are
	poisoning output.

Their wish to conceal that superabundance
slashes prices and prosperity
	is bad for business
	has foundered.

Be satisfied with free cars, they say,
free food, free televisions, free

washing machines and
toiling automatons.

A simulation shows a man
feeding his old car into the recycler,
      selecting a new one
      and driving off.

He puts all his garbage
into an orifice under the sink
      where it goes
      straight to the infrastructure.

The post office closes down
and is replaced by fax.
      Illusion closes down
      and is replaced by facts.

We see a call-up of the eighteen-year-olds
for two years' toil. At twenty
      they walk free to face
      the terrors of self-realisation.

But how will we escape with no wars?
Will we feel safe with sport,
      art, opera, science,
      social work, or yoga?

Shall we have to organise controlled
football violence? Or can we too live
      as aristocrats lived,
      content with inherited handouts:

killing birds, breeding horses,
training dogs, playing polo,
      giving huge gourmet picnics,
      parties and balls? –

devoting days and nights
to love affairs? Of course,
      those who love power
      can govern the country.

But can we live without fake problems,
or seek escape up mountains,
            or race aeroplanes
                upside down?

We may be here for millennia!
Can we spend them growing
            the sidewhiskers
                of the nineteenth century?

I must fill the void with smoke,
or the vested interests preventing the future
            will seem a family
                of delinquent primates –

and they're my fellow-men!
So I'm waiting for some scientist
            to prove that smoking
                isn't caused by cancer.

A VISITATION FROM BROTHER RICO

Brother Rico
brought his trombone
from Jamaica

and *Man is God!*
said Brother Rico:

that was why he
never cut his hair.

And I wondered why,
wondered how.

WONDER WHY WONDER HOW
(sliding that bone)
AND THE BONE SAID GOD
MAN IS GOD
(Sliding that horn)

WONDER HOW WONDER WHY
NOT OMNIPOTENT
NOT OMNISCIENT
MAN IS GOD
WHOLLY MAN
UNHOLY GOD

A trained mind muttered
to the blameless face:
If Man were God
no one would say it.
If Man were God
there'd be no word
for Man or God.
If Man were God
there'd be no Man
or there'd be no God.

But Brother Rico
shone with hOppiness
omnipotent RicO
Don't make mOnnay
need an aigent
in this cOnntray, y'know...

WONDER WHY WONDER HOW
MAN IS GOD
(the bone said GOD
the horn said GOD)
TROMP TROMP
TROMP THAT BONE
MAN IS GOD MAN IS GOD

(the being of man is God?)

PRIVATE AND CONFIDENTIAL
(1974)

NOTES ON WITTGENSTEIN

What does it mean to say *I hear*?
The piano, the air, the ear, the player?

What does it mean to say *I hope*?
Is hope a feeling? How long can I hope you come?

And what does it mean to say *I love*?
Your skin, your boots, your smell, your world?

No one says *No. That wasn't true pain.
True pain wouldn't have faded – or faded so quickly.*

Is it you I love or myself?
And are roses red in the dark?

EZRA POUND IN OLD AGE

Clouds are black and blue and white and grey-blue.
That wall of old brick has prancing shadows on it.
I've suffered history and tried to understand it
and failed. Let it explain itself then.

A child knows when it wants to cry, and an old husk
when it's finished, blown along in the light.
The candle flickers as daylight comes.
A child's right is to cry, but age's to be silent.

No one understands history. But there seem to be gods
and to walk by cypress and olives is perhaps enough
in age and in youth. Especially if the sea crashes
below on the rocks. There's a grace in being wrong.

Perhaps it's enough to leave the world with this knowledge.
Enough at any rate to make you seldom speak to outsiders.
Whose fault is it if I disconcert by staring them in the eye?
Or go to dinner parties and look into the distance?

A + B = ?

Jane was one of those happy authors
    who've no history or self.
She'd no adventures, didn't travel,
    saw little of London but much of bad health.

If Emily Prunty had coined Wuthering Heights
    would the book have caught?
The passion's consuming but isn't physical,
    and for Dr. Leavis the book's a sport.

Emily wandered the moors with Heathcliff
    opened up to her God,
proved denial of her soul was death,
    and died of consumption at thirty-odd.

Jane kept the sitting-room with her pen:
    sensibility wouldn't do.
She proved denial of the code was folly
    and died an old maid at forty-two.

SHORT STORY

The events and circumstances
in his life
conformed to his conception
of it all:
he didn't expect much or want it
or get it.

His objects,
the situations he magnetised
around him,
were part of his field of force
and choice of
which of the universes he

seemed to be realising now.
Can I blame
her? he asked. If I've chosen
to marry

a puritanical woman I'll
have patience.

Have patience.
Then he took the gun, loaded it and
put it in
the bedside drawer where he kept
condoms and
managed to forget it was there.

THE BYWAYS OF DESIRE

    1.

Who can remember Haworth churchyard,
cocked stones, November wet,
the scratch of your match, the flame,
your cigarette end red –

the gravestone beneath us, drizzled,
as we lay under night with the dead,
and those arctic sheets in the Guest House,
your pineapple eyes, yellow with carnality,

smoked or drowsing, suffering love
dredged to your pupils – and two lines
toused in one cheek that said pleasure –
but love or what it brought or might

who can remember
or what you were like inside?

    2.

It irritated your sister, driving,
that we lay in the back seat kissing.
Occasionally I saw her toss of head,
and anyway the back of her glowering.

Were we even in love? You needed relief,
a man again after your husband gone,
I to find out about love. I needed
flesh and wanted to touch it.

There'd been the blow on the spine one night
as I faced the burn in your eyes and knew it was on.
Then you looked down with a nod. But it'd been
a warning: you couldn't be rejected.

Recognition and pain: we'd be together for a while,
as if in love, and then need to be destroyed.

SUDDENLY

She ogled the dragonfly, until the dragonfly
seemed to be her, and she the dragonfly
in a feelered world: all that geology
crusted in her mind, and the dragonfly saw
the planet was an event. An owl was hunting
by infra-red: the mice glowed.
Abyss: reflected sunlight: tremblings
in a tiny brain. But what was darkness?

The wings sprayed oscillations, and she
blue fire: for the big cat the king was meat.
Suddenly there were no stars: no one was left.
A king walked over the horizon, and glaciers
iced in his brain: the planet
came with him and left with him: with him
the sun died, and an ant cantered out
groping antennae into a counterglow.

CLEAR NIGHT

August moonlight
filling the night
like a liquid.

Not a stir from the asp.

The alders begin to grow.

Galaxies, galaxies, galaxies.

On a night like this
dead people
can use the moonlight
like a telephone.

BLUE AEGEAN

Blue Aegean, yellow moon:
big inquisitive face.
A cat can look at a friend.

And out of the yellow eyes
the yearning
the learning and turning
of yellow eyes walking.

Visible the paths stretching,
astonished the waves touching,
the waves watching.

THE SINS NEVER COMMITTED ARE WORST

     In Athens, that time, very drunk –
after an evening in one of the expensive bars:
can't even remember which –
why didn't we make love?

> There was no one around to make us pay
or make us feel dirty.

It couldn't have mattered
or done the slightest damage

except to certain ghosts:

> people

not present in the body,
but watching us carefully

> as if they were devils already.

THROUGH THE NEEDLES

There are nightglows on a lake whose name I can't remember:
July midnight, in the north, the veranda of a broken hut.
In the daytime I saw the veins on a fly's dead wing.
I looked at the lake and dived in, as if it were a woman's body.
It received me with cold kisses and dashed cortisone
round my veins. Later she received me with hot kisses
and she was hot and gushing inside. All I can see now
are bright stained reds and peacock blues and an unveiled look
in her eyes she never had at any other time. She was made for love
and nothing else. I can only see her through pine boles and needles
but at odd moments feeling can seem as roomy as the planet.

PEEPSHOW CABINET

In this chamber a deformed cat
leers at a pumpkin and a mighty glass of wine:

Gothic windows open out on a classical landscape
where the tall buildings mean proportion and repose.

Yet here, everything, the crazy pillars, is awry.
Something's always telling us we die

though youngsters cling on tight in a close embrace.
Is the cat afraid, or waiting to pounce?

Or is it pretending...? Something's transparent here,
the table?... Or the chequered floor?... All of them.

They dodge the eye: when you look they look so solid.
Solid too the pillars and the beautiful buildings.

Solid and so unaccountably deceiving.

ON THE WAY TO THE POST OFFICE

As she walks her trousers act out and discuss
all the rhythms of her cheeks.

There's a slight sag to her buttocks
in that orbit of gyrations.

Involuntarily I fall into step, though
twenty-five yards behind.

Suddenly it's as if she'd no trousers on,
my consciousness is between her legs

among her pubic hairs, between her vagina
and her anus. She turns round.

Furtiveness is an important part
of an artist's life.

VENUS IS MARRIED TO INDUSTRY AND COMMITS ADULTERY WITH WAR

Venus'd been bored for years with Vulcan:
everyone knew that. But what was more,
so'd she been with Mars: all that gore.

But, looking round for someone else,
who was there? Adonis? A recurrent bore –
hunting and being hunted: bad as war.

She'd tried it with Hermes too – not bad.
But with what result? An hermaphrodite.
All that camping soon gets trite.

As Urania she was known as an intellectual.
But none of the gods was particularly bright.
Marx then? But that Victorian beard couldn't be right?

LOVE STORY

*You may forget, but let me tell you this:
someone in some future time'll think of us.*

More than two millennia later he thought of Sappho,
imagining the girl, the place, and how she said it,

out of the caves seven thousand years, with vines and olives,
and civilisation warming like an egg.

Through the windscreen the whizzing motorway, the landscape, the lights
became an arrangement in Dufy blue: it made him strong –

*Why don't you – someone – you paint that.
If I were a painter, that's what I'd do,*

he said. She was ten years older than he,
and it made her feel ten years older.

No one would paint a scene like that today, she said.

WHO?

Made from her flesh
my flesh pricks
if she starts smarting.
Let the wind go through her bones
and my bones go cold.
If she groans in her sleep,
groans walk through the darkness,
and climb in with me.
Much that she's said
and left unsaid
is said in my head –
though I'd disown it.
And who am I
being myself alone
while I groan in the body of another?

AT MIDNIGHT ON THE ASTRAL

A Lomas left a will in the Vale of Todmorden
in the twelve hundreds. No wonder the air smells
like inheritance when I'm there. But there
I never am, except at night, in the astral body.
I see the Pike's black stones and the entrance,
and I climb the black winding stair
to the balcony. Up here the buffeting wind
hits my face, and I can see the coarse grass
and the hopping sheep, dropping pills.
It's more concrete than other acres of the spirit.
I'm on the mountainside or in the stairwell,
I'm never more than twelve, and I seem alive.
Below, at the last bit of road, there's
the Fever Hospital, where my mother went
for six weeks. I stand outside in the wind.
Father's allowed in, and I'm lonely.
But Rupert's with me, barking about
and wagging his tongue, glad-eyed, loving me.
It was on that moor I realised he was ill,
and he nearly died when I squeezed his chest.
It's strange I didn't feel myself watching

even then. Perhaps I did. I often felt
there was another watcher. I still do.

PRECAMBRIAN ROCK

I travelled a long way to Finland,
not really under my own volition.
It's a morose landscape that smiles in summer
and it's friendly to melancholy people, by not
being cheerful, only beautiful.
In winter the Victorian statues turn
abstract with snow, and it's as if
the past doesn't exist. In summer
the light flitters all night long
and shifts each moment and you know
this selection of weather's the solution
of all the planet's history of climate
since the beginning, and so are you.
At times you're bigger than the stars,
and at others you're a member of
the universe like that ant, and not
very responsible for yourself.
As you watch the clouds changing in the lake
while you crouch there shaving,
you're just what you are, and then it's gone,
you're someone else.

BIRDS IN FINLAND

Mallards are clapping over the snow in an ochre sun.
If I go on looking I can imagine Estonia.
Out there in Tallinn the soviet facts
must be seeming as real as these do by now.
There are gaols on both sides of the Baltic.
All property is theft.

Who's the criminal is relative and depends on time,
like who is sick. Mallards freeze in

if they stick on the ice too long.
One's got to keep flying.
If you look closely at a mallard,
you see its got a neat white collar.

Nevertheless man's a social bird,
as well as a spirit. It's important
to know how dependent you are and still
keep some plumage. You'll never be an albatross
dipping to sloping seas and nipping up squid.
You're poised between pole and spin.

It's not much fun knowing this.
It's more fun to think you can escape
or be a bird. Are all these hundreds of people
you see in the streets, who never give it a thought,
part of the evolution of man? The answer is,
of course, yes.

WALNUT

Your little wrinkled face looks
like a bad luck gift for a man.
You're a hard nut to crack, but
not too hard – even with the hands.
A good squeeze is enough.
Then you open, and look:
inside a small dried-up brain.
Did it ever think?
Mummified now. A Chinese mandarin's
mummified cortex, with a little, bitter taste.
No wonder you look so dead.

THE STRUGGLE FOR THE SOUL OF MAN

Harry puts a bottle of JC on the table:
Finest beer in London, he says, meaning England.
Beer's your god, his wife adds.

Look at your God, says Harry. *What
about Lillian Board then? What
has your God been able to do for her then?
The finest woman who ever lived?*

Harry's face just asks me across the bar.
A dead fag points downwards
and Harry's circumflex eyebrows are pained at God
watching running girls he's never seen
running off the edge of the world.

I'll tell you what, then, says his wife. *What about it?
If God saved Lillian Board, would you give up drinking?*

His face gives no wink,
but somewhere beyond original sin and Harry's innocence
a big face looks out and winks.

MUSK

Musk seemed to whisper hoarsely, a hoarse sound,
                with a throaty burr
going right back to the deer's gland,
to the muskiest scent snuffed out by the females
                and passed on in the rank glands,
                      a single grain of musk
perfuming millions of cubic feet of air,
            teaching sexwise nostrils,

Empress Josephine's musk, impregnating lace,
                inflaming Bonaparte's
antlered passion, impregnating her walls,
a musky perfume aphrodisiac for years
                in kings, queens, rajahs, sybarites,
                      courtesans, drifting on particles,
navigating down the animal odour so maddening to
            the soft meat of feminine deer.

THE HISTORY OF LOVE

Olga Wadsworth went off to America when I was five.
        I never spoke to her, let alone touched,
                but once
        I invited her to my party.
She was desked in sunlight on the other side of the classroom,
                with golden hair and shafted eyes.
After she left I saw her in lots of American films.

Marjorie Green pulled her knickers down
        under a mac on the hillside above the Park.
            When we came out of the mac
I could see Kenneth Marshall shooting for goal down below
        in a bright jersey, free from sin,
and as we looped past the goalposts he grinned as if he knew,
        and his white pants were filthied with muck.
Next Saturday I played too and slid as much as I could.

Mary Priestley was in the bathroom when my mother came in
        and we were all looking at each others' bottoms.
            She was sent home with the rest
and my mother wouldn't speak to me all day.
            There was a turd in the potty
that Mary Priestly had left, and it looked
        warm, dirty, black and guilty.
            I didn't see her for a long time.

Then I recited a poem at the Rechabites' Poetry Competition
            and won and was invited to join their Concert Party
as a compère. I wore a wig and a velvet suit like a lackey.
        Mary Priestley was in the chorus,
            dancing with long legs and knickers,
                powdered and stamping and kicking in line.
                Those girls were never shy:
                    they made me shy.

            Once in the winter streets
        I found Mary Priestley playing at night
            and I played with her.
And later I was moved up a form and entered her class.
            She wrote and whispered *Pass it on*,
                and the note said *I love you*.
            Hot, I wrote,

     and later in the playground
  ran up to the gate between us like an aeroplane
   and threw my letter over like a bomb:
      I love you.

Now I'm married to a girl called Mary who comes from America.

HAUNTING

It's winter again: the vampires are sleeping badly.
There's a moaning in the cellars and the walls:
they're getting thirsty: old ladies
are shuffling out,
remembering.

A man looked out of the frozen lake yesterday,
showed me his fangs
before disappearing, smiling
and nodding.

Bones have shifted in the vaults, cobwebs are torn.
There's too much walking around
among the dead, and there are rumours
that when I'm gone
I shall be no exception.

Old bones in the bonehouse
will stir again.
Tall white ghosts will walk the earth
remembering.

EPITAPH

These two lovers were married a lifetime together,
fought for each other, fought against each other,
coped with poverty, unemployment and wealth,
betrayed each other in sickness and in health,
educated their children, then lived apart,

old irreconcilable folk, with angina of the heart,
in separate flats, in the same town, same part,
and died within an hour of one another.

AT THE CAMDEN ARTS

Since she's seventeen, and I'm, let's say,
much older, and, moreover, happily married,
which only makes me love women more,
and the girl's in love with the poet in the orange shirt
this evening, it's much wiser to say goodbye,
after getting five kisses of excuse, which I value,
and get on the tube at Finchley Road,
feeling, *Well, at least, I've been treated considerately.*

It's not very dignified leaving her to the younger poet
and going home to someone you love more, especially as you
would be allowed to if you wanted. But it does make something clear.
There's nothing now, nothing at all, to stop you
seeing that what you love's not veins, fingers,
rings and feet, but only these when you've got into
the esoteric hinterlands that these are the merchandise of.
It's not enough to fuck someone on a sofa one night.

Even these intelligent recondite women aren't unknowable enough
						for me.
It's you I'm curious about. Now I've landed on your coasts,
it's your rivers I want to explore, your inhabitants to trade with.
I'm entranced by your silences and cries. It's your customs
I want to study and bring your artefacts home to my museums.
There's a religion I can learn, I think, if I learn your language.
It hasn't a theology perhaps, but in its rituals I'll find, I suspect,
the sorcerous genitalia of all theology.

IMAGINATION

When I look at you, Mary, my eyes
are flickered on by a
shower of particles that
pierce my lens, tap

on my retina, wash
electromagnetic
currents up the threads of

my nerves to something that looks like a
cauliflower and weighs
three pounds. All the rest, love,
in fact the lot,

is pure imagination. When an
atom of sodium
meets a wild atom of
chlorine and they

synthesise into salt,
who imagines green gas
and white powder? I, love,

creator of brain, nerves, lens,
suddenly forget them
when I look at you
and create you

accurately as you are
at your imagined
far speculated you.

DON'T BE NERVOUS, CHLOE
    Horace, *Odes*, I xxiii

Chloe, you're dodging me like a baby lamb,
wanting her niddering mother in the empty mountains
        and ducking at every gust
    and flutter in the woods.

Whatever happens – spring coming, shivers
in the excitable trees, a green lizard
        shoving at a bramble – lambs are timorous
    at the heart and knees.

But I'm not going to crush you like a Bengal tiger
or leap on you and maul you. Give up your mama
        now, come on: it's time
    to go trotting after a man.

A SURVIVOR SPEAKS

    Horace, *Odes*, I v

I wonder who the pretty boy is now, Primrose,
that's getting your hugs in your flowery den
        muffled in perfumes?
Who are you brushing your golden locks for now

with unaffected sophistication? Oh dear, he'll soon know:
he'll be groaning about your flexibility and the promiscuous gods
and stare disbelievingly
    at the waves stripped by black winds,

though now he's clinging to your harbours and fondling your currency,
thinking it valid. He thinks you'll always be loving and loveable
        and free from other ships,
not realising that breezes change.

What a glittering stretch you are, so tempting unattempted.
As for me, I've hung up my sopping clothes
        on the temple wall:
    an offering to the god who saves us from shipwreck.

A SPRING CALLED BANDUSIA

    Horace, *Odes*, III xiii

O Bandusia,, more glittery than crystal,
I'll pour red wine in you, and some flowers, yes; and tomorrow
        I'll give you a young goat
   with sprouting horns –

a forehead bulging for erotic battles
he won't ever have: I'll give you a hot kid
        to colour your cool veins
   with red blood.

The atrocious heat doesn't touch you.
In the roasting afternoon you've a delicious chill
        for the overworked ox
   and the dusty herd.

Now you're a name to remember.
These words do it – I just have to mention that evergreen
        on your bouldery outlet where the talking
   lymphs leap down.

ADVICE

    Horace, *Odes*, II v

There's nothing wrong with tenderness for a servant,
Alfred. Even Generals have been known to do it:
Achilles wasn't used to it and thought he was above it.
        But a girl called Snowdrop got him.

Ajax captured a girl, but then she caught him.
Agamemnon fired Troy, but the virgin he snatched
set fire to him. He was as easy as Troy became
        once Hector was dead.

You never know, her parents might be rich.
A blonde like that has to be a princess
robbed of her inheritance. Anyone who can charm you
        couldn't really be out of the bottom drawer.

Besides, look how faithful she is. She'd never accept money.
I can't help noticing she's got lovely breasts and ankles
and the sweetest face too. Don't be suspicious. Everyone knows
    a man of forty's not interested in girls.

TWO POEMS ABOUT ART

1. IN THE NATIONAL GALLERY

I'm sitting in the National Gallery cafeteria
where the tinned salmon sandwiches are a trifle expensive
and the intelligent well-brought-up
somewhat artistic girls come.

Particles of sexuality are
troubling the ether like lightwaves, or packets of energy,
and it's very hot.

The quanta come off in clouds from between their legs
and gather round male trousers, insinuating themselves.

Later I might go up and look at the pictures.

2. HOT DAY IN THE NATIONAL GALLERY
after Sassoon

Everyone suddenly started taking their clothes off,
the ladies in hats and the girls in leather,
and one girl started scratching herself,
and when people started feeling each other
in front of the Rubens and Piero di Cosimos
the attendants were mute.

Nobody told the police, because of the spontaneity, the day
everyone impulsively fell in love in the National Gallery
and did everything artists had only dreamed about
as if they were all in celestial bodies on the Astral Plane
or bacchanaling around in the Elysian Fields,

with the sun shafting in through the dome,
catching water, making wine.

'INSIDE THE THIMBLES WERE THE PURPLE ELEPHANTS' HELICOPTERS'

    H. A. Gleason jr, *Linguistics & English Grammar*

Inside the thimbles *were* the purple elephants' helicopters:
they were waiting to lift off for the purple jungles,
where they'd never been but where, intuitively,
they knew they belonged.

Inside the helicopters were hundreds of green tins
of purple soup, which the elephants were going to
heat up on their violet primuses when they
touched down in the purple night.

Inside the purple jungle humped the black elephants' artillery:
they were triggered to shoot down the purple elephants' helicopters
as soon as their rotaries were visible coming over the purple trees
from the black jungle.

But if they'd known it, or thought about it, the black elephants
would have been much happier getting into black helicopters
and helicoptering off with their grey primuses and white tins of
                                                              black soup
to love in the black jungles they came from.

AFTERWARDS

    after Hardy

When I've passed out by the side-vomitory under the screen
        (no main exit for me, or short intermission)
and the poetry rat-race goes on as before, will anyone say
      He didn't have the ordinary ambitions?

I saved six hedgehogs from being poisoned at least,
      I brought up half-a-dozen cats, one dog and a hare,

I refrained from killing a lot of flies,
    except with DDT, but will anyone care?

I listened to a lot of censorious, self-righteous and snide
    comments about my poet-friends, almost nightly,
and didn't join in (though often sorely tempted to)
    but did anyone notice? Not likely.

I dare say there'll be quite a lot of people at my funeral
    who wish they were somewhere else unusual
and think coffins in bad taste. I've often observed
    this phenomenon at funerals.

But will anyone remember I'd thought of this
    when they're in the pew or the pub?
I doubt it. They'll resent me and my tactless corpse
    in spite of the booze and the grub.

I managed to like some people for about
thirty years, but defeat set in about there,
say thirty-one, and I've been forgetting more clearly what
    it was all about since then. But who'll care?

LORD SUSPENDS LAW OF KARMA FOR LUCKY LUCIANO

In 1931, the fall, Luciano, Charley,
    on business bent,
thinking the previous generation
ain't reaping the US's barley
    in the way it was meant,

takes care of 41 Italian-born old bugs
    who pioneer the Mafia,
and one and all agree
Charley can nine those old mugs
    and no one is unhappier.

But the Accuser, turning up in town
    in the natural recess,

takes an exceedingly moral tone,
says, Gee – Takes a lot to put me down,
      I'm not given to stress,

and what executive's expendable?
      But, jeeze, this two-dime
cold-eyed Sicilian dude
croaks all the most dependable
      brains in crime.

So? says God. Ain't he getting ahead?
      He eases some guys
into boxes. What else is new?
So Charley's the first cat throws lead
      in a business enterprise?

OK. Chop Charley. Who's next on the scene?
      Just who rates
with Charley in your personal esteem
for big-timing the greatest single slug-machine
in the United States?

Aw Boss, quit stalling, says Satan.
      This story's news.
Guy croaks a generation like that,
All 49 states'll go off their crate an'
      stop minding his p's and q's.

Then listen, says Dad. Get doing your sums.
      Guys gotta be dead.
The whole joint's gargling with geezers.
You want hippies and bums?
      Handouts and reds?

Then the Lord goes into a thinkhatch.
      Satan just scoffs:
You know the score, Dad. Triggers are killers.
It's not principle or scratch.
They like picking guys off.

So what do we do? Do we take them up here?
      You don't dig them below.

What do we do with these hatchets?
Just a word in my ear
    and I'll know.

What it is, sneers the Casuist, stalling,
    You like jerks that win.
These skates are playing the system.
They stop Wall Street from falling.
    The Lord just grins.

THE PAPERS ARE NOT AN INSTRUMENT OF THE RULING CLASS

Lord Northcliffe was the only man
who understood the Education Act,
    milked it
and saw the significance of reading.

He said, *If a dog bites a man,*
it's not news; but if a man
    bites a dog,
it's news. Similarly, if a country has

30 million abortions a year,
that's not news; but if 30 million foetuses
    killed their mothers,
that'd be news. In Paris

there are thousands of restaurants
that aren't news; but there's a restaurant
    where you can eat people;
that's news. They're freshly murdered

and you order in advance the parts
you want, breast, shin, brains, etcetera.
    The thumb's supposed to be
particularly good, and the coccyx. Someone who

ate there was convinced by a colour supplement
that war was fun, as well as profitable. He joined up

and they fried him to a crackling.
They found his prick erect, which wasn't news.

IN SPITE OF EVERYTHING MOST OF THE MIDDLE CLASSES NEVER GET HURT

Bombs slipped out of Nixon's nostrils.
Peace came out of his teeth
LBJ died the week before, perhaps
so he couldn't hear the news. Harry went
where he couldn't give 'em Hell.

Teenage lads leapt on an Irishman
who was drunk and happy. They bashed
his head and the back of his neck and stole
thirty p and some cigarettes. Then
they returned and bashed him some more.

Then they reported in to the police:
first they reported the man damaged,
then they confessed they did it.
The judge gave them twenty years.
He was afraid.

The boys were afraid. Afraid
of themselves and afraid of their street,
afraid of wigs, of truncheons and money,
afraid of what would happen if
they fought as their fears taught them.

They were afraid of what they'd done.
Hearing the sentence they were still more
afraid of the powerful, the confident and the successful,
men in suits and men in blue.
So afraid they had to kill.

Bombs slipped out of Nixon's nostrils.
Peace came out of his teeth.
Nixon was most afraid of failure,
more afraid of failure than anyone's death.
The majority of the Americans voted for Nixon.

'AVARICE & USURY & PRECAUTION MUST BE OUR GODS FOR A LITTLE LONGER STILL'

Lord Keynes in 1930

To get up on time for the factory
you needed an alarm clock.

It was dark: the alarm clock
needed luminous numbers.

The luminous numbers needed girls
to paint on radioactive paint.

To paint on the numbers the girls
needed a fine point to the brush.

To get the fine point on the brush
the girls needed to suck it.

They died of cancer of the mouth.
None of this was needed.

As they died they didn't think
of freedom or poetry or who owns time

or who owns the factory or why.
But when they died it was as if

they were experiencing death for the first time.

DEATH VALLEY

Death Valley's drier, hotter and lower
than any other depression in the world.

On the west's the Panamint Range, The Funeral, Grapevine
and Black Mountains saw off the east.

Five hundred arid square miles
genetically related to other valleys

slump below sea level and culminate
in Badwater at minus three hundred feet.

Precipitation's small, but despite the drouth
and the incalescence, some beasts, some birds survive.

It's a National Monument, with craggy spectacular
geography and blocks of historical glamour.

It first destroyed white men as they worked to the west,
boned by its heats on the borax floors,

walking black mountains that stood like funerals,
putting tongues in waters that tasted of badness,

a place of the limping and isolated, till they found
borax in the valley and gold in the mountains.

Then came the 20-mule team wagons and
cartloads groaning on the long haul home.

The most famous prospector was Death Valley Scotty,
financed, they said, by gold from an arcane mine.

Later we heard his speculations were promoted by
a Chicago man called Johnson, retired. But later, again,

Johnson, it seemed, was a front for a mysterious
lawyer, in business too, and name unknown.

'YE SHALL BE AS GODS, KNOWING GOOD AND EVIL'

This apple that she gave to you
wasn't sweet flesh or vegetable dew.

If Othello was fiction, Iago too,
Shakespeare's Othello is no less true.

It wasn't knowledge that made you sin
but double knowledge, two doors to come in.

Good and evil, devil's fiction,
split the world in every direction.

The way out's the way in.
The flaming sword's in your brain.

IN THE CAVE OF THE SKULL

Even through the curtains dawn is rosy-fingered
and won't pull back: I can hear the birds –
one shriek in particular, with hot sun in it:
all that's there when I'm not here.

Birdie, I'm not different from you, but one
hot sun doesn't make a world sunshine. I may not
even pull back that curtain – and I'm not listening
to the radio. Everyone else wants news of capitalism.

You wouldn't know about that: how we sell our presidents,
prime ministers and programmes the way
a fabric firm sells curtains. And unlike curtains
politicians are the cause of all our problems

and we can't get rid of them. And look, as I get up
my lamp throws my shadow on my curtain.
If I were a bird I'd prefer to buy my nest – so would you
if you understood money: giving's against nature.

PRIVATE AND CONFIDENTIAL

There's not much point in looking at the stars: we know what they are.
Except that we don't know what anything is. Not to understand stars
I rubbed them out and then tried to invent them.
I made every star like every other star, except they were different
like fingerprints or trees. Probably I didn't know
what the universe was going to do with itself.

If you go on looking at galaxies long enough they
and you go out and when you're invisible
darkness goes groping around after darkness even though
everything seems to be disappearing behind points of light.

SOUGHT

He came into the file as an intellectual enquirer:
he assumed that what high-calibre brains had discovered
before would be found in physics.

He was no judge: the point was to be objective –
to leave himself outside, untouched, observing.
He could be a tape or perhaps a microscope.

Beginning in this disinterested, detached, critical
way, divested of all preconceptions or assumptions,
he was disturbed to find he felt somehow watched.

Not only was he not entirely outside his work, it was as if
his work was inside him, and looking at him.
He hadn't expected this.

One day radiated by billions of elementary particles
as usual, he began to get a particular awareness
of being a subtle person in the bombardment of light.

MESSAGE
from the Finnish of Aaro Hellaakoski, 'Viesti'

Quiescent waterstretch
split by a splash.

Mysteryfish
swished back in a splash.

Depth message fetched
in a moment of flash
splashed on the waterstretch.

Wish I knew that fish.

BEING ELSEWHERE

Everything in the earth's made out of lightning.
Put terminals to it and it'd flash
loudly at you. As you walk about on the soil
it's easy to forget the oven underneath
and the oven underneath the oven.
Everything's cracking around like a whip
inside an egg just going to hatch out tigers.

But still, outside and inside all this there's something
cooler and more insulating than cotton wool or lambs.
If the world's an incubator, it was made by
intangible hands. You can only guess the silence
by listening to the thunder. It's the absence
that's as quiet as ultimate noise.

OLIVES

Olives
rooted with sane gestures in green peace
making their oil and bright black fruit
unhurriedly

volatile
immaterial rocks, seeming to dream,
with inhuman light behind them

water
weir-smooth, wonderful, sleeping
water silence, silence of slime and weed
gliding fish silence

water coolness and rock heat
in the shimmering air

and a very hot sun
that shines through a haze
on us and white stones

landscape
like gauze in the heat
that another eye might see through

and heat silence inhuman

and the sun like a gong

that silently makes us dance.

   Greece, 1950

PRODIGAL

At the last bit of the forest
the wanderer nearly dies,
but he sees a cottage light burning
and it just keeps him alive.

So he gropes to the tiny doorway
and he drums like a man in a cell,
but the door's wide open even before
he cries *Save me, I'm in Hell!*

And the Lord stands there with the turkey
and the Bollinger '94
and a glittering tinselled Christmas tree
and angels there by the score.

But the man just bellows *Save me!
Can't you help me! Save my life!*
So God reaches out with the turkey
and tries to give him a slice.

But he still keeps shouting *Feed me!*
So God leaves him there at the door –
leaving it slightly ajar though –
and warms His pants at the fire.

He knows it's no use talking.
He wouldn't know where to begin.
One day he'll wake again from his sleep,
and when he does, he's in.

PUBLIC FOOTPATH
(1981)

BLACKBIRDS IN LONDON

    1.

There's a scratching in the dead leaves outside my window.
A blackbird's looking for pears, making a furtive rustle
Like a hand edging towards someone's legs. Even in November
There's one rosebud on that bush, and others on bushes I can't see.

It's amazing how much time people have for boredom. If only
People were interesting as their dreams, and not alert to ensure
No one is. After certain nights, though, their beds
Look pretty unkempt and messy, especially old beds.

If you let your feelings stray to the passions under the lunch tables
Round this city, it doesn't seem to have much to do
With happiness, though. What you get a whiff of is immense meanness
In nylon tights. No one's running around naked on an island

And giving themselves unreservedly. Rather, they're thinking, *If I could
Make the boss, my troubles'd be over temporarily at least.*
Occasionally someone's happy at work and lunch because of love
And asks nothing else. And some are happy to see them.

But chiefly in sleep the wife's dreaming of joints and ovens
And the husband's raising his umbrella to his boss. Freud might see
Sex in this, but I don't. Everyone's dreams have affiliated
Into a big cruise going into the darkness without any games.

    2.

My dwarf orange tree killed while I was away last summer
Has some green shoots coming out of its base. I couldn't bear
To throw out the corpse. Water's made the stems look quite green.

This is nearly December but an indoor situation. As I look
At the Thames, the people who've looked at the Thames
Don't seem to be there any more. All those who died,

Some for a principle, more for a bit of nonsense
The state expected. Greater love hath no man:
To lay down all he could be for the easy lie.

The city used to seem to be built on corpses,
Like a church in a cemetery nourishing great yews: a darkness
Of dead presences: people in wigs pottering round

The gardens and pubs, still looking grave from
Stained glass windows. A lot of nitrogen has grown us
Into being old newspapers blown along a tarmac road

Of rubble. The tall concrete's raised on
Piles of paper falling through space. Through the blue
Vacuum the stars look clean: they're still burning.

   3.

It's dark in my college study. A little moonlight's moving on the work
Left on my desk, and on the pictures of Shelley, Eliot, Shakespeare
                                              and Hardy
Saving my notice board from notices, lighting a few of the books.

In a way I'm there, though the door's locked. Someone looking for me'd
Find bits of me there. And in few thousand students' minds too
There are chips of me lying around like old postcards once looked at.

They won't quite forget me, as I shan't forget Bud Paine or Froggie
                                                Charnley
Or Taffy Evans, all dead. I can still resent a violent unfair
Slap on the face. They showed me all their life. I can acknowledge a
                                                  tenderness.

There are things I've written I've felt people reading in invisible places.
Some I know and some I don't – they've given me their consciousness,
And fragments of my nervous system, mainly in the spine, have
                                                  wagged at it.

Here in my car kisses and handshakes go to invisible people,
Not quite collisions with those I haven't been known by and haven't
                                                  known.
No obligations: the ignitions are angelic, beginning and ending in fire.

4.

The way she walked out of the students' union,
Her nose-tilt saying, *I've not come here to be insulted
With truth,* and no one has. Come or been consulted.
And now, when Keith Douglas invites to communion
With *How to Kill*, the committee laughs: it's
Obviously malapropos for the Common Paper. *Information
About killing's normal in a young person's education
In most countries. I studied and killed in the blitz
Myself,* no one cries. Would you ever say to a Professor
*A pensioner could live twelve years on a thoroughbred stallion's
Fuck,* even though it's true? So unreluctantly, in peace,
Let's forget about ways to kill and turn to the battalions
Of positive poets and, to keep death from the Assessor,
Here's a poem on senility by Louis MacNeice.

5.

This rain I'm listening to, as if it'll never end,
Is the sort of rain and drenched birdsong Shelley heard,
Warned by his father-in-law that in their lifetime
The ignorance wouldn't end.

The lawn's suddenly emerald through the rained-down window,
                                                though when
I look again it's not glowing green romantic glass:
More radical than that it's struggling, swallowing, crass
With pleasure, killable by sun.

*We've more moral, political and historical wisdom than we know
how to reduce into practice*: the grass's more sensitive, voracious
and vulnerable than glass: *calculations outrun conception.*
Who can imagine what we know?

As long as I talk to myself I can't hear the wind. It's time
To let the rain splash on my nerves when I look at the grass.

GROVES OF ACADEME

   1.

She's not as young as she used to be – she
never was. Age's always trodden on her heel,
tickled her ear: twenty, twenty-one,
thirty, thirty-nine, forty? And always, always,
wasn't there? there was something, something
she could have done. In those days
a girl didn't ring or write to a man
as they can now and say they love him
or just want sex. Why can't she now?
She's old. She was young then.
What is she missing? She's got
a husband, a job, a beautiful child.
But beyond all that, something's
still unsatisfied, afraid. Is infinity
waiting for her? It's that infinity
in her now that wants to make her
take a man again. Infinity knows
her life's not yet begun. She'll never
have enough of life to fill infinity up...

   2.

And afternoon's a hot time for ticking essays.
Heat shimmers on the Library wall across.
A face sits behind a typewriter at its
open window. Occasionally eyes meet.

Her glasses have grease on. A straggle of hair
hangs over an eye. She nibbles her lip.
These thoughts have come out of my lectures.
How depressing. She'd like a kiss – or highbrow talk.

It comes to her that what she wants is
something in her body – but for her mind
new knowledge. Someone's eyes come out of their head –
they'd open and she'd be a person she's not.

Her legs are hot. Caressingly her hand rests there
and moves to the top. Does she know she's doing it?

She squeezes it tight and warm, folding in it, concentrating.
There's a man alone, down the corridor, working too.

But neither'll ever restore the other's body,
except in lucid dreams, where they've often met at night.
Now she goes to the loo and fills a glass with water,
she tosses her hair and drinks it, tapping her foot.

RAZMAK

My most intimate relationship with a strange Indian
was at the end of the war.
        At nineteen what seemed a
whole straddle of history had lugged me to a fortress
of walls, towers and barbed wire against red-cheeked men in pagris,
striding along, each man with his own rifle.

        Almost at once
two Garhwal havildars were thumping uphill, kukris bouncing,
like foxes, and me behind like their brush,
weakening, while soft-nosed bullets
gobbed up stones round my toes.

        Then I was a bird
hovering detached above myself, watching us all
running, ready to take off if the silver cord was loosed
and aware of a man two thousand feet away in a turban
ogling me dancing on the sight of his old
and inaccurate rifle and hoping to burgle me
of my nineteen years, reloading. He killed a mule,
his bullet inching in and cratering out.

        As my body
got to the rock and I feathered down with it and
crouched with the havildars, we grinned,
and mortars moped. I was a boy, never
quite expecting the unexpected. No one knows.
It didn't strike me then as even strange that an Indian
should take such a personal and determined interest
in an Englishman's future.

THE PAPER GATES OF JERUSALEM

For the earnest expectation of the creature waiteth for the manifestation of the sons of God... Because the creature itself shall be delivered from the bondage of corruption into the glorious liberty of the children of God. For we know that the whole creation groaneth and travaileth together in pain until now. And not only they, but ourselves also, which have the firstfruits of the Spirit, even we ourselves groan within ourselves, waiting for the adoption, to wit, the redemption of our body. For we are saved by hope: but hope that is seen is not hope: for what a man seeth, why doth he yet hope for?

ROMANS, VIII 19-23

1.

Plants are exuding effluvia
when I'm not there, and so am I.

But my cat groaneth together in travail,
hungering as for pipesmoke in his yellow pupil.

Especially that seed of soul he caught
from kneading his human mother is distraught.

Stroke him a while – he can't be satisfied:
hyperactive, prowling anxious-eyed.

Hunting's nervous: his little black head
came out hunting from his mother, hunting his need:

hunting in me now, in my eyes. My eyes
hurt him, he blinks. His famished heart rises

everywhere, and everywhere's waiting for a self.
I'm waiting for myself myself.

Yet I'm stopped at that: Herrick would be surprised
at that roadside rabbit, with huge bumps for eyes.

In an age of civil war who can still
say goodbye to the daffodils?

If I'd a telescopic gun, someone said,
I could manage to blow off the back of my head.

2.

The plants are exercised
            about a problem:
Rain: a right or a privilege?

In the back window a sign:
            Give Blood.
In the back seat a toy
            crab the colour of
            arterial blood
            dangles and bounces.
In the front seat the head
            turns: the eyebrows
            are pencilled black;
The canines are huge fangs.

When asked how he earned his living
            Dracula replied:
            I have private means.

He was painting a picture of Oxford Street.
Suddenly he realised he'd left himself out.

He started to put himself in the picture of Oxford Street
but then he became aware he was painting the picture.

He painted a picture of himself painting a picture of himself
painting Oxford Street and then he painted a

picture of himself painting a picture of himself
painting a picture of himself and suddenly disappeared.

At that moment Oxford Street disappeared.

3.

The Mullah Nasrudin saw some farm-workers burning wheat, and it stopped him picking daisies.
    Why are you burning that crop? he asked.
    It makes the catharine wheels of business go round, they smiled
    The mullah smiled. Seeing some dairy-maids, he went over and watched them piling butter in the cow-troughs.
    Chatting up the prettiest, he said, *That's a funny thing to be feeding cows with, isn't it?*
    Not for our Général de Gaulle, she smiled. *Can we let them eat cake?*
    The Mullah smiled. Then he came to what seemed a lake of blood. A man was smiling as he contemplated it.
    What's that then? the Mullah asked.
    Wine, the man smiled, as he started back to his chateau. *And those are the Meat Mountains in the distance.*
    The Mullah was shocked into his component particles cybernetically. When he'd reconstructed himself, he was in the USA, looking over a farmer's shoulder, as the farmer sat in his office riffling cheques.
    So the US Government's giving you all that money? He smiled.
    For laying off my land, the farmer smiled.
    Back by the Lake of Wine, the Mullah took out his hamburger, threw it in the Lake, took some dollar bills from his wallet and started munching them thoughtfully. Without dressing, the greenbacks rustled like lettuce. A little boy smiled and said, *Why are you eating all that paper?*
    Trust the economists, the Mullah smiled. *We're not working in the dark, you know.*

4.

It was the Western end we found the gates at,
and they were entirely made of paper,
with heads of kings, queens, dollars and pounds on,
like playing cards, souvenirs or something.

So we sat down, talked, someone played with the latch,
and there was this fool playing with a match –

and someone tried to stop him, many did, too late.
Long wait. Then someone said, *Well, let's go in?*

SENT

At Proprietary Perfumes they know as much as possible:
In their mind's nose a woman's lavishing herself
With plangent-smelling goodies, sending herself
Glaucous: the man's incidental.

It's cheering her up. (Sales in fragrance products
Actually boom in recessions.) After the ritual cleansing
A touch of perfume's an improving odour, exciting
The female with castorum, musk, civet and other glands.

Dabbing herself she feels pampered, erotically done-to,
Voluptuously touched-up and *it*... She already feels
Someone's after her. She's even attracting herself.

Though it's a strong garter of class, a sash of taste,
An aromatic affidavit of money, and a rumour of age-group
And experience, any man's perfume given to a woman's
A sexual innuendo, surely – like a woman's whisper to herself.

NEW SOURCES OF SEX

Sometimes who dreams of what it'll be like in heaven? – No fission,
But fusion of bodies, a sun, the combustion of angels
In brilliant sex: inexhaustible supply: five hundred times
The burning of all the world's fossil fuel in the graze of a hand?

I love you. And in spite of that, because of it, I'd like to
Colonise you – greed would, and greed perhaps, this same inherited
Greed in us both'd like to make new markets, penetrate you, exploit your
Raw materials, enlist the sensitive, open the interior, kill the Indians.

Solar energy, wind potency, pushing of the tides, deuterium igniting... but
I know we're all ruined. As long as we dream of heaven it doesn't exist.

When all the petrol's burnt and all our children dead,
Faces with beautiful genes'll walk the prairies of light; yes –

But now there's your body, and it still needs discovery: thank God,
Beyond your unmanageable hills the unimaginable still looks out
And doesn't look out. Out of those alarmed, indoctrinated eyes
Lust like my own is staring back, unteachably, wavering.

Discovery uncovers you: your unique musk, length of leg, brown
Discs of eyes, shifting persona, can be rifled, but you're a safe with no
Back. The closer I burgle you the more your contents vanish.
                                                                I'm a
Physicist in an atom, an aroma from nowhere, disappearing and
                                                       opening out.

A PRESENT IN THE PARK

Why keep guns out of sight of my son...
For God or the Devil or Chance came in
And crossed the park disguised as a man
And told the *au pair* he'd found this one –
A handsome curlicued six-shooter gun
With a cowboy's nineteenth-century handle on
And a stylish death-and-life for my son.

I dream of sometime going again
To the park where Fate solicited my son
And proffer a tray with penises in –
Some Lovecraft candles for other men's sons.
Arrested, of course, I'd spell to the screen
The sexual point my gesture had been:
Only the tools of death are obscene.

But I've started buying my little boy guns
To come to terms with other men's sons.
Let hitting and killing be done in fun.
The growns know how to hit and when.
Which peace my son'll kill for then
And how, if at all, it's his to choose. But a sten
Of the mind'll be needed again.

The ocean's an endlessly altering school:
It runs in the wise and it runs in the fool.

A CHILD OF THE SUN

When they crucified him to the lawn with the croquet hoops, it wasn't
Because he'd been staying up late studying Greek, to see himself
Shine at the early-morning seminar.

When he was hoping for a grant he didn't even know
Dole queues were stretching out impatiently waiting for
Champagne, with the rock bands blaring, and debutantes,
Enviously eyeing each others' flawless creations,
Clinging to young men clawing uncomfortably at white ties
And murmuring their feet were killing them.

                                              No one said,
You're here to enjoy yourself and be brilliant. He'd never met
A Master of Balliol or an Arctic Explorer. No one
He knew ran a million-and-a-half-pound-a-year
Export Company before they were twenty and so
Had an interest in Keep Britain in Europe.

                                              He didn't
Really blame this on the social system.
He somehow thought it was because he'd made some huge
Pre-natal cosmic mistake.

PERSEUS AND ANDROMEDA

The girl's quite free and naked and only seems to be chained:
She's in fact completely available and wondering what
The fuss is all about. The dragon looks like a Victorian bicycle
And is in fact a gimcrack mechanism in the man's own mind.
Yet it's real enough: the teeth could needle through
To the bone and perhaps will. The bestial killing fury in the eyes
Has come from an unimagined anguish in the man's own spine.
This is the terror that love is wound round.

He's the man with the sword. He pushes its neck aside,
But his eyes are meditative, not on its head or eyes,
But on some hallucination of a Satanic God in his own insides.
Blue is the armour, icy blue, cold leaves, quite dead.
If he looked on a maidenhead, with the hair around,
the snakes would turn him to stone. Split by that split
he turns her face on the human world to destroy it.
His power is that split mirrored in the fearful shield.

THE SIZE OF THE SEA

The size of the sea can make you sick with passion:
        There's so much of it not used up –
Much more than anyone can fit into a marriage
        However much they love their husbands,
        Unless they're spiritual athletes.

People say the illusions you experience in love are
        Illusions. The visions you have of temples on the astral,
The seashores where you run in slow motion
        With your beloved, her hair rising and falling
        Like a horse in a slow film,

The erotic pillared porticoes opening on a lakeshore
        And purple water, where you find her lying
Naked, one knee raised and lean over her, breathing,
        A blue shadow. The belief that it'll
        Begin again another morning

After you're both dead, the wish to die,
        To find those shores of orgasm, to see
The crystal eyes of the beloved as God imagined them,
        To touch her celestial body and turn
        Literal flame,

To walk floating the plains of beautiful light
        And the jewelled cities, drinking
Unknown wine in heavenly cafés. There are some who say
        Reality's only a fish-and-chip lunch, with the
        Bills unpaid, and the children obstreperous,

Yet you've only to smell the sea to smell that illusion's
        Reality, those acres of sperm smell
Are unusable up. The floating suffering it gives you
           As you watch it creaming and creaming in
           Will make you leap in again and again

For lives you haven't lived and are going to live.

HAMLET

> *Naturally, the common people don't want war, but after all it is the leaders of the country who determine the policy, and it is always a simple matter to drag the people along. Voice or no voice, the people can always be brought to the bidding of the leaders. This is easy. All you have to do is tell them they are being attacked and denounce the pacifists for lack of patriotism and for exposing the country to danger. It works the same in every country.*
>   Hermann Goering, 1946

Every generation has a ghost: suddenly
History's here, stinking of corpse-flesh,
        Calling you son,
Claiming your name and arm.

Your uncles were killers,
And it's your job
        To set it
        Right, O cursed spite, etcetera.

And every generation feels
The same. What we really want to do
        Is write, find
        Verbal solutions for the universe

Or just hang about with our friends
Making the grown-ups feel uncomfortable.
        There's something
        Rotten in the state all right,

But you are the state. And the state
Will look at your rottenness

And wonder
Should they look you up?

It's misery just thinking.
Easier to go abroad, wherever
        They send you:
    England, Vietnam, or Aden.

You may get killed or kill. You go.
Or if not, there's sleep, suicide, or
        The alternative world
    Of dreaming: Hamlet.

He at least did do the bloody deed
With his last breath, though why then
        Hand it all over
    To that idiot soldier Fortinbras?

Does every generation have to have
That ghost, and did he know it? Anyway,
        Here we are
    Still in Denmark, ogled by Claudius,

With a new Polonius, still muttering
O cursed spite, etcetera, and shall we do
        The given deed
    Before we die, and put it right?

A HISTORY OF ENGLISH MUSIC FROM BYRD TO CAGE

Every year now if I don't watch out
I'll catch him saying the same things.
Here he is with the same girl
And another face. It ends the same:
They only want to be pregnant.
We should get into them in the morning
With a hard fuck and then talk about it
In the evening with our friends.

*It's as if I'm living someone else's life.
I don't like my work. I only do it
To keep her house going. She doesn't
Get up till nine o'clock.
I've made my own breakfast. At
Nine o'clock in the evening
She's going to bed again. She
Doesn't read or do anything*

*When my dad died my blood pressure
went up from that of a man of thirty-five
to that of a man of sixty.
It just shot up like that.
My doctor implies I should leave her:
How can I expect to get rid of these
Headaches and this bad leg?
The worst is I don't care a twat.*

And I? If I'm not careful I'll tell him
The same things: *You're just waiting
For the same fuck.* How can I tell him
*You're writing the same book, with no pace,
Over and over again?* What frightens me
Is that others will see in me
As I in him the same recorded performance
Ground all over my flat surface.

He's bought himself a watch that
Only registers time, lighting up red,
When he presses a button.
It costs him two pounds a year.
It'd be worth a few pounds
To buy another that gave us
A minute of forgetfulness
Each time we pressed the button.

SERVICES

1. At the Maltings, 19 December 1976

So we're smarted up again, with our middle-class
Bald heads and silver hair-dos, here to share
Beauty and order, the opposite of sloppiness.
Does one know that person there? Where?
No, it's oneself, a suit, some genes we've never met before.

Onto the platform bounce four collectively famous, greying
Podgy and balding men who'll put together something
Marvellous and perfectly useless, making us into men
With the dedication we give to making money.
We're asked for silence, and we give a minute.

New clothes hide old cells and swish as they rise.
And the minute doesn't pass: it is. It is really moving.
He is or isn't here – and then we sit.
And the Haydn begins. A professional opens the score.
Music for an aristocrat – it's the taste of an Emperor –

With its logos that doesn't exist except in the air,
Slim value that fat men make as long as we're here.
And the expensive time's being curlicued, at three pounds an hour,
And almost at times stopped still – to start up with regret
That it's passing. We remember our records and forget.

It's the dead who make time stop. No longer alive,
He's plaintively counterpointing, two at a time, like love.
The music's almost a whimper – not for an aristocrat.
It's more like the marsh the wind goes over
Than the disciplined ways we work at, save in and waste at.

And who will there be to welcome us into heaven?
Whom have we loved enough? It's harder and harder
To believe in the stuff we've often betrayed,
Leaving our lovers behind. Love died,
Of despicableness, failed, a poor suicide,

And the only thing we loved. Beyond, those other old men
Hobble to the post for their pensions, or back to the meths
And the questions: *How long can these days go on?*

Can this order we've adored survive our bodily death?
It ends in the dark and we drive in convoy to our lighted homes.

2. Aldeburgh Beach

It's as if the half-drowned coypu they shot on the beach
And showed me his enormous teeth
Were now zipping along the shoreline, ten-size his size,
Spiralling and tunnelling like a torpedo.

Images go bounding where an eye's cutting the spirals,
As something's cutting the spirals in my eye and brain that I've
Blown up and can't do without.
I can see them on a surgeon's table, laid out like a diagram.

But who's this, sitting here groundless in the moonlight,
Aware of a vapour sitting here along and watching
The venuslight and moonlight spiralling through the window
On a unique change of the changeless sea

And remembering his birth that was spiralled on by venuslight
And moonlight? Behind another window
Someone's knowing himself. He's still not here.
The runner's only a shadow against the sea.

3. February

The waves come spiralling in athwart, peeling off
In quiffs and crumbles, khaki and white, spreading
Tablecloths flat and whisking them back, hitting
The coming-in wave. One detonates.
The shushing's an orgasmic hangsah, out of its own
Power, slung by the moon's lob, hair
On a back-and-forth head. The pushing, rumbling
And lulling's fizzing with the pushing of
Earlier and earlier waves.
                    If ever I die, my mother said,
it'll be in February, and she did, and it was.

ELEGY FOR JOHN RIDGEWELL

Drowned in the Humber, March 1968

   1.

Two men are washing a boat; shadows have wiped out their faces;
There's a boy, dallying, learning the business of living. The summer's
Extra, more than strictly necessary – the universe squandering
Its behaviour. You look at it for a second, glow, and go from it,
To get on with the job, talk about your job and think about your job.

Our cars are gassing along country lanes; we're chattering about
Prices, houses, the prices of houses, as the trees go about
Flipping the wind, photosynthesising sunlight, dredging up fluids,
Eliminating gases, proliferating cells, up and out,
Unaware of our itness in windows of whizzing cars.

It's not here, that fountain that no one's ever seen, breaking,
Spurting and coursing, that rose in the desert sweetening.
You can't forget money, but look in that windscreen: those two men
Washing that boat, glistening like lips, that boy's denizen
Eyes, scored by his death: unemployed and posed as the stars.

   2.

Millions of people have smelt the sea,
Felt lonely and then not felt lonely.
Angry seagulls have a famished eye,
Rising on the cliffwinds, shouting and crying
And fishing for the great drop to the sea
That was a mother, is and isn't,
Who sharpens the ego, then solves its
Crystal of salt: and you liquefy,
Go seagull, seagull cry.

And millions have thrilled to the suck
And guzzle of the shingle, that cobble excretion,
Pacified out of season by ingestion
Digestion egestion.
The waves can kill and tranquillise, but what
Puts to you to sleep is that usual metre and suck:
Your stones converting, nuzzling and consorting

In all this ebbing, soothed and schooled
By that rubbing, that sad mothering.

Millions become the millions
As the sea engrosses them. The sea is
Sparkling eyes in the freckling sun:
Watchers: but it's a transit, no exit,
Into new behaviour with no freckles in it:
Unimaginable as the world to a foetus.
The body you believe in the mirror
The sea makes you forget. It isn't prayer
But it's a kind of potentiality for prayer.

3.

Bunhill Fields is a quiet haven amid the roar of London... Its border flowers flame – reminding us that this is not only the Graveyard but also the Garden of the Imagination. Familiar shades still haunt it – two in particular, a burdened Pilgrim and a marooned adventurer clothed in goatskins: and there all day strikes silently on a ghostly anvil the hammer of Los the Eternal Blacksmith.
Thomas Wright, *The Life of William Blake*, 1929

Through the sunny windows
There are yellow doors,

A scaffolding of gold-edged bodies
And light and shade brandishing hammers.

It's a landscape you could walk through, like
Walking through the glass without a break.

And here: student abstractions, paper masks
Of persons, pale on a mahogany desk.

How can I measure them – the substance of lives
Or workmen sunlighting into weightless shoes?

The difference between the sky and the house:
The house so subtle, the sky so solid: ours.

Oh, through those atoms, how to feel the dead movers,
The workmen studiously wielding silent hammers?

4.

These houses keep shaking as the lumbering voices go by. They give
The walls a shaking but they're not really for you or me.
Their owners are elsewhere in other cities while we're trying to sleep.
Even awake beings with huge metal hands are craning by.

In the air on huge bows there's news of various wars we can't hear
For the great voices wheeling by. There are times you're pushing
Clean brown furrows across slopes and slopes, there's bread
In the wind, trousers corded at the knees, a blowing white shirt

And a red kerchief splashed round your neck. This is at night
And the great lights go across the ceiling. On night watch
Sea lorries are crashing the tracks of fishes. Underneath
Huge whales are opening their eyes out of sleep and nosing the currents.

You can tell where an animal is. We've been out of the sea a while.
As you watch the clouds come out of the sea they're going back in,
As if posting themselves. It won't be like that. The message
You're going to deliver isn't the one you came here with.

5.
A sandstone girl looking in a mirror – an Indian statuette, 11th century.

She's not looking at
What we're looking at.

We're looking at her bottom
And the accoutrements
That hide nothing.

Four cords at the fingerable
Delicious bump of the spine,
As her inviting buttocks begin,

Then a vertical cord slips down
The cleavage to three
Cords round her thighs

Framing the folds that
Flesh is folding inwards,
Pointing to secrets: forget.

The other thing's the great
Hole of her earring.
Then there's something like

A python dangling down
The whole of her side.
But what is it she's hiding

In her great unisex
Sage's face? – suddenly faced
By a hole behind her face?

    6.

He'd got nothing
And ten years he studied architecture
And bought and rebuilt a boat
And rented and altered a flat

He paid his own way through college
And started a new love affair
He rented and altered a flat
And there was still nothing

There was a boat for someone else
A flat unfinished
An architecture unbuilt
A girl unmarried

The moon phasing
The sun coming up
The river opening
Strangers coming

And big projects for architecture
And he borrowed a boat he never came back in.

7.

In his beard and black jacket
Cold and a little hunched
With his six-foot-seven stoop
Like a secular friar

Cold and a little hunched
After long penance
Waiting for his death
Like a longboned friar

I'm glad I looked at him carefully
Concentrated for death
That was twenty-four hours away
Though I didn't know

I'll remember him admiring the sea
Though we didn't know he was going
It was as if the sea were his
He was round-eyed, ensured

Quelled into happiness
Stating affinity of water
In the sea that's always there
Here, round us, ensuring

Affinity of water
Feeling and being water
In the sea that's always there
Though he's gone now, relaxing

In the shovings of the Humber
Tidally unmasking
The face that's gone now
Unwinding his eyes

In the heavy Humber
Smashed in the river's muscles
Taking the face from the darkness
That's always conscious

Before we're drenched
And before we're dried
In a six-foot-seven stoop
And a beard and black jacket.

WATER INTO WINE

Drawing rooms – are they ever really rooms?

There's Mr. Christy, coming onto the lawn,
Just as you're hearing the news you've longed for –
And he's feeding the birds.

                      Or you're praying,
Driving, *Why am I suffering namelessly,*
Like this? and the Word's a van passing:
Thorn Lighting. Then another: *Patience Rose.*

Mr. B, the Estate Agent, used to be
A soldier and survived. He's walking down a road
That stretches far past the office and the golf course,
Losing and winning games.

                    All this is really about Anna,
Who set herself on fire in a Volkswagen.
Had there to be one Anna, like one Schoenberg,
And was no one else willing to be she?

How far is it out of doubt that the Word
Is discovering something of His spelling in her?
And do we therefore rejoice as Christians

Or in the silence
Where we're afraid or ecstatic
Do our souls choke on the spelling of rejoicing?

                              Six weeks
She took to die, like a burnt
Sausage, with teeth and beautiful eyes.
Ruined meat draped from the windows.

Be gentle with him, she said about her husband,
As if she'd been gentle, or things were simple.
And I felt like a foetus, watching
A faint pink light, or hearing flesh-muffled music.

WELL, SO THAT IS THAT

> *...Now we must dismantle the tree,*
> *Putting the decorations back into the cardboard boxes –*
> *Some have got broken – and carrying them up to the attic.*
> W. H. Auden, For the Time Being

1.

Christmas is gone. So it's time to pick the tree of its stars,
Pull off the candlesticks, drop the planets, conceal the fairies
In the bone box with seven ways in.

Then it's Christmas again: the stars glow out of the bone,
The candles flow like a Lady Chapel, the fairies are
Flipping into the flowers and flapping out like petals.

I can stop smelling my brain.
My nose is all the perfumes.

2.

The moon's phasing behind my eyes
As if the slow movement of this quartet,
The sea's in my ears, knocking at my cells,
Swishing the generators of imagery,

All that blue space I invented is passing through me
Punctuated with stars and I've
Pricked out my body with primroses and bluebells
And dug into myself with coal mines,

Covered myself with an eczema of tractors,
Swung over myself with ogreous cranes,

Swilled myself with oceans of salt,
Dried myself with deserts and filled myself

With camels and whales that I'm exterminating in ships
That are myself cutting through the ice of myself.
Shall I be dismantled some day, stop
Believing in it and expand into *I am*.

    3.

Sometimes watching you, no one it seems is there –
No one that speaks – or faces watch out
From their own rooms and their own curtains.

And sometimes, watching you, I see faces
I'd rather not see, ogling me
With your eyes.

The furniture shifts. Someone seems to need me
For purposes she doesn't understand
And someone else will inherit.

    4.

And in the morning we'll awake again
And you'll be waking beside me.
I'll feel your hair on my pillow

Daybreak will break from you
As we come together
From the strange lovers of sleep

And I'll make you again
As I remember who you are
And you'll make me

We'll take up our novel where we left it,
Swim in the green lake, catch
The same fish, touch

The new flesh, feel the forest
In the flesh, the lakewater in the skin
And quarrel again bitterly

And leave each other cruelly
And go to sleep forgetfully,
And in the morning...

    5.
You must go on, I can't go on, I'll go on.
                      Samuel Beckett, *The Unnameable*

The point thinks *I can't go on* as it goes on,
Straightening into a line.

The line claims *I can't go on* as it edges sideways
And flattens into a plane.

The plane says *I can't go on* as it edges sideways
And swells into a cube,

When it groans, goes no direction at last
And turns time, till

Time sighs *I can't go on*, smiles
And dies in eternity.

IMITATIONS OF HORACE

    1. Palms Upwards
    Horace, *Odes*, III xxiii

As the moon emerges from the clouds' legs
Spread your hands palm upwards,
Kill a juicy pig, light some incense,
Offer the gods some fruit.

That's how the vine grows heavy:
No wind disturbs it, no blight
Hits your crops, no murrain strikes
Your new flock in apple time.

Big sacrifices are fattening somewhere
On high mountain tops for priests
With bloody knives. But no need:
A little rosemary, some myrtle flowers will do.

If your hands are right they don't require
Excessive presents. The gods will love you
If you offer a little porridge, or throw
Some salt on the fire.

2. NOT YET

Horace, Odes, II v

She's only a heifer still. You can't bend her
To the plough yet or get her working with you
On those shared duties in bed, or supporting
    The weight of a hot bull.

Her mind's still running on green meadows,
She wants to cool off in the waters
Or frisk about with the other heifers
    Under the willow trees.

Don't eat raw grapes. Just wait a bit.
Autumn's coming, with some new colours,
Including a ripe purple for this bunch.
    It's you that'll be eaten.

Time's ferocious. Remember, every year you lose
She gets one. Before you know it
She'll be chasing you shamelessly.
    You'll enjoy Lalage more

Than the unapproachable Prue, or Felicity
Of the pure skin and shoulders like unclouded moon

In the midnight sea, or even
    Jamie the gorgeous

Lad your sophisticated guests couldn't spot
Sitting ambiguously among a crowd of girls
With his long hair flowing down
    And his girl-boy face.

3. Concentrate on Loving

Horace, Odes, I xxii
for Malcolm Quantrill

It's all in the mind, Malcolm,
And our moral stance. We don't need
Sten guns, mortars, hand grenades or hit men,
    Even if we're

Toiling through the Mojave or Saudi Arabia,
Burning a draft card, asylumed in Siberia,
On safari in Idi Amin's Uganda or
    New York at night.

For instance, absolutely unsuspecting,
Trying to get a poem right, about Mary, I went
Completely off track in the forest,
    Miles from the farm,

With not so much as a stick – and what do I meet?
A mad dog, no less, dripping with rabies,
Dribbling red tongue, spiked teeth, laser eyes,
    The size of a

Billy goat. I just stared – and it ran. True.
I'd trust the ice packs and the polar bears,
Navigate Nigeria in the prickly downpours
    Or the hot gritty winds,

Hump my pack at high noon in the Sahara
With one bottle and no mess tin:
All I'd need is a thought of Mary, her
    Sweet laughter and lovely talk.

AUDEN AT HIS VILLA ON ISCHIA

The poet's still closeted with his talent,
even in the open air. Harassed, wry,
would be-relaxed, martini in hand, he'd
like to give it a holiday.

He won't be happy till its screaming stops,
and that won't happen till he's drunk and smoked
him and his talent to a good death.
His face is the map of its wigglings:

journeys of the soul on an old stone
it's his job to decipher. Meanwhile he keeps
reminding himself to keep on time,
run his accounts straight, and his talent lets him –

provided he gives it breakfast very early
and devotes a day to it. Even then it needs coddling:
the crosswords, the mysteries, the anagrams
that help the thing to overcome its tantrums.

The talent's perfectly fair: all it wants
is total attention. Get that, and it can be patient.
If it screws his muscles, never lets up,
it does offer bliss when he's been good to it:

an ecstasy – what ordinary mortals
ordinarily feel at weekends, out
fishing, or with nothing
particularly to worry about.

MINOR VICTORIANS

1. Nude Study

Nude Study, 1856. Photograph by Watson

Go on, love, put your bum this way, Watson opined,
We'll imagine your tits in the mirror. So you peep
At the glass as he told you – and it too seems peeping:
A chintz transvestite, holding a bowl of reverent flowers

Near your tweeny, erecting its candlesticks and carved
Oval face – though you're feeling the dicky bird behind.

Soft, soft you are, one of the good Queen's poor
Little boys taught sex in the streets: in doorways,
Up against walls, teasing, worrying – or did *you*
Teach them? Was it always dirty, or did something more
Ever enter? Could you love, when it was asked for?

That dressing table – they're still around; and so is
Your DNA in a lot of young students' faces:
The straggly hair, the nice eyes with no flies,
The found drowned look, igniting to a smile,
Going to bed because they're cold or just lonely.

Even your back's somehow modern: swerve of spine,
Trendless shoulder blades – strong, as your arms
No longer are: too fleshy for Ruskin then
Or camera gloss now, against a dingy wall.
Your skin expects so little. Did no one look at it
Lovingly when you were a kid? Your charms –

Sadder the lower we look: you're disenchanted
Under the waist. Your diminuendo thighs, your
Calfless, unexercised legs, not walked much, smutted
With wrinkly shadows – they make you half my
Victorian grandmother on a girl of twenty!

2. A Tramp

Photograph by Paul Martin, 1886

Ezra Pound's hat, some Whitman, some Tolstoy,
A rag of a coat, and Augustus John, his corduroys.
You're the real bohemian the artist's cords destroy.

It's a big grizzly half-Marx beard you are,
Dad, and long combed white hair,
Backed by hedges, wildflowers, and invisible birds;

Dispossessed but unsmirched by words,
Bank or factory whistle, resting your face
On a good fist and looking at – not the rat race.

What is it? An old age pension? A tip
For the photo? Your view of the photographer? A nip
Of something warming? Your next of kin?

Which ditch they'll find you dead in?
Or perhaps you're thinking of a whore?
It isn't breakfast. You'll get it at the next back door.

No: we can't connect; and he's never met
Malthus, Ricardo, Mill, Marshall, Cobbett,
Or even the poet Davies. Edward Thomas is eight. This man begs

And all the birds of Oxfordshire and Gloucestershire are laying eggs.

3. Trippers Caught by a Wave

Photograph by Paul Martin, 1892

Photographed ladies, black as bats,
Tiptoe in foam, like water-shy cats, curtained in billowy clothes;
A bowlered old waiter of a boy has trousers rolled to the knee;
        Three friskier girl-tots in risky fruitbowl hats,
           Are hiking their skirts: waves saved on pasteboard,
      Combing to crumble in industrial churchyards.

Smelling and feeling the wet salt choppings,
But not plunging in; drinking oysters instead, those minuscule oceans
Their bodies recall under clothes, and their own seasmell commotions:
        Not mill-floors now but boarding houses and winkle shops.
         What fishy improbable detail before the wave and after –
In those swelling clothes and the shocked water.

RETREAT TO THE SHEETS

My cat approves of these long slow afternoons –
A day in bed, a headache, grey outside.
These days in bed are always opportune.

Despair's close by – and who can be immune?
You need new time, to brew unoccupied,
Which makes my cat enjoy these afternoons.

Unless I can dream, I'm reckoned in a room,
But illness opens out new vestibules inside:
These dreaming days in bed are opportune.

Last night the sky was flaming with red festoons –
Which happens when a wire and rain collide.
My cat prefers these long slow afternoons.

A counterpane become a felt lagoon –
Listening to those silk pacific tides
Whose shushing makes these days so opportune.

You hit hot sand – and leisure to commune:
You're sick and draw the time your work denies.
And cats approve of these long slow afternoons.

Proximity – it brings these little healing swoons
As telepathically our muscles all subside.
Your eyelids droop on days so opportune.

Frail wings can only grow in still cocoons.
It all ends here. Why am I seldom satisfied –
Like him – with these long slow afternoons?
Such days in bed are, oh, so opportune.

LUCIDITY

In this dream I'd cleared the edge of a cliff – carwheels
Spinning in air, thousands up in the afternoon,
And death sparkling below in the creamy Alpine snow.
Bluebacked snowpeaks carolled in mountain
High above the douce green spruce we'd die in.

Life was over – and for a minute we'd know it. I turned
And looked at her. We'd neither sit by a deathbed –
Which one first? I kissed her. *It's over! Our life!* I said.
And then I was steering again, hang-gliding, swerving
Like a sleigh into a bosom of soft spruce snowblossom.

Down we go through the trees, scrunching softly,
With no sound through the branches, sink into
Soft earth, and so to sleep again. We've never woken since.
Crises are like that: you're alive for a while, and then
The lucid afternoon fades and you hunch through snow into sleep.

PERSEPHONE AGAIN

Persephone is perhaps the soul,
Or spring, or the recurrence of death in life.
A foetus dies and is born as a boy or girl.
A boy or a girl die and become a grown-up you
Or I, and they marry and become someone else.

And soon the girl my soul is turns
Lover of Hades, refuses the role
Of mere wife – or if she does revolts,
Re-enters myself as a daughter of Ceres,
Lives a new summer, and soon
Becomes a lover of Hades again.

But death is death. If I die an Egyptian girl
Three thousand years ago, seen naked
On an old fresco, kneeling with a crucible
Before a seated sphinx, or am perhaps
Dug up in old bandages in a pretty case,

My death is keen as the transition
Of a foetus. I may become a blue-chinned
Pipe-smoking accountant checking the bills
In an insolvent builder's receivership
But my sudden heart attack is death.

Something dies in me and the human race.
If Persephone's the rhythm of death,
And death's the rhythm of life, death's
A new birth each time, however often
The end happens, and whatever survives.

CLOCK STOP

She stood at the bus stop, and
The church clock stopped.

It stopped on the hour of eight
In the dusk of evening, and

Two old people limped up to the stop
And waited. The clock went on.

The bus came and the elderly couple
Climbed on. The clock stopped.

Twenty past eight. Yawning,
With her mother comes a little girl.

The clock starts, the bus comes,
And they all climb on.

Waking again in her home
She checks the clock. It's stopped.

It stops all evening. It's twelve o'clock
When she tells her doctor.

The moving consulting-room clock
Stops, starts again, and moves steadily.

Later, she meets a man and the clock
Doesn't move. They stop together.

They're always together now.

FIRE IN THE GARDEN
(1984)

Unto God the Lord belong the issues of death, that is, the disposition and manner of our death: what kind of issue and transmigration wee shall have out of this world, whether prepared or sudden, whether violent or natural, whether in our perfect senses or shaken and disordered by sickness, there is no condemnation to bee argued out of that, no Judgement to bee made upon that, for howsoever they dye, precious in his sight is the death of his saints, and with him are issues of death, the wayes of our departing out of this life are in his hands. And so in this sense of the words, this *exitus mortis*, the issue of death, is *liberatio in morte*, A deliverance in death; Not that God will deliver us from dying, but that hee will have a care of us in the houre of death, of what kinde soever our passage be.

John Donne, *Death's Duell*

ST. MARTIN-IN-THE-FIELDS

City churches aren't always easy
to pray in: there may be someone buffing up brasses
pianissimo, insistently, with cheesy
breath and a polish of rage behind their glasses,
sending almost tangible meditations
to distract our straggly congregations.

Or visitors delicately boggle at the faithful patients,
Guide Book in hand, not expecting religion
in architecture like this. Outside, the pigeons
drop little pats of white on assembled nations;
inside we pray, uneasily wondering:
whoever it is up there, is he listening?

Yet here bums in a blue-chinned Greek-looking worshipper,
pockets stuffed with evening newspapers, coat
flapping, and grabs his God by the throat:
he prays precipitately, wagging his head – a pew-gripper
pointing out to an old employer – what?
Is it horses? A tip flopped? A reproach or not?

And suddenly I'm in it: his grace has snatched
me out: over the altar the angels' faces
break the wood: they're reaching down with fact,
listening, embracing, swooping, and I'm hatched:
a broad white shell of completeness
has widened and cracked:
I'm open to sweetness.

A WAY OF LIFE

> *Is it the ghost of Miles Wetheril, the infamous Vicarage murderer, that stalks the corridors of the Black Swan Hotel?*
> *Todmorden News and Advertiser*

These rainy winter evenings make you race
Back to the first steel of rain on your skin
Even in Greenwich Park, with economic sin
Pocking the city below. Drenching the brick, slewed
Along the iron railings, down, across the road,
And up to Chesterfield's house, it cuts and cools
Your skin like something interested in your face.

The paths wind like your life now, pluvious
Corners with only the expected round them, and no
Dare except perhaps a mugging – a quick blow
Like ice in the spine at a quick footstep –
Which is only the darkling jogger. No; except
The threat the gate might be shut, there's no threat;
And a shut gate's more like a hope, a plus,

Than extinction. A dog strains at its crap
And peers back vulnerably but trustingly
Over its shoulder as you exit the gate. I'll be
Fifty-eight today, a figure suggesting
Eighty-five: a not-so-distant interesting
Fellow that's still fermenting, brewed in
The demijohns I designed from the original chap.

February seventh – the month my mother and I
Chose for our birth in, and the month my mother
Died in, as she predicted. Still, it's rather
Kinder than many others. The English winter's
Certainly the weather for reverie – a hinter
At insight among the skeletal streets. With no
Cold or rain who'd ever think or cry

Or bear death? The house we lived and live in is,
I read in the local rag, haunted. Footsteps shin
Or plod along upstairs when no one's in.
Glasses explode. One Sunday lunch
A whole tray of twenty went smash at once.
Beermugs slide along to the end of the bar
When there's no one near, suddenly go whizz

Or keel and tip their contents on the floor
Like men. Cellar barrels have their taps turned off
By invisible fingers. In the empty loft – a cough.
Heavily sprung fire doors open and shut
Though immovably draught-proof and expertly cut.
A cur sniffs and stares, hair on its neck
Hackling at a quiet ceiling or empty door.

It leaves me wondering: is it myself bewildering
The house, or my mother, or my father, deep in the quiz
Of endings – back where it ended: happiness, that is.
New places made new faces: we went mad,
Each in our pertinent ways. How much time, dad,
It's taken – to shake off the spooks that tracked from that house,
Molesting my childhood and still perhaps my children's.

DOWN THE HILL

A curtain of dusty sunlight in the street.
I walk through it and down the hill
From Exchange Station to the Kardomah caff.
Sheila Banks still
In my heart inhales the steam: somewhat –
With her cup clasped – like a squirrel with a nut.

She looks at me across the rim and smiles,
Yielding and secret, failed nun,
Ex-schizophrenic, cured consumptive,
who held my hand for fun
One afternoon at the pictures, and gave a bang
To my surprised heart, since I was young.

She tried to make me a Catholic, taking advantage
Of what she'd done. Suffering was exquisite,
Sent as a grace, she said, so felt no guilt
For giving me so much of it;
And fell in love with my friend and followed him
Meek-eyed, eager to gratify every whim.

He didn't care for her and thought her rather
Daft, could mimic her quite well,
Enjoyed his victory over me,
Was flattered by our little triple hell.
Pain was a shame to share, for he was vexed
By only loving his own sex.

We were a little crocodile from Chekhov: he
Impassioned for a blond unaware
Medical student about to be married,
I in love with her,
And she with him. I don't know where
They are now – and know too well to care.

Here's all the delivery of that blaze
Without the flame: a little pain
New suffering has raised,
Exquisitely sought out again.
Will they too go on living if we meet
Behind the curtain of dusty sunlight in the street?

IN THE VALE

Brooding finically on nine
Daffodils, shoulders slightly hunched,
Hands in pockets – he scrunches
Over to the aconites, questions on his mind.

Out of the shed he hauls the huge
Hosepipe, with its frigging attachment –
And he vanishes – yet another implement –
And the garden's perfecting: the perfect subterfuge.

As perfect, anyway, as nature ever is –
Less obviously now an enemy of our nervous race,
Sophisticated in this perfectible place:
A dekinked product of our helixed enterprise.

Does anyone ever see the place but me?
And I only look when something flitters by –
A quick flop of a jay, a lolloping clockwork magpie –
But of course it's usually he who makes me see.

And every day his garden's new:
He never steps into the same one twice:
The four great phases, and sun, rain, ice,
Minute by minute they let a new face through.

And who are they for, these eager energies?
The summer show – it's coming, then autumn the tinter,
And spring again, the imprinter; but plodding through the winter
He's making, not a garden, but who he is.

CHANGE OF ADDRESS

Some people have a lot of names:
Shirt, Shirtie, Bert, Bertie.
Lomas can be perturbing; but only
Herbert's embarrassing, deranges the who I am.

Names keep changing, at some cost, though, like houses.
Each is an ambience; you squat in it,
Display it, deploy it, housewarm it.
On parole, inhabit the language's character.

Who can abide the selves you find in the street –
The rich relations of someone who's
Long been found missing – so
Simple and incredulous and unwise

He hasn't found an idiolect in the language?
Every lover, every friend, every colleague
Creates him. It's only at funerals
People find him, calling me Herbert.

The changes of address have gone.
My visiting card's the name my father called me.

AT THE FUNERAL OF LILIAN WILSON

He tilts on the altar step, like someone at risk
On a sill of the Empire State – almost a slew –
But skips without toppling and, stick and whiskers,
Negotiates a place inside a pew.

So who is he then – this improbable Guest
Out of the choir desks, without invitation,
After the Requiem, before we blessed? –
And wobbling the whole of our congregation?

With the others gone, he asks the parson, *Why
That old service?* His quizzical nose read
The two of us, as sad birds do, and he nodded an eye.
Ah... didn't know the lady was all he said.

It's the nose and eyebrow of a friend... His stick
Picked his way through the porch – or I thought it did:
For I didn't see him go – that quick
Of an eye in the closing ceremony's lid.

The oil-rig millionaire, I heard, slipped
Some quids in the visitor's pocket: each secretes
Some alcoholic brother, a sister on the streets,
Or a time when the man himself had once been tipped.

THE GREAT CHURCH, HELSINKI

Every man who has faith in the Lord and lives in charity to the neighbour is a church in particular, the church in general being composed of similar individuals.
                                                                Swedenborg

Man has no body distinct from his soul, for that called body is a portion of soul discerned by the five senses, the chief inlets of soul in this age.
            William Blake, The Marriage of Heaven and Hell

Grazing a purple shadow in the square
The body watches, timid and half-aware,
The mind's inventions – calling them a world.
The brain lights up, funiculi are curled:
Aerial, elegant and immaculately risen,
A white bird on the wind, you pause
While the cathedral wakes and stares: a collision
Of nerves becomes transparent as a bowl.
The structure of a molecule is its soul.
In every world a vision shapes the laws.

Brilliant in its cuts, a diamond mates
The silence of the jeweller and the stone.
Pushed boiling up through pipes of rock it waits
In darkness to be mined and priced and known.
Then bringing glyptic skill imagination
Sharpens every angle and smites
A bounce of molecules into a light.
The echoing brain we walk in overawes
With clammy dragon shadows, gargoyle jaws,
But galaxies shine when the lights go on.

Raised like a cloud of vapour in the radiant
Intolerable ache of startling light,
A pile of heatwaves on its chosen gradient,
The Great Church shimmers, a weightless white.
Like all cathedrals, statues, cities – this too
Looks to have stood here always, veiling and unveiling
The stealaway or vulva where the saints
Absconded, though figured in bronze against trailing
Cloudscapes, gesturing to flying flocks, and their complaints,
With green and vigorous fists against the blue.

Crossed by the purple shadows of your pillars
We sit on your sparkling steps and view the world.
An elegant Czar makes a long-since futile gesture
(With dignity, though, and whiskers rightly curled);
A ragged man is sleeping on the stone.
Meanwhile the shape of Jesus unobserved
Expects on the lucid skyline, attentive, tall,
The occasional startled face to pause and turn;
And round the corner with your place reserved
Waits Peter's burly shadow, key and all.

ELEGY FOR ROBIN LEE

1.

People get very upset
When you take your life. You queue for it,
A warm takeaway Chinese meal, and sit,
Plate on knee, munching quietly,
With music on, so as not to be sick.

Then at the tap, a glass to gulp
The pain-killing pills, and steadily
You settle in bed, with a bottle of whisky –
And an urbane soothing voice,
Civilised on Radio Three.

The ritual includes a note,
Absolving and thanking your friends,
Suddenly scribbling faster
As the sleepiness hits you, knowing at last
You can't last –

The mistaken day is darkening –
Though even now perhaps,
Through your napping,
Something's still ripening –
But too late to tell us now

What it is you've seen –
Perhaps brightening somewhere
At the end of a tunnel of light? –
And write the single word 'angel'
In Hebrew, to tease our night.

Who'll say you weren't right?
Who even knows what we know?
Death's a two-way contract.
Some want that angel hard enough indeed
and have to try and try and try again, in fact,
and will not succeed.

2.

They find you in your bed,
In the dried vomit, the dead
Whisky bottle on the bedspread,
The Third Programme
Starting at seven *ad nauseam*.

You'll not in this stiff mood
Cling or sing,
No more poisoning,
With eight warming whiskies and eighty-odd
White tranquillisers in your blood.

You've given the last word
To a man who never met you: *balance disturbed*.
It's instead of those words
That might have come through
In the dim academic days ahead.

Your life was hard.
If so, you've annulled it.
If the sun was too bright,
You've dulled it.
The pale face in the flushed sun
Is ashes now in a darker one.

NUNHEAD CEMETERY

Unfindable as an elephant's graveyard: an address
Always difficult to recall: wild undone
Acres of estate in the sump of south-east London.
Too jowl-by-cheekbone for more arrivals, it's a mess
For vampires at night, but on brambly sunny days
A buzzing plot of elegiac haze.

Some find the blackberries stewing here delicious:
Heat from gravestones and corpsemeat nitrogen
Fatten up great black clots from juice of citizens.
Tasting one day, I was stopped by inauspicious

Nudging: old thighs and shins spread out like toys,
Turfed out by dogs, or necromancers, or boys.

No doubt cold-eyed killers have been
Laid out here as well. I shouldn't specially want
The fruit of a gangster's guts; and souls who haunt,
Slow to let go of the soil, are often mean.
Miming Oscar or Joyce, a ghost can fake,
Drag you from a séance to a psychomantic wake.

The chapel's horny and spiky; a spirited evil's
Crept into the crockets, and there's a smatch of more
Than malice in its Gothic crouch: a sore
Damned sourness, unhouseled upheaval.
Whoever thought murder a sport (a *recherché* thrill)
Could find a campus here for a quiet kill.

Idiot, I planned to work here: a sunny weekday
Afternoon – a quiet spot, I schemed,
For reverie and writing; but soon it seemed
Someone was watching, or tracking my way.
Easy to cudgel you here – a ripe place for a shambles –
And shove you in someone's grave, under the brambles.

Was there someone following me all about?
Yes: you'd think your brother in this retreat
Wouldn't be quite so careful never to meet!
I left, but when do we ever meet? Peering out
At eyes that since the playground we've loved, or fled,
Who on earth do we know, living or dead?

HOW I LOVE MY SISTER

My sister was never born.
She came out of the horn
Of plenty and back through the horn.

All my life I've been unexpectedly drawn
To my sister, who was never born.
You could say I've missed her.

Even as a tot I slipped my hand
Up her skirt, a search not planned
But urgent for her tender hand.

I also adored her and didn't dare
Touch her dazzling skin or face her stare
That watched me from some little girl's hair.

She was very close to God and is,
And so I'm dumb as I come to her school
And will always behave like a fool.

I think she's my twin,
And she's often led me into sin.
But I've had to let her escape

Back to her city of crape.
Friendship's perhaps the most
I can hope from her blonde ghost

If I want her to be a happy one,
And dark girls lead me on.

THE CHAPEL PERILOUS

As the car eased up
The long avenue past
The ruined chapel and the nuns'
Graveyard to the heat-reflecting
Rectory in the bird-whistling
Silence and the almost transparent lawn, I
Was several witnesses of myself –
Almost a crowd in the solitude.

The crowd's always there to meet me.
The lawn seeded for centuries
And inhabited, and the house
That watches with invisible people
Ready with their ordeals
I'm always almost expecting: the great beach
Glittering in the distance with its distant cream.

THE GRAVEYARD BY THE SEA

after Paul Valéry

The sea's a roof, where sails, like pigeons, roam –
Pulsing through the pines, and between the tombs.
Noon works precisely: sun forms sea from fire –
The sea, for ever beginning again.
What a recompense – after too much brain –
To contemplate the calm those gods inspire.

Such delicate action of refined lights... a fume
Of diamond on diamond of out-of-sight foam.
Such peace, quite self-conceived, or seeming so...
Now that the sun lies tranquil on the sound
(Those absolute inventions of an eternal ground)
Time gains a shine: dreaming is to know.

My stable currency is silence. It's a shrine
To Minerva – a visible reserve, a mine
Of calm. An eye too, haughtily sealing
A water of reverie beneath a blazing veil.
Ah, silence... structure in the soul:
A multi-laminated golden-cambered ceiling.

The Temple of Time – sum it up in a sigh –
This is the height I've climbed to, by and by,
Completely circled by my maritime view.
And, as my last libation to the gods,
This brilliant tranquillity serenely nods
A royal *hauteur* on Time's altitude.

As fruit dissolves in taste and sensuousness,
Turning its passing to deliciousness
Inside a mouth whose bodily form is dying,
I scent my future here as burnt-out coal;
And the sky discloses to the pent-up soul
The seashore's dissolution into sighing.

Dear Heaven – real sky – see my change.
After all the conceit, after all that strange
Inertia – though brimming over with potency –
I open out inside this shining space.
My shadow moves around this peopled place
And teaches me to move as tenuously.

My soul's naked in the solstice blaze.
I'll take your fine judicial rays
And cruel blades, light! I'll put you back
Intact on your primal proper site.
So look at yourself!... But giving light
Implies a counter-shade of funeral black.

Oh, for myself, to be mine alone, within,
Near the quick of the heart, where a poem begins
(Between the void and the free adventure)
I'll listen – for the echo of my grandeur –
In that sombre, bitter, sonorous cistern, and the
Boom within of nothingness, always future!

And that gulf of sea – feasting, tree-devouring, fake
Prisoner of frail leaves, a dazzle on the ache
Of eyes, even lidded down – does it know
This body that'll drag me to its close,
This mind that draws me to these bony rows?
At sea, a spark is conscious of my absence now.

Enclosed, hallowed, a bodiless, bright
Acre of earth sacrificed to light,
This precinct charms me, flashing in the spume,
Compact of gold and stone and sombre yews –
All this marble shimmering on all these shadows.
Faithfully, the sea's resting on my tombs.

Bright watchdog! Chase off idle idols, while
In solitude, and with a shepherd's smile,
I graze for hours my mysterious sheep,
The white flock of these quiet graves.
Keep prudence off, and all those cautious doves –
Futile dreams, the angels that poke and peep.

Here already, the future turns to idleness.
A creaking cricket grinds the edge of dryness.
Everything's burnt, expunged, faded in air –
Ascended to some unimaginable essence...
Life's larger, if you're drunk with a draught of absence,
Bitterness is sweet, the spirit sure.

The hidden dead lie easy in this ground
That warms their bones and dries their tongueless mounds.
Up high, mid-day, motionless in itself,
Is deep in endless noon-absorbed attention...
O perfect head, crowned in round suspension,
This secret process in you – it's myself.

If not I, who can contain your fears?
It's all my doubts, frustrations, penitent tears
That form the flaw that kinks your diamond side...
But in a night weighed down by ponderous marble
A tree-root-dwelling insubstantial people
Are swelling mid-day, slowly magnified.

They've melted off into a deepening absence:
Red clay has drunk their white clay's opulence.
Their gift of life has passed into the flowers.
Where are they now – their well-known turns of speech,
Their personal ways, the unique soul of each?
Grubs are burrowing where they grew their tears.

The little shrieks of girls when they are tickled,
Their teeth, their eyes, the moistening as they prickle,
Their pretty breasts that love to play with flame,
Their blood that floods the lips when they're excited,
Their final favours, shielded with fingers, yet delighted,
They all go underground, back in the game.

Ah, mighty soul – still eager for a dream
Not fabricated from the cheating beams
That wave and sun distil for physical eyes –
How will you sing when my throat turns vapour?
Away with you! Everything goes. I'm paper.
Your holy discontent – it also dies.

Slim immortality, black and gilded,
Consoling hellhag, laurelled and bewildered,
Forging a mother's breast from death and after –
Pretty perjury and pious fraud!
We've come to know them, so they get ignored –
The empty cranium, and the deathless laughter!

Pensive underground fathers, uninhabited heads,
Loaded down with piles of soil from spades,
You *are* the earth that grabs us by the knee.
And the famous worm is biting, irrefutable,
But not on you, asleep beneath the table:
It dines on life – and never lets me be!

The gnaw is Love, or is it rather Hate –
Self-hate? Its sneaky tooth can penetrate
So intimately, any name will do.
It sees, it wants, it dreams, it touches.
My meat's tasty: even in bed Love clutches
My flesh. I only live for it to chew.

Ah, Zeno, Zeno of Elea, cruel Zeno –
Reaching me with your nifty arrow
That hums from the bow, that flies, yet never will!
I'm a child at the sound, and the flinthead kills.
The sun's a paradigm. A tortoise shadow thrills
The soul: Achilles sprints while standing still!

No, no... Get up. We'll live in our own time.
Body! Shake off this Thinker's mime.
My lungs are drinking... A gusty breeze revives,
A whiff of freshness skimming off the sea –
It gives my soul back! – the salt, and potency –
I'll dash to the shore then splash back out alive!

Yes. Swingeing, delirious ocean,
A million tiny icons of the sun
Are dotting your panther chlamys, torn in the onrush
Of your hundred mouths, snapping their own tails,
Giddy with the swig of your blue scales,
In a tumultuousness that's almost like a hush.

The wind is rising... We have to try to live.
The mighty air goes riffling through my book, waves
Ejaculate on the white-flecked rocks.
So fly off then, completely dazzled, pages.
The waves crash in. Smash with your lucky rages
This quiet roof where sails like pigeons pecked.

WITH THE PIKE BEHIND HER

The end of the expedition:
Brown eyes, like a fox's, keep
Unbeatable lookout, not quite
Human now, retreating under light,
Hearing perfectly, but I thought she was asleep.

A hand crabs out from the bedclothes,
And I hold it: slightly moist meat, a crone's
Fingers, blotched red, a forehead grown
Like Shakespeare's, greying at the roots, knobs
Protruding from her collar bones.

I sit quietly and pray: what comes
Is her spry person, in her kitchen, frying,
Smiling in the mountain house above Shaw Wood,
With Stoodley Pike behind her in the twilight,
Making me feel wanted without trying.

She knows I'm here – she asks about my children –
And who's looking after me tonight?
And, *Don't you know anything then?*
So I tell her what I know – a mite
To the tortured body: all that's trite.

How my children often nag each other raw,
An ill-matched affectionate couple, both mules,
And flibbertigibbets; that my mother-in-law's
Married again at nearly seventy – nice deal;
And what we think of their schools.

Time ends, and I bend to kiss
Her damp forehead and, leaving, acquiesce
In death, blowing kisses to brown eyes.
She says, *I've been listening to a lovely story,*
Blowing kisses back, more like a mistress.

And all the time we're talking, outside a window
Some children and a dog or two
Are laughing, barking, with a bouncing ball
In a sunny park, in a bubble of light, all
Hanging like a bathysphere in the dark blue.

ROUND AND ROUND

The Sun's the same Sun
In Green Leaf and Blue Sea.

The Sea's still in motion
Though the Rivers are flowing
And the Vapours going.

The King knows who's King
And behaves like one.

The Child knows without remembering
Who his mother is
And behaves like a Son.

STRASSENBAHNEN

Over the Square swank the ideal creatures:
They don't move – unlike our trams,
Our nosing cars and tearable figures.

Two towers tower like randy rams
And peer, watching with their clocks
The aimed footwork in the traffic jams.

To them we can't seem planned
By man or God or nature: a providential
Random shuffle of pullulating semen lands

One agonising wriggler of potential
Into the digesting ovum's little box.
With something like a sperm's persistence

In and out of the tunnels go the trams
Beneath the sign of Light from Osram:
HELL WIE DER LICHTE TAG.

And all we folk will one day light
On life within a wooden ovum
Under the Mason's ideal humans

Surprised at last by their non-existence.

SAD COWS

Horses have a sense of humour, but these cows
Do not. Their slow gait has the float of hopelessness.
One hoists from the field like an old-age pensioner
Who's called again to the loo and plods slow-motion,
Humping, as if to a gas chamber, leaning
On shoulder-bones towards a place that's lost a meaning.

It's as if they were in mourning for the sorrows
Of all cattle, enduring in the *anima gregis*
Their ancient failure of a purpose of their own,
Their beautiful-eyed uncomprehending indecipherable
Dossier of offspring slaughtered for some mysterious table.

THE GHOST OF A ROSE

He was conceived by the Landscape of the Summer Solstice,
Gestated in the National Film Theatre
And delivered one night, rather late
After something to drink and inner debate.

He'd a year to live. He knew he was dying
In the B Minor Mass and the walk back
Past the Film Theatre, with bells
Against a livid sky in a John Martin Hell.

Death came as the car stopped.
He cut off her stiff upper lip
And she cried at last on his shoulder, and he
Cried without letting her see.

Life after death was three days
And then in agony the second death.
The new man will watch her game
From the touchlines – mixed hockey –

And cheer her on. He'll take an
Interest in her score and escape
To the new landscape,
Exploring his immortality.

THE DEW DROP INN

There are jokes you laugh at
Not because they make you laugh
But because they don't.

There are people like that,
Except that those would if they could,
And these won't.

It's difficult to idealise
Those you know
And this applies
Only more so
To your own torso.

She came in a flood of tears
And a bath chair.
She felt his fingers (like a buccaneer's)
And her despair.
He was the source of all her fears
And wasn't there.

Sometimes perfectly ordinary very nice wives
Will murmur 2 + 1 = 5,
And, as you stare, you have to admit
The equation's less mathematical, has wit,
And even resembles our lives.

But as you drive away
You think with your heart
That often the sum of the parts
Is smaller than the whole, not more, or
2 + one or two more = less than before.

TWO NOTES ON THE LITERARY LIFE

   1.

Loving a girl in every nook,
That's the story of Herrick's book.

Chaste I lived, without a wife –
That's the story of Herrick's life.

   2.

Cavafy sloped
Into Heaven
At a slight angle.

God heard a rumour
but said: *OK –
I've changed
My pneuma:
He can stay.*

There'd been some delay
On His Judgement already,
Scoffers would say.

*A thousand years?
It's a day. I'm infinite.
Don't think, when you think,
I hadn't thought of it.*

In fine, the Lord flashed,
*There's been so much
Judgement passed, I want mine
To be the Last.*

THE BRIDGES THAT MATTER

The bridges that matter to me aren't the silky gleams
Engineered over leagues, the glassy slivers

Of light, or nervous ligaments of mist, deftly
Flexing over rivers,

But the thundering viaduct of blackened millstone grit,
Always dripping above the slaughter-house, and the chippie,
And through it the seedier streets, the boys' club, the park,
The prospect of Burnley and the Hippy.

A bridge is nothing felicitous – no mathematical six-lane flow –
But a louring and whistling, rushed at by trains, a soar and a rise
You undergo to a possibly promised land. I remember
The doggy tenderness in a calf's eyes

As a knife went into its throat: trust and dread
And a sad glazing before the head was spoilt with red.

FAILED ANCESTORS

*Donne deserved hanging
For not keeping of accent.*

Edward Thomas got a pranging
From friendly fire, a

Whizz bang his own side –
Or maybe the Huns – sent.

Hopkins was snarked
By the exams he marked.

They were all nullified
At some tether.

It's not pride
But huddling together

That keeps you identified:
All thought failures –

Put on the shelves –
Not least by themselves.

EXPERT BEYOND EXPERIENCE

Is anything older than a child's face?
Old as mine was, photoed, in its day,
Not deceived into thinking of disgrace
As merely childish: face of an old *habitué*:

Experienced eyes, brown rings,
With a dog's sadness: face of a sick composer
Terminal already in how things
The mind conceives occur to the decomposer

And art merely enhances. No remedy
Except enduring. Can't do his decimals –
Does it mean he hasn't grieved all day
Or felt the rain's incessant lancing parallels

Or all that Dante knew of suffering,
Love and death? Isn't any father's son
Expert beyond experiencing?
Love is incessant once the life's begun.

MOTHER SKIN

That arctic fox my mother used to drape
Around her bosom seemed to snuggle in
Its tail, nipped with a clip beneath its chin.
She'd fluff it up and nestle it round her nape
And over her pearls and cleavage, scented shapes
Like the brylcreamed bowler, father brushed with firm
And cleansing swipes, before she took his arm.
I loved my parents through these smells and drapes.

Furs and hats are soft and hard, furs speak
Of mother skin – any fur will reek
Of powder, graze the cheek, or touch the veil.
Smelly monsters every infant breeds
Make for a hundred hairy grown-up needs,
Though furs have meat stripped out and bite their tail.

I AM WHAT I AM – YHVH

Iago: *I am not what I am*

Wordsworth observing himself
wandering lonely as a cloud

began dramatising himself
wandering lonely as a cloud

and soon was describing himself
wandering lonely as a cloud

and then flashed cloudlike
on that inward eye that is the bliss

of solitude and then was dramatising
that inward I... and then he was... revising...

Later all these I's go out
in the night and I watches them going

and we all go out in the night
and I watches us going.

WHY IS THERE SOMETHING RATHER THAN NOTHING?

He didn't tend to think of himself as an accident.
Yet, another evening, the telephone, a surprise –
A tadpole flick – and another sperm might win:
He might have been a girl with chocolate eyes.

At certain hours he dreamed he'd been invented
Just as he was – or made himself: his turn
Had come before the love began: the place
Was right, he chose the lovers and rode the sperm.

He yearned at times for a timeless feel of self –
Tail-twisting back to the booming Word
Whose frequencies scored the gas and dust,
Riddling logogriphs in the inert Absurd.

And he thought again of a photograph they printed:
Abstracted majesty: a black man in the Chair.
Mechanics stooped around his loins like tailors,
Each with the expert's concentrated stare,

Putting last touches to electrical connections
In the art of death. And it was clear
The man had gone already from the Chair,
Listening to distance, far away from here,

Knowing with surprise how he is loved, not where.

AFTER THE SEMINAR

It was curious: I'd been invited
To the Staff Seminar on a poem
And there in the bar was the bard.

Beery, corpulent, he was being eye-caressed
By two sycophants, proud to be impressed
By the most prominent poet in England,
Pint in hand.
                It was clear
This was a daily rite, to fill
The void he stoutly faced in his verses
With pints and admiration till
His belly swagged.
                In the next intense two hours
We said goodbye to the exploded past
That terrified with hell and read the score.
The dome of air that turns dark blue to white
Was lifted off like a greenhouse and we saw
Endless radiation unstained through an empty glass.

GREECE 1950

    1.

In those years the Aegean was a solution
Of lapis lazuli where
Brindled fish stared
And finned though filtering light like fish in tanks.

You plunged in – and took a nostril-shock at how
Epochs of tiny
Lives can flash and flow
Along you in a blanched rush of flailing shanks.

Tasting thick salt, you know them with your skin –
And pump up breathless,
Head-jerking, chin
First – smacked by some mountain in the blue Peloponnesian ranks.

And the terrain's new again: it's a face or tomb
Lit by a church window –
Or someone made love to
By a woman whose mother's dying in the next room.

    2.

Two people will
Always be sitting
On the island of Spetsai.

Over their shoulders
Hydra turns purple
As the indigo sky
Goes dark.

In his kitchen Stavros
Is frying their
Camel steaks.

If there's a way
To a forgotten life
We must have been seeking it
When we went so far away.

SUNDAY JOINT

> ... there is no conceivable similitude that could make Sunday stand for coitus...
> Michael Riffaterre, *The Semiotics of Poetry*

Sunday's when the week goes to bed
And wakes up Monday
Postcoitally dejected.

On Monday the secular and divine
Are impotent with each other, but on Sunday
They consummate in the bread and the wine.

The whole creation groaneth together
In travail and complaineth
Until the glorious Coming –

The Yea of those who play
On God's Day.

EMMA LAVINIA HARDY

Wed to the pessimist poet, I'm *démodée*
As a writer, and a wife, but know
Some things he doesn't know.
The day we married was a perfect marriage day,
September's autumn show,
Not brilliant sunshine but a softly sunny
Luminousness, just as it should be.

Various adventures I've had, intriguing
Some, sad others, others gay
Since that luminous way,

But as one sees the happenings, unhappy happenings
Too, a queer unearthly ray
Flames pale on him and me with a soft sunny
Luminousness, just as it should be,

Even though my husband's darkness is complete,
And nowadays we hardly ever meet.

MURDER IN THE PUBLIC SECTOR

Hemingway had already killed
A hundred and twenty-two –
The sures besides the possibles –
But the last was worst:

Let me take him – with
a fast grab for an M1.
The blast gets the boy in the spine,
Tours through and out the liver. The Hun's
About the age of Patrick, Papa's son.

Papa gives the kid his morphine –
Nothing can be done –
And his bike to an orphan
whose own bike's been
nobbled by the Huns,
with *Get the hell away* –
Back to the estaminet.

The last man Papa killed
Was actually himself. He rose
On Sunday before seven, pressed
Both barrels of a Ross
To his brow, rested
The butt on the floor and drilled
Out of the entire cranial vault.

In my dream Hemingway was skinned
On a sierra in the wind
With a white beard and a worried face.

Back and forth, back and
Forth he passed
A cut-throat razor through his neck,
Unable to understand why he was
Unable to die.

Winston Churchill planned
To finish six cities
And three million folks
With a dose of anthrax
And let Germany be
A sadder and a wiser land.

A romantic pragmatist
He'd no time to spend
On *these psalm-singing defeatists.*

Anthrax is a form of cancer
That makes your skin like rubber.

Churchill took a time to die
Even after he started.
Was he blocked at the Styx
By the crowds still going over

The Guinness-and-champagne
Black-velvet waters
Across the fosse
To the plains of light
Where the only V-sign is a crucifix?

ROSES ARE BLOOMING IN PICARDY

The Sudanese grips his enemy's balls,
Shrills victory, spits on his opponent's prick
And slashes the scrotum, which, conscious, quick,
Ejaculates in death, as a hanged man falls;
The victor's semen spurts on the softening genitals.
For warriors like these, a battlefield slick

With slime and bleeding men is like a picnic
Of deflowered virgins for heterosexuals.

Owen wouldn't speak of the delight of war
To those at home who didn't pay with blood –
But knew the rabies of battle: the toreador
Alone – and curse the impresario – should
Taste the fine delight that fathers more
Than normal taste for sex has understood.

JESUS AS A PROPONENT OF *REALPOLITIK*

The Pope puts his hope
In proscription of contraception.
The sanctity of life is such
That we need much
More of the human race
To keep pace
With the IRA
And the CIA.

The best must sell guns
To the worst
So the Other Side
Won't sell them first.

We all need to kill
If only by proxy. Better
Proscribe the pill
Or the pox-free French letter.

Our own Church's wisdom
Is the Just War.
Render unto Caesar
The things that are Caesar's.
One law for the reprobate
Or private sinner,
Another for the State.

The Kingdom is inner.
Jesus showed us
There were good ways
To be as shrewd as
Herod, Pilate and Judas.

HAWKS STONES, KEBS

These stones are what we lift our life out of.
It's stiff stone to lift, for if
It's not stiff it's not life,
Nor your own, the stone.

We grope up mountains to be born.
And the wind cracks: *Change or be back.*

On these moors, or graveyards,
Even the worms squeak for elegies.
Curlews curl over the snow,
Beaks to the wind, fly
With a shout from the egg.

Somewhere, where the grit ungags,
There's another cry.

WEALTH

for Father Murray Bodo

In Assisi St. Francis was still there.

He was taking an interest in everybody,
Including the pigeons, and he said to me:

What I like is cheerful people
With a sense of humour who
Ought to be laughing politicians out of power.

It's crazy: I knew I'd always be rich
But who can eat while children are hungry?

The trouble is, the more I tried
To give it away, the more
I had it: that's how it is.

Since it's all being given away all the time
Try to persuade people to take it.

DEAD RECKONING

And you've rusted in the belly of the whale...
Through your own minginess timidly pulled out,
Exported a talent to sea, bargained abroad – for sale
Where the work would pay, slipped down the gullet.

You thought – and thought again, in the whitening
Digestive juices of the mammal, delivered to its liver.
Hardly surprising, is it, if it's unenlightening,
In the stale must of thought for ever and ever?

And then you were out and you let yourself down.
Well, the prophecies change. Naturally people scoff.
It's the prophet's lot: the huge gourd's grown,
And then the tinkering grub will kill it off.

And yes: you've doubted your streaks of illumination.
The wind – it's suspect even to clerics.
It's hair-raising too. Remember: hallucination.
The mind's a liar, delusive, prone to hysterics.

And yet it comes to you still, if you're quiet:
An angle of sunlight – specially for you;
Soft through a window, picking you out,
For the new affair at the sudden rendezvous.

The café's warm at your smile; the proprietor notices.
The touch of a hand's a sauciness on your shoulder.

It opens your hope like a secret; you're a sunlit lotus.
She's laughing at you. The sight of you older

Makes her feel tender. Why had you got
So ready to suffer without her, neglecting to call
Her presence inside you, in the not
Quite normal quietness that unexpectedly falls.

THE BAPTIST CHOIR

   Photo of a day's outing at Foot's Delph, 1890

Moses wouldn't be more weird than these elders.
We conduit water from the struck rock for millennia,
But these moustaches against the huge cracked crags
Are too like baboons on Monkey Hill for comfort.
With their watchchains, waistcoats and more dignity
Than rock has lichen, they answer no questions
About why blood flows at regular intervals.

But the pubs rocked with comic turns, the parties
Were cracked with kidding and old stories.
At school my uncle wrote, *My pet is a rabite,*
And wen it ops it punces with it back legs.
Another lad said, *Sir, he's gone and putten putten*
Where he ought to have putten put.
Our lives have flowed out from such solutions.

WHAT SHE FINALLY SAID

Early August: acres of forest roast
In a cold moon, and two log cabins blanch
On neighbouring rocks. The ghost of love's our host

And night famishes on. We try to stanch
The flow of sex-hunger that makes our eyes
Bark at each other, makes your arms branch

Like shrinking laurel, and your shooting thighs
Rise from the chair: anger burns with love,
Feeding a blow-lamp in your eyes' surprise.

Their Botticelli blue will now disprove
They ever loved – too late, too late, too late –
Because you did love; and yet the fierceness of

Your face makes the cabin dissipate
Into vacuum in vacuum, a bathysphere of space
In endless space, a bubble of no weight.

I see the earth's transparent face
As if a foetus witnessed from the womb
A grace beyond his little belly-base

As lighting sees through a set. A little room
Is less than everywhere. And now you cry
What is it? and I watch your face assume

The look of someone looking at the sky.
Something splits and opens. You shake your hair.
I ask you if you think you're going to die.

We go to sleep abashed, ghosts everywhere,
Patrolling the moonglow on the lake, inveighing:
Stop hurting yourselves. Nothing anywhere

Is what you think, least of all here, dismaying
Though you make it. Love while you can. At dawn
A knock on the door, a door-framed face is saying

What happened last night: *Elsa has died.* Drawn,
Can it be, to the nearest friend, do ghosts bring news?
What she sowed at birth, she says, *that seed of corn,*

Is now a head. The stalk lies out of use.
It's not the hell I feared, or heaven. It's far
more wonderful, acquitted unaccused!

Our wake, as we row, is a low-roofed corridor
Till our boat knocks on her rock and a smell of flowers
Acid as vegetables. She's a corpse, and here we are.

There she lies, a girl now, slipped from the hours
And out of her moles and wrinkles, posting through
In packets of moonlight news of new life and ours.

Later we sit by her box in a boat that will do
To ferry her stalk, as we nose towards a warehouse
In a city that, in time, we all go to.

FIRE IN THE GARDEN

   1.

...per una selva oscura...
                     Dante, *Inferno*, I. 2

The room's so quiet it seems audible.
I'm here, in the sane words of a mad poet –
Recalling my fear of madness that
Made me ordinary. Perhaps madness
Is our natural state if we get free.
I certainly spoke to God, in spite of badness,
And he, I thought, to me: grew up in three
Short months – nearly getting me asylumed.
Still, as we know, no man's an island.
So then, just having a job, a toiler's fee,
A place to love, someone to help,
A disguise, to be more or less a self,
Accepted as part of the crowd, seemed,
Though never quite completely, the meaning
Of being human. It's death, though,
We call madness and are afraid of, so –
We know our preoccupations have to go –
Into a room so quiet it seems audible.

2.

...si che ogni sucidume quindi stinghe...
                                    Dante, *Purgatorio*, I. 96

The garden stiffens as it listens to the fire.
The live branches hit staccato blaze
And the man crouches back and forth with his
Deformed hand and pirate beard. The garden's space
Is being cleaned, enhanced: do they know –
The slightly hunched trees – as they undergo
Their pale winter survival at the purchase of so
Much evergreen pain? The whole glade's
Assuaged as the sun breaks. It deducts our gaze
From the man. We'd like to think about our roots,
But the crackling spits and snaps and the tongues unsmother
Trying to get at the sun. The garden shrinks
At the man pitilessly making it beautiful.
Even in the sun there's an air of funeral
(Though the fire's ecstatic) before the drinks
Go round and the family rediscover each other.

3.

...la concreata e perpetua sete...
                                    Dante, *Paradiso*, II. 19

Just to be still after the life of work
Is a good death: the flavour of viaticum –
Bouquet of wine in the rush-hour dark
Towards fields of daffodils and clockless nights,
The stretching insight of elysium,
When the cigarette smoke in the committee room,
The bagpipe of one's own voice droning on,
The nuances gone and the thing ill-said,
The queuing years among red tail-lights,
The monoxide drive towards the amber loom
Of whisky, the fall on the bed, the evening gone,
Die, and the soul flies: a paper bird
In the garden, after the parrot is dead.

LETTERS IN THE DARK
At Southwark Cathedral
(1986)

Ma tu, perchè ritorni a tanta noia?
perchè non sali il dilettoso monte
ch'è principio e cagion di tutta gioia?
                    Dante, *Inferno*, I. 76-8

1.

I lay awake writing letters to you
in the dark – so I got up, felt alone,
and put on the light. I need someone.
There's a kind of intimacy that's closer than the bone
and can sometimes get into letters, more than anywhere.
It's communion with the dead, or more like prayer.
The dead are somehow refined, or are being refined.
When they answer back it's in disembodied voices
from which all static and chatter stored in the cells
have been magnetised off, buried, or even burned.
In the purgatory of the small hours the person
God might have first imagined stirs on the rock,
pushes the vulture from his liver and begins to turn
his anguish into intimate words, or at least
disembodied expressions of love disguised
as chatter and sent to a disembodied love.

2.

So here I am in my usual pew, between
a supine Shakespeare – crapula must have struck –
and generous John Gower, gaudy as Blackpool Rock,
and stiffened flat, it seems, with atropine;
and slightly in front, the spastic lady's got a sticker
on her wheel chair: *My Other Car's a Porsche.*
She can read me: her senses are quicker
than ours, and she corkscrews at my applause –
which is entirely in my head.
                                                The Ghost
is close to the distressed (I know) and she
can bless without trying, easily understands.
Tears embarrass my eyes: I have to see
through wet refractions our filtering blue host
astride the world like glass, with doves for hands.

3.

Outside the competers: competent and virtuous
(often ourselves); here – incompleteness; screening glass
chequered with flesh but letting stained light pass.
Worldliness to the rail – all words superfluous
and inexact, who hardly know what ails us.
That's why we're here. We're usually crass
or stony with good and evil, yet the Mass
invites the knower to be dubious.

It's our goodness and our knowledge he can't use:
they make us so benign – put us in a class
apart. Stiff with restraint, how messy if
we get crushy with love and play the silly ass!
Behind the unreadable fool the unspeakable hieroglyph –
and hermeneutics here would merely confuse.

4.

Insight is sousing in: grizzly mist on the horizon.
My sea's very upset: as if it can't
decide to ebb or flow – yet the sun's
quite tense, like a discus – or poised for a sprint
from cloudhole to cloudhole; rack hits salt, and everything
inside me tastes of brine – and there's so
surprising much it seeps over in tears, stinging
gladness, gratitude, unreadiness – sorrow!

Listening carefully to the sea – those huge hugs:
following its wriggling fingers, eeling down
and beckoning along drifting strata to the tug
of intense cold deep down below: shown
something quite different from anything you've seen before –
steering fishily up from an unknown floor.

5.

A week ago, what should I see but two young swans
Who'd found each other; asleep in a ditch; full-grown
cygnets, brown on a green marsh mattress
of duckweed; dismantled wind-up gramophones...

Their beaks tucked back under a wing
like fold-up needle-heads – inward-bound,
as self-contained as two pies, till she felt me
looking and unsheathed her head, peeking around.

Then he woke too – quizzing more carefully,
solicitously, more protectively than she,
but, seeing no danger, turned a serpent's gaze
and studied her with deathless agape.

They considered sleeping again but felt a need
had come to paddle on; so, with slow care,
each tested the stretch of a brown wing
as if to know the gear was in repair –

and made two partings down the duckweed,
not parted in their partings. I had to know
swans love with inseparable love, and so our birdselves go
treading the water, not knowing on whom we feed.

6.

Shakespeare buried his actor brother
here, next to Massinger,
who neighbours Fletcher,
his honeyed collaborator
who might have lived longer
but for a septic delay
in plague-ridden London
to visit his tailor.

1607: Edmund Shakespeare:
Just a year after
King Lear.
The sibling joke
about the bastard wicked brother
might make a brother choke
as he stood where we stand.
Those family names:
Hamnet died like Hamlet.

But Massinger, Fletcher, Shakespeare,
Henslowe and Alleyn,
men of this parish
who swashed and buckled for gain
have parted from their profits,
actorish or bearish,
and their names,
which we cherish,
their quibblings for King James,
and sprung to that perpetual spring
where no benumbing cold or scorching heat
can diminish anything
of what hangs here for ever
suspended in this air:
what men endure, the life of prayer.

Famine nor age have any being there.

   7.

If the brain's the mind's rind
that we grip through the many senses, and striped wasps
sting and build as they do from a habit
they use like a pension, which works, though it keeps them
little machines, with genes for mastermind,

and man's the timeless but evolving kind, the least
grabbed by habit, copying, creating, hawking
new science and new solutions
that clock and alter his heart and will in time
draft how his body will officiate and feast,

not part goat, part ghost, but
an outward and visible cipher of an inward and spiritual
contriver, why does an old man polish brass
and peer from a door, as if for his life, wondering
why it never arrived, or trail his foot

past a funeral parlour that says *We're here to help you?*

    8.

Yes, you will smile, *but does the mind exist,*
the spook in this machine? But does the face –
broadly, that is, as we think it does, in space?
Looking at what we call a brain or fist,
who is it that perceives? Not that little cyst,
or camera, the eye: no actual image or embrace
pulses up the nerve tracks to race
the dendrites and tell you you've been kissed.

The brain is something we've imagined.
Our ganglia jerking, electricked
into ecstasy, who crooks this underpass
of input into insight? The flesh is grass,
an adoring face, or a twitching skin of conflict,
but who concocts these molecules into man?

    9.

The hoisted leg and waddle of crows,
as if they'd no business with the grace
of birds – just a job to do,
eating, practical,
claws on the ground – except when they
lengthen out their finger-ended wings like hawks
and waft slow-flapping off
to another dung-heap.
                        These undertakers
seem so much closer to
men than a blackbird.

10.

I've forgotten the scruffy intellectual I once was.
Can I admit the divine man in friends,
in the hips of a camp Indian, in fag ends
of toothless tramps, washed policewomen, or the cross
in a class snub? It's my loss
that I'm one of the clean who condescends.
I scare the needy – my clothes can stink of dividends.

What God would want to know me? Though I'd like
to praise him, I stare out of a bay window
at a chirping garden, a holly tree, conker spikes,
a knowingness of late roses. They could imply
a mask of sorts: the passivity of this show
can blink like a face – everything in it an eye.

11.

The pelican hacks her breast and suckles with blood:
guilty pap of fledglings of the good
who badly devour the edible breast – the musky silk
that circumvents with luxury our milk.
Wagner touched silk and cunt – smell and love of skin
that dies with love of death. The nectarine
and curious peach call up the ticklish nipple, even when
men prefer gardens. Yeats's famous interest
in death was but his longing for the breast
in Eden gone: he pressed and was impressed.

And how to let him out – the child inside
who knows no time, our nosy cause and guide:
love would disinherit him: he knows what's best.
Babies nurtured at their mother's breast
dream in unison with her, as if in the womb,
even when they sleep in a separate room.

12.

Innate science:
a martin inherits a technology
of clay pellets: a genetic testament.
Caspars don't build houses with their genes.
People learn what they can, repeat and imitate,
if pushed invent.

Words we have – almost like causes.
But a new elusiveness smiles
from our new names,
which give us power to shake
the land that's barren now and cursed
for nomenclature's sake.

13.

Lionel Lockyer claimed his pills
had been distilled
from the rays of the sun:
they'd keep the agued carrying on
in fogs and the contagious air.

On his memorial bier
he seems to have a migraine
and a bicentenary grin
as one by one year after year
the tourists peer

at his well-wrought epitaph
and laugh.

14.

There's something we're always missing among
these antiquated people. They're strong
on only baring themselves to their personal sex.

They finger their thoughts by themselves,
with whisky bottles behind bookshelves,
and phantom touch, no fondling to perplex.

What could be fairer than their class
dues, but the upper upper are crass.
All kin are not brothers, or lovers.

At odds with bodies, they're cowed
by actual pricks and breasts, though proud
at mirrors, quick to see spots on others.

Find them attractive, give them a hug, and they
rise to you, but quick – they pull away,
to bespatter you later out of rectitude.

Yearning for those shudders and delights,
they have to cope them in accepted rites
that prettify a calculating attitude.

One perfect intimacy: nothing else will do.
But it doesn't. The lies prick through,
and sweet imperfect loving is subdued.

    15.

Ave verum corpus: we're here – and halt –
because we're feebler than others, rock salt.
We limp with sclerosis, a stick for senile thighs,
an arm to help these lightweight brittle bones to rise –
and each audacious step a precipice
of hospitalisation yet again: indignities –
flat feet, arthritic shuffle, sheer
ugliness, incontinence, smelliness or beer.

The first Adam was a higher primate.
We creaking hairless gorillas malinger
to be cuddled, old dogs caressing our privates,
pressing our itching ears to kissing fingers.
Yet each has been called to be something else:
he calls us out from ourselves like funeral bells.

And the golden face looks out from the icon and glows,
supporting all this dole with God only knows.

16.

The lake crazes into splinters, jaggings, chips:
a wind like an artifice orchestrates the trees,
screams quietly, crescendos to a wheeze,
comes cracking down with thunder, lightning blips
and rain: a tremendous tutti, then diminuendo slips
squalling away. For ghostlier ears than these
a wind of no coming has knocked men to their knees,
rocking their standing with apocalypse.

My boat stops on a glassy lake, expects.
Light shines inside me vertically, thrown
through my head to the centre of the earth:
a husband comes inside through love, not worth –
face witnessing face and subject subject.
Amongst a world of glass who knows we're known?

17.

Hagar's in prayer – but breaks when the angel comes:
she didn't really expect it – or the sudden landscape
beyond the carnally twisting trees: how to escape
the non-molecular rock, the thumbs
on her ears, forcing her to look
at the river she knows she's got to cross,
that motionless boat, the fishers, the final fosse,
and the bridge weathering to original rock.

It crashes on her head – the great dismay:
no rules, no way,
no place to hide, and this that's just begun
now solider than the soil she's clung to. Pregnant today
but not with what she cannot bear, she spawns
in the desert a wild ass of a son.

18.

Oaks: nervous systems
against a December sky.
They tickle my dendrites
as my axons try
to escape infinity
for when I die
I'll feel vacuity
stretching like sky
and the tree of my body
left to lie
as I ask emptiness why
I lost identity
unless it was to try
as I do now
to rediscover entity
after pitching myself away
and learning to deny
in my hard way.

19.

This fly was born in this attic
with no food. What can he do but fuss,
plod up a pane of glass, fall,
buzz, plod up again like Sisyphus.
He was here yesterday, and the day before,
now he's got to the mullion, crawls
along it, round the corner, excelsior –
on a higher pane above. Outside, climatic –
all that the glass is blocking him from meeting.
I open the window. Retreating
upwards from the space above the sill,
he needs some coaxing with a pencil,
then side-slips into coldness that will kill.

20.

So here's the alarming silly tale again:
our father Abraham's call to murder a son –
hearing a voice, like the voice near a Bradford grave
advising the Ripper to dekink casual love
with hammer, axe and sharpened tool:
gouge and bash those girls just out of school.

And the father's needed sacrifice,
provision for a life, has had its price:
provision for a death. And for the son –
priapic expensive manhood's just begun.
So boys must learn their life on burning wickets:
rams caught by horns on convenient thickets.

Yet Abraham's caught by the horn: the mind can lie:
inwit, the great I Am, insights his eye.
We Israelites, the wandering heirs
of a bewildered dervish, are taught distrust in prayer.

21.

Brown in the autumn time, the grass is blown
and brittle, rustling dry, like the wild boy's hair
who's guessed though not quite known despair.
Wind feels the bones of the whistling son
who whistles by the church and the shuddering trees, down
by the slugsmeared arch, on some new scheme.
The viaduct drips and echoes on its stream,
each drop a flash, you can't guess where, then gone.

Alone, alone... a stony watered echo
boomed by the mossy archway deep down here.
A train shrieks overhead, and he must go,
hooting for pleasure, liquid, hollow,
till suddenly in his fear
the lean wind grips him, twisting his curling hair.

22.

St. Cuthbert's hopping – a cassock on the shore –
at two ravens rooting with their beaks
in the thatch he's heaved in the North Wind's roar
to top the hospice on the lonely isle of Farne.
He can't believe their cheek.

That's a nest you've got in your craw,
he shouts, but the ravens scoff. *In the name of Christ,*
he cries, *it's for my friend, St. Herbert! Yes, caw –*
but come here again, and you'll get my boot, not straw!
He's never been like this. They flap off fast.

Yet one comes back regardless. Cuthbert, bending to sow,
studies the trailing wings, reads what the crow will say.
Beak at feet, he bows, his croak is slow,
screwing his neck at Cuthbert and starting to go.
But Cuthbert catches his eye and grins: *Well… stay.*

They both fly back, lugging a present of lard –
a gift you could grease your boots with. And by and by
he lets them live in his yard,
where they look askance at their saint – and doubly hard
at the hole he's built in the roof to watch the sky.

23.

All my most intimate talkers – they've been
men and women of inwit I never met:
survivors, inhalers, whom the threat
of the matter that matters or chore of citizen
compelled less than a whiff of ghostly oxygen
their nostrils flared at: Lawrence, Rilke, Herbert,
Wordsworth, Blake, Hopkins, Brontë, Dickinson:
abundant life's seductive martinets.

No, it's not back-suction to the womb.
Just the opposite: it's the whack
of the little beak that pecks the shell. Whiteness
glows through the crackable walls of the once big room
that's shrunk to a bag: one peck,
and a great slit opens onto brightness.

24.

Now here's a cosy photo:
two seekers who look like fun –
both of them holding roses
and with curious costume on.
One is a mystical lama,
the other a lunatic don.
Both are bedragoned with visions
from *The Tibetan Book of the Dead*,
though the whole thing is loaded with dread
and may well have been once a con.
But something's gone right with the lama,
and something's gone wrong with the don.

25.

William Austin looked on his mother's face
and thought: *As the clear light is upon the holy
candlesticks, so is the beauty of her face
in a ripe age.* William was melancholy,
unsure about death, though he joyed in a well-writ book,
a picture and a song. *No beautiful thing
is made by chance,* he thought, *but even of learning,
as of wine, a man may go on hungering
till it make him mad. Shall there be nothing
left me but the grave? Shall I at last
no other dwelling have?* But till we come
to Thomas and his confession we have no Christ.

26.

All thoughts are parrots, pretty mocking birds.
Twitter about God's a cultural activity.
Does it show more than intertextuality
to shuffle packs of metaphysical absurds
or crap out concepts like a Luther's turds?
Reading the Bible's normal creativity:
the reader is the writer: each subjectivity
fabricates a Jesus from a text of words.

Your God's too human: those signifiers
were organised by stone-age Jeremiahs,
linguistically ingenuous desert bards...
who felt the Word was broadcast out of silence.
Whispering in the syntax, truth interlards
the structuring brain's concocted violence.

27.

To be sponged on
and neglected,
to have people take
and give back cheek
is, if you catch the joke,
to be Godlike and grin sheepishly
as you sense the shepherd coming close.

It's in these silly
moments of blissful dying
that, elect with God
in your neglect,
you recognise the Host
and swallow without trying.

28.

O God, prayed Andrewes in secret every night,
save me from making a God of the King. To observe
the grass, herbs, corn, trees, cattle,
earth, waters, heavens, to contemplate
their orders, qualities, virtues, uses was
ever to him the greatest mirth, content
and recreation – held to his dying day.

Shakespeare had little Latin and less Greek,
while Lancelot had a lot of both, as well as
Hebrew, Chaldee, Syriack, Arabick, Aramaick.
*Your Majesty's bishop is a learned man
but he lacks unction; he rather plays with his text
than preaches it. Andrewes can pray as no
other man can pray, but he cannot preach.*

Yet if there were two saints of God in England
that summer, they were surely to be found
under the roof of the Bishop's Palace at Ely,
alone with their books and still at work with God:
abandoned souls, prostrate in the scholar's litany.
Casaubon and Lancelot Andrewes doubted they were
true scholars that came to speak to a man before noon.

*On the Real Presence we agree with the Romans;
our controversy is as to the mode of it.
We define nothing anxiously nor rashly.
There is a real change in the elements. But the death
on the Cross is absolute: all else is relative.
Christ is a sacrifice – so, to be slain.
A propitiatory sacrifice – so, to be eaten.*

But Privy Councillor to the royal pirate, fattening
his favourites? To dine at the court of flattery?
To be carried about, feasted and amused
by the heathen poor, who had to find for James,
Laud and Andrewes, horse, carriage, royal board,
or feel the wrench of a rope around their neck?
And your Devotions slubbered and watered with penitent tears?

His Lordship kept Christmas all the year.
Come and transfix a buck with me. I am
not well in my solitude: the hand that writes
these lines is ill with ague. Let me see
your dear face. If Stourbridge Fair, the finest
in England doesn't suit, I have beside me
a Matthew in Hebrew to make your mouth water.

A more servile and short-sighted body of men
than the bench of bishops under James the First never
set a royal house on the road to ruin.
Lord, I repent: help thou my impenitence.
Who am I, or what is my father's house,
that thou shouldest look upon such a
dead dog as I am. I spit in my own face.

But who cursed the hanged and dismembered Gowries
every August before King James? At least
one commandment must have exceptions, as we're
the first to admit: our public executions
are marvels of technology in the Middle East
and help the Exchequer; the saintliest then
admitted the King's enemies should be hanged.

And so. if persons nowadays feel squeamish
about hanging, here at home, to say
nothing of drawing and quartering, it tells more
about the fashion of the age than about
an individual's virtue or conscience. Saintliness,
after all, is vicarious redemption, inviting grace,
not a capacity to see beyond your own time.

Andrewes prayed with dust on his head, a rope
around his neck: in great calamity we exercise
great devotion. A knighthood might be had
for sixty pounds, but only nothing will buy off
the irrefragable accusation of our lives.
Kings' benevolences are malevolences indeed.
But God hath not turned His mercy from our side.

29.

By the standards of Parliament
Jesus was very naive.
It's not that we're not all agreed.
We know what's rational:
It's that rationality's not compatible
with powerful interests and greed.

The world's very old,
much older than the Messiah.
And more modern.
The way things tread and science
between them
have trodden and trodden and trodden.

He didn't know
how the world wagged,
the politics of size.
To realise his ambitions
or even survive
he needed to compromise.

If he succeeded
in ruling the world
it'd have to be thanks
to the Roman Empire,
the Sanhedrin,
or nowadays the banks.

Unfortunately for him
He'd thought all this out
and got it wrong
in hallucinatory argument
with the Devil,
who loves the strong.

30.

On the cover of *Honest to God* there's a depressed
thinker. Perhaps all thinking is depressed.
Depression makes you think. Is it because
our faith's too cheerful that we miss the wit
that only those who know the truth's always
absconding can hit? The Bishop's face
is blithesome and halcyon. To have faith in God,
even if *'God', perhaps, is not a word*
we should use for a generation, is faith
in more than truth, for jesting Pilate was inspired
to ask the question of the Way, the Truth and the Life.
The joke was on him, we presume. *A reluctant revolution*
is dying daily: difficult to admit
that what we know to be true is no longer true.

As we stand on our dung-heap of ideas and crow,
he slips away whispering *I Am*, to break bread
just when we're discussing his non-existence,
as we know from time to time but not in time.

And Bishop John Robinson left his scholarship,
waiting to see what he would learn from cancer.

31.

Elizabeth Newcomen once sold milk,
and Dorothy Applebee married a brewer.
The money in their legacies for beggars
and the schools they built
serialise immaterially
in children not yet born
and those who don't know where their luck comes from:
even goldener than the gilt
of Dorothy's candelabrum
still dangling like a rumour from the tower.

32.

The shark survives
although he doesn't chatter
like whales or major in science.
The *quality* of survival
doesn't matter.

We're pickled in our own solution.
The murders we watch on the box
we think we have to do.
History's watching beside us.
The skeleton that knocks
in the pipes is fossiled here inside us.

Is there a leap we're still not trying?
The dog that groans in travail on the floor
is waiting for me,
whimpering and sighing,
and feeling unspeakably more
not less than I,
as he twitches with loving fear.

I'm always saying goodbye.
He's always here.

33.

You who have bitten to the core
and cannot taste the apple
may stare in new confusion at your pain.
It's not enough to feel the ripple
of a twisted thigh within your brain –
you must feel more.

For those who tenderly build your prison
can split the walling skies to clear your sight,
and agony that killed your crimson pleasure
reveal you newly walking, hair now bright,
the ecstasy of heavenly seizure
in the plains of beautiful light.

34.

We look for chocolate wrapped in silver paper
or Father Christmas, in from the planet Venus.
But he lives in sin and points to wounded feet
and hobbles round in distant labour camps
or dies unnoticed in a neighbouring street.
He whispers kindly when we start to eat him
and peeps at us from eyes of smelly tramps.

And, peeping back, we feel we're smelling death
and turn discreetly from distracting life.
His scripture is the dirt we're often doing.
He points our noses at our petty strife,
demands the loaves and fishes from our pockets –
provisions we're withholding from the war –
but adds to those who never feel accepted

Accept that you're accepted, as you are.

35.

At the summit of St. Thomas's Hospital
I felt no doubt. Easy to imagine
the buses and formicating cars
queuing for regroupment over Lambeth bridge
were the last glints of a world I was leaving.

The Thames winked, and as the optical day
staged its illusory matinées of light,
the incredible stained to credibility, like
God's love at a canine remove, transferred
from the pack to man, dogging with joy and healing.

Infants who've known every passion
before they've met the grown-up blows
they'll not be wise to when they happen
show the unwrinkled skin of those who've
heard the story *before* they thrust
their hands inside the slits of the bloody wounds.

36.

We meet again at the kneeling place
we plod to without emphasis,
where it's no disgrace
to face another face
as psychic invalids
with lowered eyelids.

In every lowered glance
we find provision
for the journey we're on.
Grace whispers grace
to his own face
through all these faces.

37.

Midnight Mass: Mervyn tells us
divinity desires a world like this burning tree.
The choir carols from every coign in turn
of the semi-darkened sanctuary,
tuning the stones
and topping them up with that plangent wine
the ghost mouth tastes in every graceful shrine.

I read the prayers from the lectern
and from all those bowed heads
an almost tangible breath has begun to flow;
my heart turns red
in the expanding now
and vertical as a chimney
I feel their flames go through me to the tower.

38.

Listening's dissolving. After I go –
surprise: I'm still here. I grasp for my I
and find my I ungraspable. I know
me, but I eludes me. I am, identified,
becomes the person I've just been, a me inside my head.

I am in endless space, aware
of watching as I'm watched. The me is a bugged cell
with a one-way mirror, which is everywhere.
I watch a bright screen in the dark, but, light failing,
the emptiness reminds me I am here.

39.

Dear God, though I'm sweating round the park for death,
it's not because I'm not with every bronchial breath
running for life. Slow turnings make the book
seem seamless. It's only when I've lost the track
in cracking thunder, thrashing through flashes
in comminating streets, with no house, or friend, or hope of sanity,
no wife, no child, no end, no faith, no charity,
that I see the face I've been turning to ashes.

Yet deaths like these are not what make me say
death breaks new tracks. The black
doors grieve open and, yes, I see the Easter Day
breaking like spring – your remarkable way.
Because you come to meet us in your Mass
and make us see through wine as if through glass.

40.

Whisky's a risky aspect of the Body:
a distilled divine. All sacraments are risky.
Ecstasy can booze you to the devil –
the Dog of God: *Deus est diabolus
inversus*: the Hounds both hunt the world

as a team (see *Job*) and often it's the Dog who pads
with the prey to God. Whisky killed my dear
old dad and that's what drove my mother mad.

Death's certainly the alcoholic's mother:
those first erotic bubblings at the bottle
or breast are gaspings of our love of Her
or Him or Both, all Three, met shuddering as we rattle.
How long will it be before we find Cockayne,
where the whisky rivers flow, so stilly flow,
like every poison from the flesh of God,
with peaty water, heart of gold, an amber glow?

   41.

Imbecile to the wise and sane, our baby divination
is milky eyes staring at bosoms to be hugged,
not clouded in concepts: an infinite sky's plugged
into an infant's irises of contemplation.
Impatience
at lugging Moses' stones is right:
the yoke must be easy, the burden light.

The lost are often first.
Sprinting from God
they won't be coerced.
They see him at the winning post,
give way to a crush,
and fall like fools while the prudent only plod.

   42.

I hardly ever meet my brothers and sisters.
Here perhaps on holy ground
is the proper place.
But what we pass around
is the shining handshake, called the kiss of peace.

What can I do but intercede for the publicans
and drinkers, not here, but my actual friends?
There must be, I suppose, quite special roles
for every Madeleine. Who knows what He intends?
And is the kiss impetuous in cautious souls?

My cronies are didactic: one showed me
a film of far more breathless peaceful kisses:
These rather lovely girls and ugly chaps
had overcome the prejudices
that make us buy these films and watch perhaps.

They seem to be quite enjoying what they're paid for,
so prodigal and naughty with caresses;
but surely it's the Producer
who asks for tender smiles and licking kisses
and makes each woman long for her seducer?

    43.

Bore men if you must,
but must you bore God too?
demands Isaiah:
Mervyn's plainly-stated
maiden sermon text
to fluff the dust,
knowing it might backfire.

Or take a homeless pair
out of the fifty thousand,
and their baby, and an ass,
to construct a living crib
in Trafalgar Square.
The plods on the beat don't like it.
Nor do the brass.

We've got a crib already –
next to the tree… and hark!
The carols are starting up
on St. Martin's steps.
Mervyn and Trevor plod
with mitre, crook and nod
to a legal plot in the park,

a nook where no one'll see
their demythologising cot but God.

    44.

Of hem, that writen us to-fore
John Gower is erst in loves lore.
Tho he be dede and elles were
We thenken on his presens her,
Tho other worde of hem nought is,
Aperte fro thet he writen has,
Then mariage lisens and his wille
And tomb that stondeth to us stille.
A squere he was and born in Wales
And wened it gode writen in tales
Somewhat of lust, somewhat of lore,
Tho loves lust and lockes hore
In chambre accorden never more,
And leved he in time of blody kinges
And civil warres and tresons swinges.
But Gowerlond, tho fond in Wales,
More sothely is a lond of tales.
Ther ben also that seyn he was
In Yorkshire born from Conquerors,
And otheres seyn in argument
That he was born and bred in Kent,
But as a Suffolk man minself,
Tho adopted so, boghten in by pelf,
I wene he was a Suffolk man,
That leved in Multon manor a span,
And atte leste hadde frends in Kent
And eke therto establishment.

Dan Chaucer was his poete frend,
A yonge prentice, of hem ytrened.
He preies for Charite, Merce and Pite –
Kindenesse herd to finde in a cite –
His hair hath roses intertwined
With ivy – tribute to his minde
Versed both in bokes and science,
Of which he made an holy alliance.
But Godes curse had yfallen on
His lond in gret confusioun.
He wended out to gathre flowres –
Insted he sawe a lond of hores
Chaunging into forme of bestes:
Swine in the cite atte theyr festes,
Asses weninge they weren horses,
Dogges that licked the children's sauces,
Oxen proude of dragones tailes,
Venus lost in a lond of wailes,
And so his *Liber Amoris* sholde be
On how men moten love joiesle.
Swanne at his necke, at his fete a lion,
His sawle hath victore oer angeres scion.
Preie for his sawle, and as your guerdon
He boghte thousand dayes of perdon

45.

My chest crackles with bronchitis –
and I ask myself, *What is it then in me*
that's so unhappy with the air?
Air: it goes to my blood, it's everywhere,
It's deeply intimate with my terminal skin.
Cloud teashops, lakes of anodyne,
they float up there,
and here
her breast and her vagina –
the air's been teaching how to breathe them in.
My lungs are touch, the kiss of the eye still finer.

Enclosed in stone, I breathe through stone like skin.
The cathedral's ribs and groins
can splice me to all space –
another air, another psychic terrain
extended by the cinematic brain,
sustained by grace.

46.

When I was thirty-two I got cancer:
probably a proxy for something else,
but it took me by surprise. Time was unhurried
in the specialist's ante-room. To me it seemed
clouded with witnessing comforters. I imagined nuns
spilling their love in prayer for the sick and worried.

The specialist ogled it through a tiny lens
like one I'd had at school. He didn't think
it was cancer. Better to have it off, though. No
innuendo – but doubtless truth in that.
Two weeks later I'm taut on a clinical table,
waiting for stitches out and ready to go.

A houseman came in first in a pure white coat,
with high heels, and leaned against a wall,
hands folded behind his bum. His smoky eyes
were observant I knew to see how I would take it.
The specialist bustled in, with a hand-wag,
assuringly: *It was cancer*. No surprise.

He'd examined every cell. There was healthy flesh
all the way round. The nurse was looking embarrassed.
Who'd not heard of people cured of the dread
disease, and only a year later – they were dead?
Melanoma, a beautiful name for a fast,
distorting and painful killer when it spreads.

So I needed a little treatment: 'belt and braces.'
Regular visits for radium: massacre the cells
in case a wild one escaped. And so I rubbed
shoulders with the dead and dying. I remember a lady
carefully lipsticking lips before a mirror.
My reprieve could make me somehow feel quite snubbed.

The scar will always be mine: it makes me nervous
with women: not gold, but the size of a silver guinea –
and a wound in the side – but the other side from Christ's.
It'd be rather fun to lie: *a piece of shrapnel
got me here*, instead of my cushy war.
It looks like a brand on a pig about to be priced.

It only exists in my mind. I conned a surgeon
to carve it out, leaving merely a long
white scalpel line like a sabre wound.
On the beach it won't raise questions: more discreet.
I remember a friend in a pub and remember thinking,
He'll be kissing the girls when I'm long underground.

Dead now. I'm here but in his club.

   47.

Somewhere there's a man who took me fishing
and kept me sane. I don't even
remember his name. Stephen…
some saint's name: unintellectual, observant, well-wishing.

This useless work has risks. Near to splitting,
Rilke thought his grit in loneliness came
from glassy Capri evenings, all the same,
with two old deck-chaired dears, watching them knitting.

One of them sometimes had an apple to pass.
A tiny ugly dog with sorely swelling boobs
craved for his eyes in its solitude. The sugar cube
he gave her was a wafer in a private Mass.

48.

Perhaps those childish ecstasies of terror
when midnight pulsed on midnights of blind hate
and vampires hung behind the stirring curtains
alert for children's eyes to close and sleep
were deaths we might have had or can anticipate.
How we need to have an expert mother
to sit beside us, spreading unconcern,
and mock the terminal illness in the corridor
and tell us that it's not our turn:
the custom-built disease has gone next door.

Perhaps in every aged impotent craving
the child we were is still inside us, crying
for a rocking knee, and not believing
what we heard can never be,
though finding mother's presence near the sea:
to feel the lift from fifty fathoms
and know annihilating pleasure
of sea absorbing self in sea,
far greater than the logic
of non-acceptance on the certain shore.

49.

Some day I'm going to have to meet my mother
again. I'm not sure how it will be.
Will she be splashing that arctic fox she wore
for the sepia studio plate they had of us three
a month or two after my birth? I must feel kin
with those still girlish eyes and lenient lips –
pleased, my father proud. I'd find her smooth skin
and neck attractive, her kind intelligent hips
seductive, her Parisian costume and pearls, and her
silky hat all that could make a baby purr.

I can hardly pray for her soul. I feel meagre
because she died before she died,
too soon for me, and recouped as one too eager
and helpless to help, in need herself. I sighed
for an intellectual love, all *nous*
without the feeling. I gave her the best books
to read; she read them greedily. It was
too late. The lesion had been scored. The crux
now was: survival meant to disregard
the conscience she gave and find a new mother instead.

November, the month of holy souls. I'd like
to feel gratefully for those first baths,
her cherishing hands on my skin, those grey eyes
so tender even in my stubborn wraths,
my baby safety under it all. But misgiving
had made her need me more than I needed her,
and what I feared most was her fear of living.
The day she found us infant boys and girls
exploring bums in the bathroom was the worst.
She wouldn't speak, and both of us felt cursed.

No, the worst... Yet is she listening now? Who else
could understand her like her only son?
And who could understand me like herself?
She knew me even if her mind went wrong.
She wished me well, though neither of us knew
the way to the other's happiness. Surely now,
sophisticated in another life, she can review
more expertly than I. She must know how
to nurse me to myself when I too leave behind
all the crazy blocks that pave my mind.

I'll need some friends who've been there when I go.
As my breath scratches the last scribbles, and I write
The End, letting go of everything I know,
I'll need a helping hand in those streets of light.
Can anyone love the glaucous eyes of weakness?

Though I've got through life with the back of my head
turned to most neighbours, trusting in obliqueness,
the mother will lean one night by the cot of dread
for my sensible eyes to close in sedative calm
and the moment when I perceive who I really am.

   50.

There's no abiding city here.
A gentleman's
enfranchised everywhere.
But to be at home everywhere
is to be at home nowhere.

The Son of man hath not where
to lay his head.
Even the dead
have laid their heads
where they're not.

We've had far to go
and have farther.
There's no emptiness
like where home was,
and it won't get less.

In the tale the prodigal son
staggers back home
and sees his father running.
We've gone farther –
We're not who we were.

Our Father's stranger too, no longer
in that Old Folks' Home.
We might not recognise him –
or, shocked, try to revise him,
perhaps disguise him?

To meet an old friend
after forty years, though,
is to know
that what you've lost in going
doesn't go.

   51.

People that swim clambered
onto the land.
Fins elevated into wings
and became the status quo
for excitable birds.
The tiny ampersand
that was crouching on to man
had far to go.

My patriarch was a man
called Australopithecus.
He bounced inside his gland
the sperm that quickens us.
And did he have a soul?
Or when the angels scanned
the daughters of men
and saw that they were beautiful
did something non-indigenous
scintillate inside that skull?

When One had made it all he saw
it was beautiful and true and good.
Adam's law
has split us into two.
And was the splitting tree
that fruited on the spine
of Neolithic or Cro-Magnon man
a breaking awareness of a larger brain,
or was it law
to help the ploughman to retain
the bread his sweating brow
had toiled to win?

Round good and evil
winds the Devil,
our Accuser,
with gifts of clothes
and the *felix culpa*,
trading lust for love,
with loss of Eden, all our woe,
and Cain's
war for grain.

Since Satan's a lawyer
and a gentleman judge
how can he tolerate
that the first Adam,
a stone-pitching primate,
can be the second
in a Paradise
of forgiven vice?

Through the gate
the Scandalous Word
conducts each malefactor:
past the flaming sword
and the elder brother
with his unprodigal grudge.
Unfair –
the love that makes
the lost and last the heir:
last here, first there,
inheriting without merit
an Eden of brotherhood
and incompetence for good.

Beyond the scenery
the in-itself
and its particular machinery
still elude us. But
whatever everything is
it still includes us,
eyeless creatures prodding

at an elephant's toe,
or a foetus in the amniotic fluid,
listening to a mother's
internal radio.

Mother science is
the prodigal one
the Father welcomes in
with healing and revealing
learned studying among husks,
finding in the musk of swine,
especially there,
the absconded divine.

If moments occur
when blind eyelids
seem to open,
eyes even then
have to learn vision.
These overarching arches
are the womb of Mary.
We look towards the hymen,
the eastern light
stained blue like sky
or blue like Mary
against the particular night.

   52.

Invisible reader, impossible God,
there are times we dream you back to being
an irascible blustering Yahweh, haranguing
a gang of bedouin, but not too often.
I try to listen to your presence
quietly as an astronomer, an absence in the room,
the mother and father I imagined in the dark

when I was sick, who never came.
You're the pebble on the beach with spread
arms and a navel, the fearful passage
past the graveyard, a thorn in the flesh,
the psychiatrist who buggered off while listening,
yet in spite of everything somehow managing
to see me too in my deliberate vanishing.

TROUBLE
(1992)

I: FEUX D'ESPRIT

TROUBLE

I will be no trouble to you. I sleep all day, go to the theatre in the evening, and at night you may do what you will with me.
                                            Marie Duplessis to Liszt

That summer's lakeside cabin makes me sigh:
that manic horse, too, with its madhouse eye –
in love with you, as was I.

As we trailed to the farm for milk, he ran like my heart
thudding across the field: nose over gate;
and once – did he vault it? – out in the night,

he'd nibbled your drawers on the line. Ass!
An edge of dissolved-in-saliva grass
greened the last shreds of your silkiness.

When I cracked a window, at your wish
I rowed and sprinkled the splinters: a dish
for the water sprite – and we never lacked for fish.

The ancient pike I caught's huge jagged
crocodile snout scowled, as it rose and wagged.
And now your hatred, even, that's almost flagged.

GREENWICH PARK

Spring's come, a little late, in the park:
a tree-rat smokes flat S's over the lawn.
A mallard has somehow forgotten something
it can't quite remember. Daffodils yawn,
prick their ears, push their muzzles out
for a kiss. Pansies spoof pensive
Priapus faces: Socrates or Verlaine.

A cock-pigeon is sexually harassing
a hen: pecking and poking and padding
behind her impertinently, bowing and mowing.

But when he's suddenly absent-minded –
Can't keep even sex in his head –
she trembles, stops her gadding, doubts
and grazes his way. He remembers and pouts.

CHANSON TRISTE

The leaves on the lawn under the chestnut
are suddenly shocking
like something squandered.

His aching head
will rest in summer moonlight's lap
and the poems he'll read
will make her *prima vera*
high summer and autumn all at once.

In her melancholy eyes
he'll drink so many kisses
so many caresses
he might even be cured.

Or is he drinking with so much pleasure
the old illness
through the new kisses?

A piano made out of water
and clouds
and sunlight
is taking a golden glamour
into its greyness.

For years
one can rely on
an imaginary love.

REMEMBERING ADLESTROP

I too remember Adlestrop –
that hot compatible weekend in the car
when all the birds of Gloucestershire
seemed intoxicated by tar

and dawdled on the road. I slowed
to let them loop away. *Adlestrop
must be here, I bet,* I said.
And then, towards dusk, a sudden stop:

a signpost: *Adlestrop!* I cried,
not really having looked, and turned.
No railway: just the station sign,
yellow, conserved; and I somehow yearned

and grieved as a blackbird sang.
Had I an inkling even then that now
I'd hear it with wringing pain,
knowing your love had stopped, not how?

OTHER LIFE

She was a burning glass.
A little sun inside had passed
through her from a hotter source.

And yet she was opaque.
Made from a childhood ache
that dark as particles could flame and shake.

She was dark, dark
and almost out of sight: a watermark
pressed in the paper of her book.

The book was all she'd been,
child, mother, slut, queen,
and all she'd ever done or seen.

If he'd read her,
He'd have learned to dread her,
certainly never dared to kiss her or bed her.

SHINGLE STREET

Someone lying on the deserted beach
appears to be lying on someone else.
She lowers her head
and drinks him slowly,
holding him by the ears.

He's completely not-there,
and she, with her black hair,
is a bee-sucker
after nectar
under his grey hair.
They must know I'm coming,
but they don't care.

It must be illicit,
nowhere else to go,
not going to be stopped
by my possible stare.

Rules are overnice
in Paradise.
Though no one marries
or gives in marriage,
their bright ice,
great seers say,
melts in the solar flare
of their fusion and confusion.
That's how they feel each other there.

Who doesn't wish them well?
Perhaps we too
in some afterlife

will find some angel
to give us fugitive love
when ordinary women no longer find us
worth the worry of.

FIRST KISSES

The best kisses are the first.
First mother's kisses, and after that
the kisses in the Botanical Gardens
stolen among flowers.

Then there are the kisses when
you think you'll never be kissed again.
Kisses in foreign cities:
perhaps in a flat, perhaps in a rainy street,
panting because illicit.

And then, late at night, comforting
someone in tears. Perhaps it's because
she's so hot with suffering, or hasn't
used her kissing mouth for almost years.
But probably not: she just has a talent
and like so many talents, it's
been buried.

                        Like her breasts
with their talent for being looked at and
looking back, it's a hidden address.

Not for everyday visit or caress.

ASSISI AND BACK

It's the train from London to Assisi,
a sort of pilgrimage:
in the diner a dark girl
is staring: I feel my age.

It's the train back from Assisi, and the same
dark girl, suddenly aware:
so she smiles, sits close, intensely
close, and deplores her stare.

I'd like to say, *You're lovely, but*
as I'm old enough to be
your daddy, a man
must keep some dignity.

But on the platform at the end I give her,
unexpectedly, a kiss.
Her friends shriek, and she
wanders off in, apparently, bliss.

It's pleasant enough
to remember her now.
'I' seem young and naïve –
she showing me how.

But why was I afraid of her?
Is it cowardice? And this
convergence? Surely not
a hint from St. Francis –

knowing so much more now
than under his vow,
joined properly with poor Clare
up there?

TWO-HUNDRED-MILE-AN-HOUR WINDS

Sometimes a friend can disappear
completely out of the crowd:
a silver finger
points out of a cloud.

Two people and a donkey sailed away –
Tornadoed – miles in air –

let down later that day,
alive, but stripped bare.

Wonders occur to every doubter,
your friend not noticing, though, or caring to:
but you don't feel the same about her
after, or she you.

REFRACTIONS

*We can do no great things
but only small things
with great love,*
says a mother in Calcutta.

An old man kneels
round his wife's grave
hedge-clipping grass:
to serve, to grieve.

A dead seagull in a flooded ditch
on a dark night
has one wing raised
as if for flight.

An elaborate lamp
reflected in the window might
make it seem
as if there were no night.

IN SPITE OF EVERYTHING

In spite of everything, I think
mainly of you, even though
this is the century of mass death,
gas, squandering of resources,
and pollution of the future.

Though our grandchildren curse us, as they will,
limping and tottering with diseases
we dumped on them with war research and waste,
and millions are lying belly-bloated in Africa,
I think mostly of you.

Though trees are dying, I think
mostly of you, almost all the time, wondering
if your smile is an acid rain, or if
you really love me, and I can't have enough
of your unattainable presence and perfume.

Most of all I long to know
what you're thinking really, and this
obliterates the kneecaps blasted off in Ireland,
the profits from sophisticated weapons,
state terrorism, daggered idealism,

big dealers lobbying the government,
the investment of labour and wealth in futility,
the expense on defence on a planet
that's been indefensible ever since
the last of England were singing *There'll always be an England*.

UNACCOMPANIED VOICES

An imitation of Eugenio Montale's *Mottetti*

1.

You know it: I have to lose you again
and I can't. Each act, each cry,
snipes me, and the blown salt too
swilling the harbour mole
and making the sombre spring
of Sottoripa.

Region of ironware and rigging –
a sort of forest in the dusty evening.
From out there comes a long rasping –
grating like a nail on the window.
I look for the lost sign, the single
token you graced me with.

    And I'm certain of Hell.

    2.

Many years, one somewhat harder: an *agon*
on a foreign lake burning with sunsets.
Then you descended from the mountains,
bringing me Saint George and the Dragon.

If only I could print them on the banderole
the north-east is whipping
in my heart... And through you enter
a whirlpool of fidelity, immortal.

    3.

Frost on the windows; together
for ever, the sick, and for ever
apart; and, at the tables there,
the long post-mortems on the cards.

The exile was yours. I think again
of my own, the morning shock
of that bomb, 'the ballerina',
blasting off among the rocks.

And they dragged on, those night games,
that fiesta of artillery flares.
A brusque wing brushed and checked your hands –
but no: the card wasn't yours.

4.

Though far away, I was close
when your father entered the shades
and gave you his goodbye.
What did I know till then? I survived
all that in the past only through this:

that I didn't know you and had to.
Today's shocks tell me – bringing back
an hour down there, Cumerlotti
or Anghebeni: the shellbursts,
the groans, and the charge of the cavalry.

5.

Goodbyes, whistles in the dark, waving,
the coughs, and the lowered windows. Time to go.
Could be the robots are right. How they stare
from the corridors, walled in!

Does the faint litany of that intercity
make you too remember
the dreadful precise cadenza of the samba?

6.

The hope of ever seeing you again
abandoned me;

and I wondered if these things that cut me off
from all sense of you, these sort of movie-shots
in the street, were symptoms of death
or past shots of you: distorted and fleeting
flashes of pastiche:

(at Modena, for instance, between the porticos,
a liveried servant dragging
two jackals on a leash).

7.

The black and white swoopings of swallows
from telegraph pole to sea
are no comfort to your pierside sorrow,
will never take you where you no longer are.

Already the elder is spreading its fragrance
over the diggings: the squall is dispersing.
The clearing sky is a truce, maybe,
but your sweetness is another threat of rain.

8.

Behold the sign, nervously printed
on a wall going gold:
a jagged shadow of palm-leaf
burnt there by the shine of dawn.

Dawn's gentle pace
down from the mountains
isn't muffled by snow, is still
your life, your blood in my veins.

9.

Suppose a green lizard, darting
from the stubble,
under the great whip –

or a sail, fluttering out
and sinking
by the steep bluff –

the noonday cannon
fainter than your heart, and
the chronometer
striking without a sound –

and what then? It'd be vain

for a lightning flash to change you
into something rich and strange.
You were made of different stuff.

   10.

Why delay? In a pinetree a squirrel
is whipping his torch-tail on the bark.
A half-moon is dipping its horn
in the sun and being snuffed. Day's begun.

A gust startles the sluggish mist:
it recovers at the spot shrouding you.
Nothing will end, or everything, if you
come flashing out of the cloud.

   11.

The spirit that polkas
and rigadoons at every new
season of the street feeds on
locked-up passion, finds it
intensified at every corner.

Your voice is this diffused spirit.
By wire, by wind, by wing, by chance,
by favour of the muse, or some machine,
it comes back, happy or sad. Talk supervenes
with people who don't know you, but your imago
is there, singing on and on: *doh ray me fah soh...*

   12.

I free your brow of the icicles
you picked up, traversing those high
nebulae; your wings are lacerated
by cyclones, you wake with a start.

Mid-day: the medlar stretches a black shadow
across the square; in the sky a chilly sun
persists; and the other shadows, slipping
round the alley corner, don't know you're here.

13.

The gondola that glides in a great
glory of tar and poppy,
the sly song that rises
from masses of rigging, the high doors
locked on you, and the giggles of the masqueraders
who scamper off in swarms –

it's an evening in a thousand, and my night
is still more pregnant! I'm roused with a start
by a pale tangle writhing down there,
equating me with that rank
aficionado, eel-fishing on the bank.

14.

Is it salt or hail raging furiously down? –
massacring bellflowers, uprooting verbena.
An underwater tolling
like the one you induced
is coming and going.
Hell's pianola is speeding up, reaching
higher and higher registers, by itself, climbing
the spheres of ice... – brilliant as you
singing *Lakmé*'s 'Bell Aria'
with that trilling coloratura.

15.

At first light, when
the sudden rumble
of an underground train tells me
of trapped men in transit

in a tunnel of stone
lit by inlets
of mixed sky and water –

at first dark, when
the woodworm that tools through
the writing-desk doubles
its fervour, and the tread
of the watchman is coming –

at first and last light those stops are still human,
if you keep threading them together.

    16.

The flower, repeating
from the edge of the gorge
forget me not,
gets no sunnier or gladder tints
from the space thrown between you and me.

A screech of metal, we're lurched apart,
the steady blue won't come back.
Through an almost visible sultriness, the funicular
is taking me back to the already-dark far stage.

    17.

A frog, first to try his vocal chords
from the pond of mist and reeds, a sough
from the cluster of carobs where
a chilly sun is extinguishing its torches,
the slow flowerward drone of beetles
still sucking sap – the last sounds,
the greedy life of the *campagna*....

                      A breath of air
blows the hour out: a sky of slate
is getting ready for an apocalypse of bony
horses, with sparking hooves.

18.

Shears, never cut that face,
that fine listening look of hers,
and make an everlasting mist
of the only image I clearly remember.

It's getting chilly... A hard cut:
and the pruned acacia sheds
a cicada shell
in the first mud of November.

19.

The reed softly moulting
its red fan in spring;
the dragonflies hovering over
the black water running in the ditch;
and the dog panting home
with something heavy in his mouth –

today, no hint of recognition
for me here: but where the reflection
burns fiercest in the fosse
and the clouds lour, beyond her
eyes now so remote, just two
strands of light form a cross.

                And time passes.

20.

...Well, let be. The sound of a cornet
converses with the bees, swarming in the oaks.
On a shell, reflecting the failing light,
a painted volcano cheerfully smokes.

The coin, too, locked-fast in the lava
gleams on the table, holds down a few
loose leaves. Life that seemed so immense
is briefer than your handkerchief.

II: ESPRIT DU SOIR

We are survivors, in this age, so theories of progress ill become us, because we are intimately acquainted with the costs. To realise you are a survivor is a shock.

Saul Bellow, *Herzog*

SOLVITUR ACRIS HIEMS

    An imitation of Horace, *Odes*, I iv

Stinging winter dissolves. At the sweet swing of spring
    and the west wind, dry hulls trundle to the shore,
sheep bleat at the fold, the shepherd leaves his fire,
    and the fields unfreeze their frosty white.

Venus brings the girls out dancing under a hanging moon,
    with all the Graces, pounding the earth,
and Vulcan stokes his huge blazing furnaces up,
    eager for the summer lightning.

Now it's time to oil our hair, prick ourselves out
with tiaras of myrtle, put on flowers from the melting earth.
And now's the time to remember the gods in their shady groves
    and give them a lamb or goat for good luck.

Death's white face looks impartially at the pub door
    and the palace gate, O Terry, the lucky, and kicks at both:
the sum total of anybody's days is short, so hopes should be:
    ghosts, nothing but names now, crowd round you, and night,

and the thin exile of Hell. Once down there, no
    shake of the dice'll make you the gracious host.
No ogling of pretty boys then, whom everybody adores now
    and the girls'll soon burn to make a pass at.

THE WILD SWANS AT ALDEBURGH

Some days they look like outsize geese
with no secret, seen
waddling across reclaimed land

to a ditch. Thirteen:
my lucky number. But one, hatched out too late,
is without a mate.

The trees are in their winter grandeur.
A line of pine trees stands
aware of me as I of them –
children holding hands.
We watch a ditch ruffle like elephant skin
and the sun whiten and thin.

I track a curlew in a cloud
by its call: fast headway.
The thirteenth swan has taken off:
an immature grey,
it creaks a low flight, then stands and walks alone,
feeling its half-soul gone.

Pathetic these fallacies our lives fatten.
Forty years are lost
since I first read Yeats, yet I never see
a swan without his ghost.
A swan in death and I in life both read
the bobbin, rewinding the thread.

December sunshine brings white joy,
a milky hole in light.
These weeks three friends or almost-friends
have taken that silver flight
to some new pond or ditch or reclaimed land.
As souls, or swans, we stand

in a place of no giving in marriage.
Aware or unaware,
a leap through inarticulate light
defines some strangled prayer,
leaving us stripped, deciduous winter trees,
hand in hand, or on our knees.

SEA LADY

Someone's crept out of the sea,
lying on the pebbles, in pain:
like a crippled labrador.
She raises one arm, a lady
in a siesta, languidly,
though night's falling, and this January rain.

Hearing my crunch on the shingle,
she's turning bitch-soft eyes and whiskers to vet me.
I'm coming too close,
and she growls, hisses and whispers,
tensing my tail with her speech,
though I know she can't get me.

Hurt? Perhaps she's tired?
But I'm too close, so she levers her spine
and flops down a shingle bank, enters the ocean,
periscopes twice with her head,
then hoists ashore,
crutching her legless rear up the steep incline.

Who'd be sick, if they lived in the ocean?
And who'd bark
so hard after fish, they'd give up the earth,
lose hands and legs,
freezing the warm blood back
to the cold, to feel after fish in the dark?

I sit in my lights by the fire, listening to Mozart,
reading Gibbon.
A Diocletian legionary, an old lag
looking for loot, found
a beautiful leather purse of priceless pearls.
He threw the swag away and kept the bag.

For what's no use can have no value.
And in the morning she
who loves the waters I left behind
is gone like a piece of flotsam,
a bag of pearls,
that is and always will be far out at sea.

SUFFOLK EVENINGS

   1.

Evening's always a favourite time,
a lazy man's time, and autumn a favourite season,
for those who know they're living in failing light.
And failing light's internal. Sea and night
toil on but – it's more
of a vocation than a task. A ship snores
out of the scud, honking of risky work.
I turn to the fire and a different kind of dark.

An atmosphere close to pain; it implies
that all you've ever done, even your lies
and cruelties are invited: evening companions
to sit over tea or whisky and teach you sums,
equations once unteachable. Too
incalculable a calculus. On the pebbles, in a shampoo
of greening sea, bottle or log comes back in surges,
always erasing us, of selves.

To the child who still hurts me it was hard to believe
in a time of no canals: so like rivers:
no barges now, but heavy with frogspawn and duckweed.
You dive off a lock into ink. From the balustraded
balcony at the back of the house, you could see
a water-rat launch in a widening and widening V.
The navvies are all dead, and what they left is a clear
stretch of almost stillness that's always been there.

   2.

The tiny hands of rain on the window
rap a rainy Pennine childhood
in an eighteenth-century house
of pre-technological people: a grandma
born in the 1840s, an aunt
fifty already, my mother forty.
I crawl by the big black fireplace,
with the blackened copper kettle on the hob
that sings quietly by the flapping flame

as if we were wintered-in at Grasmere.
The huge kitchen's always dark:
lights burn by day; the only window's benighted
by the high bank glooming the yard at the back.

My dad's preparing himself a grog
in the stained-glass bar, I'm
on my farm with the lead sheep, drawing up
the drawbridge on my flagged fort,
or reading *The World's Great Books in Outline*:
pictures of Dante and Beatrice, my mother's
name, and *A Midsummer Night's Dream*:
Fuseli's vicious fairies: subfusc landscapes
with holes of light, no different from
the darkness under the table with the cat,
or the days of rain drenching the valleys,
or the watery window, where tiny hands are picking
and knocking and running down like tears.

    3.

A ship snores out of the scud,
honking of risky work.
I turn to the fire
and a different kind of dark.

Evening: thoughts slip into night:
the flash of a lightship
just out of sight
has a name I've never found out.

A brass shoe dangles from my lamp –
bought just before that
cancer-test: a gipsy called,
and told me I'd live to be old.

On a sunny afternoon
the door crashes open,
a guitar string snaps; the cat sees
a nothing there – screams and flees.

A man on the beach,
with a gold umbrella,
taps it like a white stick: not only
deafened but blinded by the sea.

For another the sea's his mother:
She's telling him something serious
that makes no sense, as if
she were a piano, and he the audience.

   4.

A white ferry strolls the horizon line:
a floating hotel, crystalline.
So much light and so much going.

Light as paper, seagulls
shriek and dip,
comparatively grey and dirty
with their angel-wings.
Sunset seeks the ship.

The other selves are creeping close tonight,
studying me: they made the choices
I didn't make. They lived promiscuously
with strangers for years and years,
becoming stranger to me,
with different wives and different lives,
taking the faces of strangers into their own.

A lightship
over the horizon,
invisible by day,
winks in evening wrack,
and, as I look,
signals knowingly back.

A ship snores out of the scud,
honking of risky work.

In the room there's an almost stillness
That's always been there
and tiny hands are picking at the window
and running down like tears.

HERON

The crematorium sits quietly by a river,
bosky, bird-haunted, willow-fringed.
At this double rendezvous,
fishing is dawdling by water
with apparently something to do.

Success is cruel: a fish flaps,
aghast at the thing in its mouth,
the net round its scales, the pain of air.
Yet a sharp smack on the back of the neck,
and the pain's not there.

The heron angles with no licence,
but glimpse a watcher, and he's off:
an awkward contraption with a glued head,
long S of neck, and a dangle of legs:
or a child playing airplane, arms spread.

In water he strides circumspectly,
not to tread on something sharp,
his knee at 90 degrees.
Feels down softly in the mud,
with his claws and his elbow-knees.

Apparently asleep or thinking,
he listens for fish. Long beak
pokes, gobbles, and his swallow
is quick. Stowed, he stands and meditates
and his flap away is slow.

Now in another place he works alone
somewhere beyond all this,
while the other watchers only wait,

scanning us from a new angle,
silently interested in our fate.

A herd of snipe are grazing:
hungry Chinamen
prodding chopsticks in a stew:
I'm absent; but once a lapwing
looked in my binoculars as if he knew.

ASHES

> *i.m. Geoffrey Castle,*
> *6 April 1898 - 8 February 1990*

The sun's bright: it's like a shopping trip.
It's the young man's lunch hour, but the ashes wait
gravely on the desk: metallic-brown, a cheap
plastic concave-sided mini-crate,
with an oilcan screw-top and an awkward fit
of a named and numbered self-adhesive chit.

Can you return it, please? Believe it or not,
they cost seven pounds. About as hard to make,
I think, as a detergent bottle. Why not depute
a fruit jar? – be cheaper and less fake.
I hold it tight and, trudging to the car,
my stomach tingles, feeling he's still there.

It occupies the mantelpiece and shapes
the whole room round it. Our lady
comes to clean, sees it and escapes.
He sits there, waiting his day: martinis,
gravlax, fillet, dual-coloured mousse,
a wine. But first we let him loose.

The wind's keen from the north, grooming the coast;
a pewter sea pours oyster waves.
In the evening sun a gibbous moon due east
looks somehow prescient, unduly grave.
The ashes pass from hand to hand; we three
watch, as one in daffodil waders walks the sea.

And the ashes pour like milk or sand.
Back, his bosun's whistle pipes three times.
And do they come, stand airily close at hand?
The stage is set – for invisible mimes
or empty coulisses? All's in reverse:
we speak to the stage: they don't converse.

The world is our idea. Turning from the mind,
we crunch the pebbles. The weathervane
points north: from behind that wind
the dead supposedly come. And now the main
has a different constitution, its whitening hue
white ash, like the waning man we knew.

I asked him, if he could, to let me know.

IGNORANCE

I sit in the great ignorance,
in a vast church in a city of doors.
Workmen bang and boom: a restoration
beyond a bewilderment of floors.

In the nothingness where I sit
circling buses and taxies peal,
like the peel from an orange
that's eaten and once was real.

Empty space always amazes, the something
that nothing was, with wrapping moods.
And later, locked in, unnoticed, I thump
twin doors: they burst, and the lock protrudes –

a tongue, but whether for insult
or kiss, or whisper, it's difficult to say.
But tongues remind of love
and love is suffering today.

My friend is dead. The glass is broken.
Emptiness remains without its shell:
and emptiness speaks, and silence,
though neither speak well.

NIGHT FEARS

Clambering to dark on the top-floor corridor's
row of moonlit rooms, you meet those eyes
and bony legs stalking the draughty floor.
You snatch the switch, to exorcise
the creaking boards and the paper faces
that ogle through the walls their old grimaces.

You sleep in shirt and pants, too scared
to be exposed or dowse the light.
Why was it no one cared
to tuck you in or say goodnight –
or noticed creased-up pants, the smell?
Why were you too afraid to tell?

And what to dream of in the dark? At times
You're a crew, wrecked in the arctic sea,
slipping their dinghy, to die betimes,
not linger in mist: choosing to die,
you know that moments later a ship will find
the man who chose to freeze and stayed behind.

Why this fear of the dark, this reluctance to tell?
New islands shine, new fauna and flora
emerge, mature, ripen, swell
and rot. Still at the tiller, there's Horror,
but you, strapped to the mast,
tune to blue night, coming, and coming fast.

KEITH VAUGHAN'S LAST JOURNAL

I thought last night about Boulanger, baker
of warm new bread, his own: those pearly nipples,
and that navel – another pearly acre.
Legs straight and strong, no bulging muscles.
I kissed him so many times. We had no sex.
Held him in my arms and touched his head,
breathing gently against each other's cheeks.
And six weeks later, Anzio Beachhead,
blasting to bits his lovely wine and bread.

That listening Japanese: beauty like the meat
of a wild cat: lotus lips and hawked
eyebrows; olive skin, widespread thighs, neat,
though little showing between. Stripped,
strung, slightly plump, by his wrist, naked
to a high bar, with a whip cracking, a fist
between the thighs, could I crack
the marble open of that smug conventionalist?
Ah, Boulanger, the hot bomb you kissed!

And life after death? Just guesswork. Oblivion!
Back, back to the state we had before
our birth: that beautiful death. But am I one
to do it at night? For then, happily, I snore
in my cups. Nothingness: what sleep can be –
what I itch for in the morning. But if the blood's
empty of drink, will the drug bring eternity?
I must be practical: death hardly could,
once the decision's made, be left to a mood.

The mask of Tutankamoun: the inorganic
universe of rock and water: onyx eyes,
gold, tear-stained cheeks. The kick
as it sees right through you. Childish, wise,
sad round the mouth, how understandingly
the face would make you go on trying. If God could woo
that way, I'd love his power, turn devotee.
The artificer of that mask certainly knew
and loved the godlike face that's peering through.

The camera reveres what's there: it can't
imagine the unseen. Those pursing lips
are poised to open, to receive. Eyes slant,
and – possibly – venom to spit. We strip
to meet a naked god: BC, three thousand-odd,
and yet it's Christ. He judges not. You
look at a king and he keeps looking: a god.
Even I could be happy, should I do
anything as beautiful as you.

Rock's where we come from and where we soon
go back: the kingdom of stone and water. And so:
viaticum, the capsules, the whisky, and the swoon.
How unreal, no bang, no wrists. I know
I'm dying yet feel no different. A bright
sunny morning like those so many die in.
I feel so alive. I feel no fright.
I do fear death but want it, let it come.
I might of course wake up. I did some...

MEETING

When I was supposed to meet you
to discuss my breakdown
the pub was full of drunken Orangemen
on their annual screw of the town.

I knew I was there on my own
but not why.
Had you put me there
to make me feel more alone?

My poems are all written to you,
even the scurrilous things:
especially the scurrilous ones –
trying to test your meanings.

You've sung to me in a pop song
and it's you who invented play.
If your cards are close to your chest,
I know you're not what they say.

Every day's a different story,
though I don't always see it as new.
I'm not always listening,
at least not always to you.

Who thinks they're far out?
Let them listen to you.
You're utterly outrageous.
You've seen everything through.

You saw it before it happened.
In the pub you were really there.
You know I can never be without you.
You invented the notion of dare.

GROWING UP IN THE THIRTIES

    1.

What day of the week was it – a Sunday?
He heard his father's shout upstairs and ran,
smelling the gas. She lay on a divan,
fishmouthed, unbeautiful, a face of whey.

She's still his mother, he loves her still.
And yet her face – it's like his grandma was
in the coffin, her sharpened nose and toes
when, forbidden to peek, he did for the thrill.

Or Antarctic Scott in the white film of those
losers in blizzards, drudging from the Pole:
cut off from affluence, the dressed-for-dinner role,
they pass their dead friend's grave and icicle nose.

Outside: flies heatstroked on the burning flags,
the boy next door bouncing a ball, trying
to dot them. Now he must hide his mother's dying.
As flies to wanton boys – school-Shakespeare rags.

   2.

She can never pass a mirror. It feeds her greed
to know she's there, suddenly grey: a gaping beak
famished for herself. Yet sybil, matriarch,
Rochester's wife: medium and mother in need.

Bony hands are clasping, can't stop wringing.
Legs must pace. Insufferable energy drives
the suffering machine: handwashing wives
can act the Lady Macbeth, neck-tendons stringing.

Set books at school are all about his home:
Paradise Lost, the sulphurous lake,
Rochester's secret, the visions of Blake.
Quo Vadis makes the room a burning Rome.

Out on the Rec, the click of a cricket bat,
a shout, a cheer. On the swings Harry's
doing his Harry Roy. His crooning carries:
This is yer old watcher-me-callum, flat.

   3.

Ruth stood among the alien corn,
loving to play her Haydn; also bright.
Not a great looker, or the sort to bite –
that the local lads'd feel and get the horn.

He loved her in his way, perhaps because
her life was not a matter of mere survival.
Himself, he summoned Beethoven, felt the arrival
whenever he beat C minor chords.

At the Gaumont he hardly dared to touch
her hand in the flickering black and white.
Her head's rigid as a sentry's, it doesn't seem right.
Oh! fear of rejection, oh need to clutch!

In the carriage back it's so difficult to chat.
Packed close with her's enough to make him hot.
Then down the train, a shout from a drunken sot.
It's Dad again, pissed, from a night out.

    4.

Outside the house, the usual gang of cheerful louts –
one in particular known to have fucked a pig.
The grammar-school cap can make you look a prig.
A chip off the old potato! – the usual shout.

Dad knows they spoil the street and hates
the prick to his pride still more: he stalks out,
and they break into cackle, scuffling about.
The beast's on the street. It only waits.

Hard at his sums, he hears his dad brought in,
K.O.'d by the boar that's married to a sow.
Right's on that side, for Dad is snoring now,
death in his breathing, slaver on his chin.

The newsreels know the ghettoes: mugs like those
can smile and smile: now the fact of race
smashes a world of glass, or a mother's face.
So should one be a Charlie, thumb the nose?

THE LONG RETREAT

> *One day in the Long Retreat they were reading in the refectory Sister Emmerich's account of the Agony in the Garden and I suddenly began to cry and sob and could not stop.*
> Gerard Manley Hopkins, *Journal*, 23.12.1869

Dear father, when I remembered your tears,
as I sipped some wine on a calm evening, I peered
out at my garden where a ravening blackbird
was picking for worms and a holly tree's
spikes seemed to be twisting its spines, and I
wept some tears like yours, knowing that Christ
is lovely in eyes and lovely in limbs not his,
eyes and limbs pierced in quiet places,
under the hammer, where no one hears,
and the choice is made when no one notices.

III: JEUX D'ESPRIT

> *Nowadays all we can tell you is this:*
> *what we are not, what we do not want.*
> Eugenio Montale, *Cuttlefish Bones*

ECONOMICS IN ALDEBURGH

> *Fundamentally, there are only two ways of co-ordinating the economic activities of millions. One is central direction involving the use of coercion – the technique of the army and the modern totalitarian state. The other is voluntary cooperation of individuals – the technique of the market place.*
> Milton Friedman

Living here, between a nuclear station,
and a sea-wall tides are slowly battering down,
everything's privilege, peace, stagflation.
Easy to be content with this little town –
content! No sign in that of economic health:
one ought to be chasing utilities and wealth.

Economists know that man's a maximiser,
his aim to maximise both wealth and pleasure.
War's fun, utility, and makes us wiser.

To give's not human. Enough's no treasure.
Freed man has learned the way to be humane:
The market maketh man and makes him sane.

The myth of a mixed economy's evasion.
The market has no need of public pelf.
Coercion's inessential to civilisation.
The market's free: you're free to sell yourself,
be sold, or unemployed: it's funny
how people hate to work but do love money.

A maxi-miser: man's a mini-miser in this locale –
miser of his uneasy, guilty luck.
The only defence he needs is against the real:
a sea wall, death, failed life, his love unstuck:
no money for these, unlike the planes and tanks
he buys to fight the reds or please the banks.

ANCIENT WALLS

The ancient walls with their patient lichens
are filling the graveyard with patience.

The poppy has chosen this little grave,
and the rhus spreads red leaves.

The horse-chestnut drops little polished
knobs: new brown shoes.

The old man's face and the girl's face
make the avenue of yews a frame.

In the Sunday distance a towering
hazy-morning steel crane is abandoned.

Dives comes out with the congregation,
and a wino Lazarus asks, *Any change?*

THE SLOW MOTION OF TREES

Hawthorn-soldiers
in their diminishing rank –

is it their spine or mine
crooked by the prevailing wind?

Or those slow
chestnut-meditations on roots –

is it their wine or mine
draining and winding down?

And oaks gesticulating
blindly in no wind –

is it the acorn in the heart
that makes their growing

a fisty centuries-long grind?

THE OPERA LOVERS

In Act One
the opera lovers
discover each other:
history stops;
eternity begins.

In Act Two
the lovers discover
how the earth spins
on history's sins.

In Act Three
history wins
and the lovers discover
how history stops
and the overture begins.

MATHEMATICS

Mathematics could always induce
an incalculable window-gazing curl
of glazed looking – to blush from, if questioned,
like caught red-handed with a girl.

And still a guest can glaze him through the glass
to tug with starlings, tails in air,
officious for something delicious
they're nippy for down there,

or to feel the wintery feeling
of the double-boled bow-legged pear,
or the down-in-the-roots horse-chestnut,
or the holly tasting the Christmas air.

HOLY LEISURE

> *Make all your life a holy leisure*
> St. Francis

His voice is the cat-purr
of a man trapped in a cell,
planning his escape.
He's a gambler: in the funny
business of buying and selling money.

Drink is out: his stomach says no.
His wife's hoping to make enough bread
or call it dough
to let the butterflies out of his stomach
and play round his boat instead.

She's frightened of him waltzing off
with the perfumed lady with
the leisurely alternative life.
Death frightens him
even more than his wife.

He pads stealthy, soft-pawed,
as if cased by MI5
or hoods on contract:

a cat that's been watching
thrushes all day, hunchbacked,

and now feels ogled itself
as, squeezed by jungle,
in obscure need of pardon,

it picks its way
out of the garden.

THE LONGEST SENTENCES

Pour dire les plus longues phrases,
Elle n'a pas besoin de mots.
Baudelaire, 'Le Chat'

In these dreams he's often teaching students
who don't want to come. They stroll in late,
won't settle down, titter, knit. He gets in, oh,
about five minutes of the proper stuff before
they're packing bags and ready to go.

In Blake's Visions, he explains, *a virgin's sweetly*
concupiscent, and sets off to find her lover, but
meets a cynic on the way, who rapes her by surprise.
Now here's a short story or novella,
but Blake makes his characters philosophise.

Conrad speaks of 'justification': make
your characters philosophise to taste,
so long as you plot a plausible premise
for your people to analyse their case.
The class is drifting off in fantasies.

And then, to his hot shame, he's weeping tears.
Teaching's a vocation, he breaks and cries.
You've taken the joy away. They shake their curls, they
rush to him in gusts of kind dismay.
They warm to his self-pity. They're girls.

AT THE SEMINAR

In the seminar room the sun
is shining on the desk more than anyone
can feel or say.

Isn't there, he wonders, *some way
to get his students to see
how displacing a shine can be?*

Even the poem's about
how signifiers can throw out
all capacity to see and be.

Instead of all this pother
if only we could just gently get together
washing and massaging each other.

EGG ON A MANTELPIECE

Some parchment-skinned Chinese
painted these boats, this pagoda,
this high peak and these
incomprehensible characters
for a pittance
on this eggshell.

In bad taste as well.
So thin a duster could break it,
and given in love,
it's lasted for years.

All history resides
on a souvenir
from a hen's insides.

HARD

It's hard to forgive the trivial things,
the dirt, the incompetence, the self-neglect
and the shambling practices.

It's difficult to forgive the smells,
the tobacco, the drink, the violence,
the need to be in control:

the desire to be top bully in a little world.
It's difficult to forgive them your snobbery.
It's difficult to need so much forgiveness,

to be ready for a heaven where there are
mothers and fathers and uncles and children.

WAITING IN WET

The metal bird appears to be watching me.
The old dog is bored by the puppy's attentions.
An ear-nibbling only makes him
sad, with the sadness of dogs.

The irritating persistence of rain hums,
and clouds curl round the would-be sunny ridges;
a cock crows occasionally, unconvincedly,
round the hill: boredom's current images.

The flies must know the sun will be coming out,
for they're coming out themselves. Or is it lunchtime,
and do they know? A carhorn crows down the valley,
with a frustrated wailing.

After a thousand miles, one rests
in a kind of driver's convalescence. The map's lost,
I've no watch, and action is stopped
by the steady downpour. I yawn and cannot read.

Even the olives are depressed.
The rain they're used to they don't need.
Into their second century, they're not going to
accept a drenching without a droop.

Into the second chapter I droop
but don't complain. In England there's a drought.
At least the wine here brings no headache.
Later I wake without a headache to the rain.

BY THE LAKE

A red pinebole glows like sunset
and I hug my arms around it.

A roach's eye glows in the lake:
a ruby. It sees my eye;
we watch each other.

Past the adder's nest
I met an elk:
we stared; he strolled away.

Two hares come boxing
on hind legs through the forest.
They see me and panic.

One part of my mind's a hare.
It's been dominating the rat.
Now the rat's eating the brain of the hare.

HOLES

There's a hole in the atom, between
electron and neutron, as distant
as Lords from Sydney.

I hoard gold inside me, with
sulphur, silver, the rest,
and holes leak my insides out.

My head's a hole in space
with no splash; a neutrino
quarks two holes in me at once.

There's a hole where someone was:
a hole in a mirror:
itself a hole in the wall.

Grief makes holes in a face
and so does laughter. The womb's
a hole, the soul's a hole,

and Felicity's the name of a cat
going through a hole
just wide enough for her whiskers.

NOTES ON LAO TZU

After the long silence with no one listening words split
                                        the beginning from the end.

Told he was dying, he said, *Ah well, that's life.*
However much he breathed, there was still more air.
Turning from the mirror, he was someone else.
He praised the dead, for no one envied them.
The tree let go its leaf without relief.

Without means meaningless, without end he was endless.
He evaporated like water and fell like water.
Too much was more than enough.
He led from below and got a head.
The hole in the clay made him a pot.

If he went into the hole in the ground he'd never fear death again.
He suspected a takeover but in the end the company just kept going.
The hidden was making secret investments.

His heart ached – there was so little at stake.
Too much light was making him blind.

He knew his mother's wishes were not his mother's.
His only hope was to escape from her advice.
When his father went to gaol he found he loved him.
A fool among fools, his only hope was to obey the rules.
Crossing the ice his step was precise.

His anxiety when he wasn't succeeding was only exceeded by
                                          his anxiety when he was.
Not at home even at home, he became inconsiderate, which made him
                                                                less at home.
His apologies were inexcusable.
He tried to admire himself and failed.
Everything was so strange he walked along listening.

He travelled effortlessly under gravity.
His temptation was to reject the easy way.
When he meant what he said he didn't know what he was saying.
Like the drunk in the street, he slept with his head away from his feet.
He never got too far in advance of the cookhouse.

Waste was bad, even of people.
He made a killing and it felt like a funeral.
Not knowing he needed saving he couldn't save anyone.
The ruler of the world had always ended up in a bunker with
                                                     a woman and a dog.
History was the history of discontent.

It wasn't easy to leave people alone.
Giving the people bread made government a piece of cake.
When the government was bad the people were happy.
By their prime ministers they knew them.
A good leader was invisible as the retina.

Although there was enough to go round it didn't go round.
The fat country had a thin country inside.
Reading the paper he knew more than he could understand.
The people were divided up among the loaves and fishes.
In his dream he remembered what he hadn't noticed.

If he'd invented air we'd all be gasping at the price.
Asked to choose between his big toe and fame he chose his toe.
It was too easy to find a reason for everything.
To make an omelette he'd needed to cook sensitively.
He didn't want to hurt the con-man's feelings by noticing.

But his problems acquired confidence.
He couldn't spot the beginnings before they happened.
The deepest vacuum was the biggest draw.
The best of the bargain was the worst.
Goodness was badly paid.

Flowery words yielded to seeds.
In the Old Folks' Home people were growing.
The man with the smile was a crippled roadsweeper.
Comfort was an oyster with no pearl.
The old soldier took his time.

The air was more secure than the balloon.
His absence was more than a presence.
What happened inside him happened outside.
Those doing the same thing weren't doing the same thing.
The starter was a loser.

Ill-bred, he tried to breed the well-bred.
There were more ways of eating than with a knife and fork.
Since he'd never die, he wouldn't multiply.
The generous host wasn't respected the most.
The truth made him laugh.

But he said so little they thought *We did this ourselves*.
The sea curtseyed, retreated and then swallowed a church.
It was hard to decide about death without knowing what it was.
Even if he'd known the map he'd have lost the way.
Unlike the wind, when he started blowing he had to go on.

THE SANTA SOPHIA OF AIR

> *The great forward movements of the Renaissance all derive their vigour, their emotional impulse, from looking backward.*
> Frances A. Yates, *Giordano Bruno and the Hermetic Tradition*

In the lantern of the upper air, sun
breeds a tropic. The conservatory
of gases turns the warming on.

The first big bang was silent: the ring
of quiet clogged into sounds we hear:
Alpha heard a crystal Omega sing.

Justinian thought he'd invented the new:
four arches, a floating dome of let-in lights.
Solomon, he said, *I've triumphed over you.*

But Hebrew prophecy, Roman and Eastern design
moulded the spandrels, the marbles, the glass mosaics:
lacy predictions of the Florentine.

We too anticipate the past: night
is our hemisphere, but domes diagram
half only of our balloon of light.

The cold blue radiations of space
make an architecture of refraction:
fake-solid spectra of place and race.

Aping faces gape from the gas and dust.
They mop and mow and crunch the forest mast.
A connoisseur keeps the best wine till the last.

SELECTED POEMS
Unpublished Poems
(1995)

VISITATIONS

1. The Child

At midnight I go down to the lake
and watch the light on the water.

It's stained glass: greens, reds
and turquoise hang among the trees.

A naked child emerges,
perfectly-grown, a foetus,

navelstring and placenta
still in place, dangling.

Ignoring me, it walks the bank
and turns, to sit watching the lake too.

I sit beside it, hoping it'll speak,
at least acknowledge my presence.

But it belongs elsewhere.
I say, *I'm sorry*.

It looks reproachfully at me,
then smiles, floats back into the lake.

First it seems to be swimming,
then slowly it disappears,

creasing and smoothing the surface,
like an aquatic creature.

2. The Face

The face pressed to my bedroom window
is only a face. It slides into my room,
flops on the floor.

Its black hair and eyes are full
of tender longing. It creeps into bed with me
and cuddles, slimy and rather smelly.

I feel uncomfortable: it's so alien,
slippery and rather creepy and,
being very sensitive, it notices.

I apologise and say
I can't help being human,
It's in the genes.

Delicately, it slides
out of bed and under the bed
and finds a chamber pot.

It drinks the pee and becomes
a beautiful woman, climbs
into bed with me, and I'm

strangely comfortable with her
even though I know she's
really a black slimy thing

that came out of the night.

3. The Man

When I open the door
the same man's there,
in his trilby.

He pushes by, walks upstairs
and sits down in the drawing room
in his coat and hat.

He still has no face and, when he
takes his coat and hat off, he's
invisible under his suit.

I sit down opposite
and wait for him to speak.
After a while he says,

I'm waiting for you to speak.
I say, I can only speak to myself.
Because I'm here and you're not.

He gets up silently
and disappears, leaving
his coat and hat on the chair.

DESPATCHES

   i.m. V. S.

   1.

I see myself driving
these eager streets
as the I that vanished might.

Do I still walk
Piccadilly with
the white flash in my cap?

I: a long trajectory,
beyond kin
and comprehension.

   2.

I look her name up
and it *is* in the directory.
Surname. Initial. Hers?

Spectres of spectres
who sat in the flesh
at Gielgud's Hamlet,

we were ghostlier
than the Ghost:
the silence and watch

of eternal love
in transient bliss
with the taste of an afterlife:

all that stage violence
our spectacular paradise,
Hamlet being ourselves.

   3.

Later,
in a salad restaurant,
it's lettuce, lights, smiles.

Forgetting passing-time
we outstay our curfew!

Outside, in the blackout
and explosions, she knows

a certain window, and,
for me, unbelievably,

the sentry's off for a pee!
I tiptoe upstairs in boots

in my Baker Street billet,
able to see her again.

And two years later, when I
call at her barrack, she's gone.

   4.

Time brings
absence. Demobilised,
we walk as exiles

in unspeakable history
from unspeakable childhood
and the invisible partner.

Queer inked-over photographs,
thinking we're living
the lives we're living,

we didn't exist, except
*one enchanted evening
across a crowded floor,*

putting our truly great trust
in gas and dust and mist
and the invisible partner.

    5.

Name in a telephone book,
who was the girl in the khaki skirt
and forties hair still haunting

a blacked-out street,
a lighted club, and a life
we never went to bed with?

FAUSTUS SPEAKS

*pecca fortiter, sed fortius fide...
...sin boldly but believe boldlier...*
                          Martin Luther

1. PURPLE HERON

Suddenly it's there –
before we know it –
the purple heron.

It sits by the reeds,
neck erect, not necessarily
watching, but listening.

A bird's always alert,
with that impersonal
ruthless eye,

feeding and mating,
tender with the young,
obeying the laws of God.

What law do we follow
when illicitly we find
we love each other?

Isn't illicitness
somehow more generous
than possession?

So many in matrimony
are asunder, whom God
hath not joined together.

2. Faustus Today

My car radio's playing Liszt's Mephisto waltz
with diabolical tritones, then Dutch baroque music,
then Liszt's fantasia on Don Giovanni.

Liszt is one of my presiding spirits.
Only the fantasia's wide of the mark.
Anyway, even if I'm dancing to the

alluring music of youth, you're no Gretchen.
Sophisticated, intelligent, witty, humorous,
you know what you want and what you're about.

Here's two on's are sophisticated. Alive,
though, with the old unsophisticated sigh:
I want to love and be loved!

It's not so easy to be loved, though, is it?

   3. Fly

Is every fly
an emissary
of Beëlzebub?

They vomit on your food
then stomp on it
to suck up the juicy pulp.

Whenever there's
one fly in the room
there are two of you.

It's not certain who's
more important in God's eyes
or Beëlzebub's.

The fly has skills:
walking upside down,
flying sideways,

avoiding swipes,
knowing when it's
snack or mealtime.

When will we learn
to accept our blackness
and the buzz of our black hearts?

4. Passionate Friendship

Since what we have
after a false start
is a passionate friendship,

I've understood
how far we are
from where we started.

Do I see in you
the integrity I've lost?
Do I see in me

the integrity you haven't found?
It seems a pity
to spend a whole lifetime

becoming a candidate for Hell,
but we grow
and we grow corrupt.

And corruption is the compost
growth grows in.

5. Sunflowers

I stare at a V-sign: sunflowers
fallen off a barge
on a canal at Amsterdam.

I read the entrails:
yellow petals
with an umber heart.

Just as I, speaking,
don't always allow
for your swiftness

you, in your presentation,
may not have allowed
for your audience's slowness.

But if they don't grasp
your point or your pun
they'll grasp your brilliance.

It's raining.
The sun's out of sight
but no less brilliant.

Then, in the evening,
I'm getting slightly drunk
on duty-free Black Label.

There's a distant piano.
I'm weary of time and
counting the steps of the sun.

When I'm dead and you're
famous, perhaps I'll be watching
from behind the sun

or beyond the sun,
counting your steps.
Perhaps I'll be younger than you.

6. The Purple Heron Again

Growing old, the phoenix
sees a girl like a funeral pyre
and, turning body to sun,

burns himself out,
rising from his ashes
nine days later.

In Heliopolis
the hieroglyph for sun-worship
is a heron-like bird.

The sun dies in his own fires
nightly, and every morning
rises again from Egypt.

Life is the
ritual sacrifice
of a purple heron.

7. Earthly Paradise

I lived alone, feeding on
light from the stars.

At the end of a thousand years,
knowing death was nearing,

I descended to Phoenicia and built
a nest of spices in the tallest palm.

At dawn, lifting my voice,
I sang a hymn so beautiful

I knew I was a poet and, that instant,
the rising sun stood still.

Sparks from its flames lit on my nest.
Instantly I rose from the ashes,

lifted up the aromatic dust
and flew to Heliopolis.

I placed the ash on the sun-temple altar
and winged towards my distant Paradise.

Thousands of birds followed me,
in friendship, singing.

8. Why He Wants to go to Bed with Her

You want to know,
Did I want to go to bed with you,
and was that why I liked your poetry?

No: I watched and heard you
reading your poetry
and I loved you and feared you.

I wanted to go to bed with you
to overcome my fear. When love is
become perfect, it casteth out fear.

Would I have loved you if you were fifty?
How can I answer a question like that?
What I do know and can tell you is this:

I feel a lot safer with women in their fifties.

9. THE HEALER

You yawn with that little
owl-like hoot that's so charming.

Or your eye criticises
your look in the hotel mirror.

Are you dressed avant-gardedly enough
for a conference on *The Connected Body?*

You're perfect: just yourself,
as if your mind had clothes on.

I can see you're turning healer,
and I the child.

I'm decades too late
to be the lover you deserve.

As you sense my insecurity
you become more secure.

Perhaps my weakness
is given to help you.

But help you to what?
Am I becoming your mouse?

10. Bells

Cracked bells ring the St. Anthony Chorale
before twelve deep notes.

One, you don't love me.

Two, you seem to need me.

Three, you only think you need me.

Four, sex is easy for you.

Five, you gave it because you needed me.

Six, if sex would have made you lose me,
You'd have withheld it.

Seven, your security about sex
makes me insecure about sex.

Eight, your feeling of the unimportance of sex
is incomprehensible to me.

Nine, if it's unimportant,
why are you withholding it?

Ten, for me sex is love,
and that makes it difficult.

Eleven, for you sex is not love,
and that makes it easy.

Twelve, what is it that's
brought us together?

In the dark silence I wonder,
Why do we want to talk to each other?

11. REDEMPTION

Profane as we are, poets must,
like St. Paul or St. Augustine,

tell what goes on in us
against all reason and morality.

So we both bring our best and worst
to our love, and our love

wrecks the journey, displaying us crudely
one to another, to ourselves.

Near Ghent there's a fire on the line.
We change trains and miss the ship.

Later, at night, we entrain for Victoria
and a man's killed under us on the line.

The tube from Brixton announces
Victoria is closed: the fire brigade's there.

In the small hours we taxi to a coach station.
Later I ring, exhausted, frustrated and drunk.

I rang to see if you'd arrived safely,
but I scare you with my paranoia.

12. SKIN

An inflammation on the skin
can be a sign of sin –

not sin done,
but sin undone –

some act of love,
licit or illicit –

immoral grace
in the place

where fingers
ought to visit.

13. SEHNSUCHT

Yearning's better in a foreign language:
the word obliterates that look of familiarity.

Sehnsucht's an agony stronger than sex
only assuageable by the connected body.

Have you any idea how precious
your bits of paper are to me?

For you, hasty missives,
dashed off to save a letter,

for me, presences of inadequate handwriting,
standing in for the presence I long for.

The agony of being alive is so strong,
nothing can assuage it except your body.

Sehnsucht's an elongated agony
parallel to eternity and going on for ever.

14. THE END

It was sad to see your sheets
revolving in the washing machine.

I shan't forget your breath
coming rhythmically on my shoulder

and your breath on my mouth
while you were asleep.

It's a privilege to know you're prettier
with your clothes off than on

which isn't true of everyone.
I know where your moles are,

what your toes are like
and I love your teeth

and your long nose.
I know how sweetly you smell.

There are moments when I can
look right through your hazel eyes

to the person looking out.
Our eyes are in touch with

transcendence. Some day
shall we be together?

A USELESS PASSION
(1998)

CALLED TO THE COLOURS

Through my birthdate, a couple of typical military cockups, and a coincidence or two, I had a cushy war. I was in Dover during the shelling, but I wasn't personally shot at till the war was over, when a Pathan tribesman whom I hadn't joined up to fight tried to kill me.

Some people I'm very fond of went through the thick of it, and so I find it slightly forward to be publishing these records of the boredoms and humiliations of soldiering. Nevertheless, what's a writer for except to write? And since bullshit rather than heroism was the lot most of the time, even the heroes had to go through it.

Many of the items only aspire to the condition of poetry, and some are trivial, but I hope they justify their place in this minor historical narrative which, I'd like to think, carries its own poetic logic and might remind others of the tomfoolery, the comradeship, the cruelty, the fun, and what it was like to be young then.

LINCOLN, AUTUMN 1943

1. Pissoles

Yer eyes are like pissoles in snow.
Sergeant Birkett fixes us
with a seagull stare.

Six weeks, and he'll crack the same joke
to a new intake. This too is a stage,
and the old jokes are best.

Last night we drank three pintfuls
of powerful Lincolnshire cider.
It cost a day's pay.

The bugle sings reveillé, at O six hundred hours –
a new kind of clock for
a new kind of life.

Then a cold-water shave in the ablutions,
with no light, though now there's
light enough for the officer to check our shave.

We ourselves are hot khaki pissoles
in the cold snow
of defending our country.

2. Students

My fellow former-students are wallowing
in this charade: this is the life:
playing soldiers.

In the evening they settle down happily
to dura-glit their buttons and their mess tins
and blanco their webbing.

I sit in the bar drinking cider. I imagine
cracking a person on the jaw with my rifle-butt
and my bayonet going into his belly.

I want out – to visit the cathedral –
out of this farcical detention camp
for the defenders of freedom.

Supposing I were a conscientious objector.
Would I work on a farm, or sit
happily in prison?

Since I volunteered to be a hired assassin
I must endure the immediate nemesis
of boredom.

3. Lincoln Cathedral

An invisible energy
hurtles through space
and is incarnate in air.

Flying through the oldest glass
in England, it's a
great rose eye

under whose largeness my
small eye watches me
wandering in darkness.

I'm a light myself under
my bushel of khaki, only
occasionally aware.

Even my air is paid for
by the work of breathing,
but light is free.

Tinctured and enriched
with these stains
I'm a wealthy St. Francis.

MAIDSTONE, WINTER 1943

1. The Regimental Sergeant-Major

This Mr. Hyde has a face of Punch,
hellfire eyes, a horn of a chin,
and the energy of a fly.

Even off parade, even to the Naafi,
arms swing shoulder-high, and
the carborundum throat's about to grind:

Left-roight, left-roight.
The swagger-stick whips and points and plies:
Head back, that man, thumb up, and shoulders square!

The joke's on us. The only enemy in sight
is this familiar, blessed with the right
to have a voice in how we go to shite.

2. First Booze-up

None of us have learned to drink.
A glass of port at Christmas, a stolen pint,
but now we sip a whisky, a sherry, and a gin.

Who was this khaki girl I was kissing?
Somehow back at camp and up at reveillé,
It's a vomit for breakfast, not my first.

Dawn is dawning: getting canned
requires the skill and wariness
of a night out in *No Man's Land.*

3. Defenders of Freedom

Wire surrounds our free time too.
We're on parole and owned by someone else.

And how to get a girl? The pay's too low to feed her,
the girls in sight callipygous, coarse, unread.

We all believe there's bromide in our tea.
Army life unmans you, but eyes can docket

sweet fruit behind an ATS breast pocket.

4. Vera Lynn

We'll meet again, don't know where,
Don't know when, but I know…

whom will I meet again? Myself perhaps?
And will it be in heaven?

5. The War Office Selection Board

Here's a glimpse of a lost civilisation.
The food good, beds comfortable,
officers courteous.

The table's for ten. I choose a place
next to the captain. Rumour has it
that it helps to get you in.

I take good care to sit up straight
and neither hunch nor shovel. I fork
a morsel gracefully to my mouth.

The captain's handsome and finds me,
apparently, entertaining.
I recognise good breeding.

Even the tasks are to my taste:
simple psychological tests
in comfortable classrooms.

A picture of a motherly-looking
lady at a rural garden gate.
A world that's gone,

I write, *yet still
worth fighting for*. Bullshit's
what you learn, and not for nothing.

There's a mini-rugby match
on an obstacle course. As former
hooker for the first XV I'm footsy.

Now I must manoeuvre
three men across a road of mustard gas
with duckboard and rope.

Right, you men! I say.
Any suggestions?
I get them across

but am not accepted. Sent back
for three months, to grow up.
I joined the Corporal's Cadre yesterday.

6. The Lance-corporal's Cadre

More battle drill, and the same old stuff:
two hours bashing Napoleonic formations
about the square.

The instructors are the duffers.
Who can – do,
who can't – teach cadres.

Lieutenant Atkinson's a lanky mouse
with a dingbat mad-dog look –
camp as a khaki tunic allows.

Rosy-cheeked, with an epicene
giggle, a silly grin and
dead-keen determination,

he plans a march, four days, a hundred miles.
Day two, his feet are bleeding in his boots.
Maverick, sado-masochistic, all smiles,

He's no hermaphrodite.
Day three, he shoulders a Bren-gun.
Like us, he's really out of sight.

7. Lance-corporal

Now I boss recruits around,
straighten rifles and salutes, inspect
shaves, adjust the angle of another's feet.

I roar them up and down the barrack square,
jolly them at the bayonet bags, shout
Kick him in the balls as I was taught.

I teach the secrets of the Bren,
how, with the middle finger, to slide
the catch back underneath.

I don't say *You'd soon find it
if it had hair round!* Could I
find something with hair round myself?

8. Corporal Cosgrove

Cosgrove's a matchstick version
of the RSM: same height, or smaller,

but legs like straws and boots like Mickey Mouse.
His black Brylcreem has a white crack like surgery.

Mincing up and down before the ranks,
he stamps like a guardsman on the turn,

salutes, and his arm swings up, a railway signal,
vibrating at the eye. Even in our room,

he parades the floor, halts and smiles triumphantly
at the punchline of his favourite joke.

His arm's a hard-on: *Wallop! Red hot cock!*
He smiles to himself, repeats it once or twice,

and I'm watching in the certain knowledge
he's never been inside a woman either.

DOVER, SPRING 1944

    1. Dover Beach

I share a first-floor billet
looking out onto the harbour
with Lance-Corporal Dalrymple.

Some people would pay a lot
for a room and a glitter like this
if it weren't for the shells.

In the night we hear them whumping
but the salvoes are short
and we hardly wake.

The few townsfolk left
sleep in the white caves
but bed is better.

Some days I feel Matthew Arnold
looking over my shoulder
at the Sophoclean sea.

We must, he says, *love one another*
and I'd like to
but I've no one to love.

    2. Arris

Arris is absent without leave much of the time.
Much of the time he's in the Glass House.
He's dark, almost black, with a ferine gleam.

His teeth are sharp, white, seen between
trees in a jungle, his wink's demonic – *Oo,
soon slip up and down inside er…*

Women are easy meat. They love him. Even our
dour major has a soft spot, smiles, would like to
rehabilitate Arris. Guts, I see, gain you admiration.

I visualise him on a dark night, creeping into
an enemy trench, cutting a throat, and creeping away
unnoticed. Men made for killing don't take orders easily.

   3. TRIPLANE

An air-sea rescue triplane's in trouble.
Parked on the promenade, it needs
protection.

The lance-corporal and private detailed
to stand guard are easy meat for Calais.
A shell hits them

and the two men and the plane explode.
Someone in authority
ought to have realised

that people
are a poor protection
against high explosives.

   4. THOUGHT IN THE RANKS

The infantry makes you too fit to think:
muscles use up the blood intended for the brain.

But the brain's sluiced by sea air. It recalls
a you you were, as you witness seagull and sky.

One by one, nearly the whole platoon
has taken me aside and told me their story –

their childhood, how their wife betrayed them,
and I wonder, do they tell it to everyone?

Do they sense I'm bookish, wondering
what to write? Never sure what constitutes

good writing, I sneak to the Dover library,
study *Horizon*, share the little

fat man's self-absorption in my own swap for a life.

5. Roll Me Over in the Clover

Out of the cold channel-wind, and the blackout,
and roasting by the fire in the pub,

I watch a three-chord man banging at the piano
with a permanently-renewing pintglass on the lid.

The ATS contingent's even hotter than the blaze:
Roll me over, they're roaring, *in the clover,*

Roll me over, lay me down and do it again.
If only they were appetising, and I fancied them.

I do want it. A corporal asks me, *When you do it,*
do you pull it out or like to let it soak?

I ponder. I've never been inside a woman.
I like to let it soak, I say. He grins and winks:

We're in the same team: *That's it*, he says.
The only way. Just lovely. Let it soak.

6. Shells

The CSM is marching us up and down
the sea front. Over in Calais
a Hun is studying us through a telescope.

He lays a clutch of eggs
inside the harbour wall, just inside,
and we start to duck for cover.

The CSM doesn't like this show of arse.
He stands up straight and calls us to attention:
Parade, shun! And the roll is shouted.

It'll be nice to know who was here
when we're in heaven. And Britons
never never let the Hun see arse.

More eggs are laid
in the centre of the harbour.
Then more, now closer still.

Then silence. They've no shells left.
In my mind's eye a Nazi officer's dancing:
Dummkopfen! Donner und blitzen! Scheisse!

Later, the CSM is posted to France
and is killed at once. He was short on
using his loaf and the indispensable cowardice.

Or, could be, his own men killed him.

7. War Literature

Lance-corporal Dalrymple's a potential officer:
bespectacled, courteous, quiet and pimpled.

We've a luxury boarding-house view of pebbles and harbour walls,
with twenty-four hours on and twenty-four off.

We guard the coast, and it gives us time
to talk about books in our little arbour.

Lance-corporal Dalrymple's smoky eyes glow
as he nurses and recommends Howard Spring's *Shabby Tiger*.

I can't work out why it's not a good book, or why
the dirty songs we sing on marches aren't better than Wordsworth.

It's the first popular novel I've read, and the worst,
since I suffered through shelves of Rice Burroughs at the age of twelve,

loving an egg-laying Goddess of Mars
and fighting her red wars.

8. June 6

The ditches and roadsides
are lined with soldiers,
all quiet, resting in full gear.

It's as if legions of angels
have suddenly been summoned,
though they smoke and drink tea.

They know where they're going
and it makes them quiet. Soon
we know: they're splashing and falling

up the French coast and we're a transit camp.
One of ours puts his rifle in his mouth
and blows his head off with a 303.

9. A Red Light in the Night

June 12, 1944

Duty corporal, I'm nodding
as my sentry alerts me.
There's a plane that's coming
and showing a red light.

Sure enough, up there
in the night sky
there's a red glow
and it's not on fire.

Who's this, haring from France?
Hitler with peace terms?
Someone escaping –
knowing it's not working?

Over our eyebrows
it buzzes inland,
till suddenly silent.
Long pause: a loud bang.

Whatever he wanted to say
he won't say now.
I wake the company CO.
He believes me and rings HQ.

It wasn't Hitler, we hear,
but a plane with no pilot.
Now we call it the buzz bomb.
It's when it stops its buzzing that it stings.

TRANSIT, WINTER 1944

   1. Pre-octu, Wrotham

Wrotham's a famous waste of time:
Two weeks' driving and maintenance –
hardly enough and, anyway, infantry officers
aren't allowed to drive.

It's just a transit camp. These old-iron
double-declutch fifteen-hundredweights
are meant to keep us busy, and they do.
My instructor fears my driving, and he's right.

And now our draft is picked for time in India.
I cough, and the doctor discovers there's been
of course a cock-up: I should have been Grade Three.
Chronic bronchitis, but somehow I'm right now.

Is it the doctor, or was it that Dover air?

2. Dancing to Victor Sylvester

Off to a couple of days of Mersey fog, and then
entraining back again. Back in London,
our billet's a convenient Baker Street hotel.

This is the big city of illustrious names,
punctured by sudden bangs. I dance
in the Nuffield Club in Leicester Square.

Across the floor, above her khaki collar,
I spot warm eyes I know can feel and think.
And now she's in my arms. She's plump and warm,

a person through the khaki, with breasts and breath.
A year of scratchy blankets without sheets
has led me to be foxtrotting with softness.

3. Escaping Curfew

Is love a coward? Her celestial flesh
is daunting. I feel her shoulder

touching mine, as we watch Gielgud's
dashing Hamlet in the Haymarket.

Ours is a love of blackout and big bangs, kisses
like strawberries and cream, but where to go?

In a restaurant where they serve just salads
we remember ourselves and forget our curfews.

And yet she climbs in by a regular window,
and the sentry at my hotel door has somehow gone!

I tiptoe up stone stairs in army boots,
lie on my creaking bed and breathe relief.

So is this history? We move in
clockless dimensions where miracles happen.

4. Unidentified

We ask no questions and are told no lies.
She comes from Austria, and is Jewish, I guess.

Like her, I have no past, I have no relatives,
and any future's hypothetical.

She does have friends: a naval officer,
outside a London club, notices, I notice,

how we're together. As for me,
I'm a prince with a white flash,

no longer an ignorant provincial boy.
My blackout's complete.

TROOPSHIP, DECEMBER 1944

1. Inside the Whale

The hammocks creak as they swing,
soothing, in the night, to the
throbbing foetal heart of the big ship.

Being cadets, we're on the least desirable deck,
six storeys down, an intestine of netted bodies,
dancing cheek to cheek, snoring and farting.

There's adventure in the belly of the whale,
nosing out of a benighted foggy Mersey, with an
invisible convoy and God knows what out there.

2. Sea-gale Mathematics

In the Bay of Biscay, it's living in a lift:
I toil up three steps, trip up another twenty.

At breakfast the table's set for twelve,
but only two have appetites. That's six eggs each.

3. The Mediterranean

Past Gibraltar our convoy's visible
with its destroyers and corvettes – nervous
nannies, nursing and fussing their flock.

Sea air charms the lungs. It's life in a film:
witnesses of ourselves on location, in a war at sea.
The occasional tentative depth charge tries the deeps.

With nothing to do but play pontoon and think,
I tell my fellow-cadets the brass prefer
latently homosexual officers: they love their men.

Remember Sassoon and Owen, I say – *and
Graves's battlefield strewn with bloodstained boys.*
Someone's heard. *Do I think it's true?*

Oh yes. I look at him solemnly, and he
looks at me with interested speculation.

4. Port Said

Men in kaftans lift their skirts, raise a fisted
forearm from their crotch and do a dance.

Boats are bumping alongside, trying to sell. There
it is: the blueness, sand and heat we've merely imagined.

Not allowed ashore, we can only picture
the woman fucked by a donkey as we line the rail.

5. Wild Life

In the Red Sea we're invaded by locusts,
corn-on-the-cob contraptions

with grasshopper heads and live antennae.
They whirr about inside like model planes.

I sleep illegally on deck: sparks of light
are flashing from the prow, and dawn flying fish
skim the blueness like a squadron of swallows.
Escaping predatory jaws? – or is it joy?

Life aboard is a clockless discourse.
I lean or sit and watch an unfolding text.
The happenings are made by sailors and politicians.
The purpose of my life – will I know it in the next?

OTS, DEHRA DUN, JANUARY 1945

1. BOMBAY

O city, city – city of spectacular
cripples. A legless trunk is swinging,

arms for crutches. The streets are nested
with big-eyed beautiful children.

They clutch and stretch like new-hatched beaks.
Vultures circle over the Parsee cemetery.

So many things to see – stupefied
by misery and humid heat.

Parents cut off limbs to give
their child a trade, and we are here to make

more cripples, or be made. The train's
squat-bog is showing my first scorpion.

2. DEHRA DUN. WATCH YOUR SALUTING

Our CO's handsome and a wonderful wit.
He makes us feel the army's terrific sport.

Narayan Singh, a Garhwali,
is proud to be my bearer.

In khaki drill, with a forage cap,
he looks a soldier, which is high-caste.

Every evening a zinc bath of hot water
waits in my little room, by clean clothes.

I find I'm good at squash and relish
clean white shorts and my 1st XV school blazer.

War seems far away. I keep a map of Europe
and mark the progress of our troops' advance.

One night, our CO falls asleep with a fag
and is nearly burned alive.

3. POETRY

Major Cooper's dark, chimp-eyed, gung-ho,
bushy-moustached and a little callipygous –

with all the traces of appreciative
teachers and fond womenfolk.

When he realises I've an Auden in my kit-bag
He's a trifle awed, even wary.

He writes a lot and has a poem that starts,
What glory is in sound of Kanchenjunga!

I don't know what to say, because I like him
and he almost seems to hold me in esteem.

4. LEARNING URDU

My munshi is a poet. Mousy,
plump, beaming, civilian, with a shiny-eyed

modest good opinion of himself.
I'm always floored by people who say they're poets.

Being a poet, I can see, is a state of mind.
I put it that the poet's is a rare calling.

He tells me everyone in India's a poet.
I sense a criticism of England,

but what does he mean? He must mean
a life lived in the light of samadhi?

Right or wrong, on the path it gives him
identity in a country's crushing disasters.

Golgonooza, thought Blake, is built by every
poetic act. Nothing anonymous is overlooked.

Perhaps my little munshi will be glorying in those
gold and ruby streets and diamond houses.

5. Infantile Paralysis

I'm in the sick bay myself with dysentery
when Stringfellow's brought to the next bed.

He's studious-looking, a sixth-form swot,
with almost white hair and wire specs.

On the edge of frightened tears,
he tells me he can't move his legs.

I've hardly spoken to him before, but I feel
guilty when, two days later, he's dead.

6. McCulloch

I don't know how he knew it was my birthday.
He bought me a box of cigars.

Not very good cigars: more like
brown paper, but it's the thought.

Dry, fibrous, brittle, a hot smoke,
they slightly burn my mouth.

Nevertheless they're a luxury,
redolent of affluence. I loll in my chair

and smoke one in front of him. I can see
from his face it's a good performance.

I blow smoke rings. But the gift embarrasses me.
I find his friendship cloying and tend to avoid him.

When he was sick in hospital, I didn't go.
Our platoon-commander told me how ill he was.

Now McCulloch's dead of a bug, like Rupert Brooke,
and I, like a pie dog, have my tail between my legs.

7. Religion

Narayan Singh can infallibly tell
a converted sweeper from a real Sikh.

When we go on an exercise to the Jumna
he begs a canteen of the holy water.

We can see the sacred Himalayas, which even
Englishmen want to climb because they're there.

Mountains, however dumb, speak
spectacularly, of ice, of holy heights,

intoxicating air, and the force of
continental shifts that folded them.

I gave up God for war, but Nanda Devi
Doesn't seem to have given up me.

LEAVE IN TEHRI-GARHWAL, SPRING 1945

1. Guests of the Rajah of Tehri-Garhwal

Our trucks wind up passes and traverse gorges
with rivers whitening the rocks.

The terraced slopes are giant staircases
in a wilderness of former chieftains,

each with his *Garh*, his fortress.
But Ajai Pal subdued them

and made a mountain kingdom
in the days of our Bluebeard Henry.

Three hundred years go by,
and then the Gurkhas kukri the king.

We war down the Gurkhas, restore a king
and recruit Garhwalis, each with his kukri,

his head shaven, and a tiny pigtail
that angels can pull him up to heaven with.

2. Killing

I can still hear it crashing through the branches,
the thump as it hit the ground.

The size of a large dwarf, thickset
with powerful hands, it's quite a weight.

I look in the ape's wise face
and the bloody hole in its heart.

The killer has a quiff, a 303,
and a face like banana fool.

There are those in this war
who can't wait to do a killing.

We hide the body in the undergrowth.
It hasn't happened.

   3. BORDERING TIBET

Dark kids dip in our dak-house pool,
and dart out like otters.

Tibetan traders trudge, mules loaded with
borax, yak tails, herbs, and the underwool of goats.

Robed in saffron, a sadhu
strides down the path, giving me a tiger look.

Out there, the priestdom of monks, magic,
buttered tea and polyandry is living in peace.

I try to imagine a circular city
less than a mile in diameter,

where, above the huge ski-jump of Potala Hill,
flat roof, tiered windows and balconies,

they have explanations of me
and the legless man in Bombay.

They look out serenely on a cosmos
where desire and life are the only problems.

I stand here with my whey-face
in a mass-production war,

dressed in the colour of dung
and training to kill.

JUNGLE TRAINING, SUMMER 1945

1. Saharanpur: Our First Mess

Get it wrong here, and you're a flop.
This is the one thing you've been trained for.
This, you could say, is going over the top.

One false move, and never again
will you be anything. Do's and don'ts
are endemic to gentlemen.

For Mencken, a gentleman's
easily defined: he never strikes a woman
without provocation.

At grammar-school we
defined a gentleman as one who
got out of his bath to have a pee.

While I treat my knife and fork with exquisite care,
a delicate hand on my shoulder makes me turn:
I meet a simian stare:

sultana eyes, vampire canines, wide agape,
hairy arms stretched out for crucifixion.
It's Albert, our female gibbon ape.

2. Ringworm

Here, in our jungle muddle, we've the monsoon.
In the pouring rain, booted and gaitered,

in jungle-green trousers and Garhwali hat,
bare-chested and festooned with ringworm, I look,

in my violet medicament, like a balloon.
I stand in line for the visiting brass

who invariably fail to pass. All the generals,
not unkindly, look me up and down and frown.

3. Albert

Albert knows she's the natural mistress
of soldiers famished for womanflesh.

On the ground her fingers dangle.
Best she likes to be sailing through the air.

We grab her hands and send her flying
over the Mess to another lover.

A drink too many, she misses a hold –
and smiles her single grimace:

bared teeth and raisin eyes.
Funny, those female arms around your neck.

4. Military Exercises

Our schemes are schemes
of discomfort, doused by
power-showers of lukewarm rain.

Cutting our dripping way through jungle,
mucking along, and scoffing cold damp
curried spuds from a plantain leaf,

we sleep in wet beneath our bivouacs –
groundsheets strung like tents between two trees.
Pointless they are: they keep us watered.

A captain seemed to think that,
fresh from OTS, we'd be teaching
the latest gen on jungle bivouacs.

Studying my groundsheet on its string,
swelling the raindrops even larger,
I try to invent a better tent but can't.

5. Horses

The battalion's three retired chargers
go for stately walks with a gaggle of mules.

The days of ha ha among the trumpets are gone by,
but a ride'll trim his figure, I propose.

He doesn't agree, liking his grub and club.
Astride him, my legs spread like on a hippo's back.

Getting him out is the hard bit – he
strains his big neck backward, knowing better.

I show the beast who's boss, and
more or less haul him with muscle out of camp.

Then I turn, and he's off. I ought to be
the boss, but, hunched like a cowboy,

I duck the jungle branches,
evade the flying tomahawks and the arrows.

Days later I've got him trotting,
when a lightweight lorry flashes from behind.

The fool panics, skips onto the road,
slides on the wet tarmac, falls

and galls himself. I'm thrown.
I reflect, as I ride him back

to his scandalized groom that
horses are beasts of action.

Cows are intelligent: slow
contemplatives, curious to know.

6. RALPH

Ralph got ratty on leave in Gulmarg,
and one evening I fought with him.

Now he squats barefoot,
in underpants and shirt,

chatting up the dhobi.
He gives a sunshine grin.

They ship him back to England.
Is he really round the bend,

says Len, *or is it a con?*
Who knows, the lucky bugger!

7. SEPTEMBER 1945

Six weeks in the rain, and I'm posted to Burma.
Next day the news comes: it's This Bomb.

If what they say is true, I scoff,
the war's over...

That week we're summoned before
the little major-general with the big map.

I suppose, he clips from his foxy face,
you chaps think you're in for a cushy time.

Well, you're not. The next war's
with Russia, and we start training for that now.

The map unrolls on the wall, and we see:
Russia's almost poking Waziristan.

My ringworm's livid, but then
they change my posting, to Razmak, in Waziristan.

THE NORTH WEST FRONTIER, AUTUMN 1945

1. Razmak

The Mahsuds, with their light skins and ruddy cheeks,
stride along, each slung with a rifle,
dagger at belt.

Here it's Hadrian's Wall.
Our troops peer across the stone battlements
or out of towers, like legionaries.

Saturday in the club is the click
of snooker balls, Indian beer, then
Sunday hangover and a curried morning.

The nearest woman's cantonments away.
Captain Scott's 'Tiger' is too manky to fondle.
Nightly we stand on the verandah and spray the lawn.

2. Second-lieutenant Pettit

Pettit's fatal move that first
lunchtime in the sixth-battalion mess

was asking half-shy, half-sly, for a whisky
when we asked for sherry.

Posted two weeks later, he's Colonel Hewson's oblation
to the God of Worry for his hard-drinking mess.

3. Out of the Body

Scampering and skittering up stony slopes
we bag our coigns of vantage on the hills
and sit in this thin heady oxygen.

Scampering and skittering down,
I find I'm racing for a rock,
bullets bouncing round my boots,

and I'm in the air, watching,
aware of life, aware of death:
equally possible, both waiting quietly.

I watch what seems like
a former self racing for a rock,
which he reaches,

and then I'm one with his crouch –
grinning at two grinning havildars –
while mortars whump.

Tubby Sen's binoculars
study the sniper's ridge
from a steel car. A mule is dead.

Later Tubby, glum as a pike,
studies me without binoculars,
as Fet cackles

and I know I'm accepted and can die young.

4. INTOXICATION

After dark, within our temporary drystone walls,
I sink to the bottom of my slit
and feel my steel-framed campbed
bouncier than a bed with springs.

Up there the stars are drinking oxygen
and burning brighter. My lungs are ecstatic.
From the bottom of my little room
Everything's extending for ever like an expanding attic.

5. NIGHTS IN THE SIXTH BATTALION MESS

There's a shortage of good whores in Mobile...
Oh the Ball, the Ball, the lovely Ball, the Ball of Kerriemuir...

The songs are new to these nine KCOs
in our stone camp surrounded by barbed wire.

We get pickled on Gibsons:
little white onions in the gin.

Major McFetridge is egg-bald like the chaps,
though without the pigtail: a white egg.

Short, always chirpy, balding,
he was glad to complete the job

and be like them. He sighs, though,
gives rueful glances, as if fending off

endemic melancholy or clinical world-pessimism,
grins, bird-shrugs, and caws his version of

Drinking rum and coca-cola...
Working for the Yankee doll-a-a-a-ar.

6. In the Sick Bay

We're the only patients this weekend,
this captain from another camp and I.

We're bored. The orderlies must be skiving.
I sneak to the bazaar, get Gordon's and a rye.

Drunk, he tells me about a barmaid's kiss.
You break a glass, it seems,

and dab the jagged points in someone's face.
And now I see he's trying to break a glass.

I look at his narrow head, the clean white parting,
the killer moustache, the ironic yellow pupils,

and go. I lock his door, circle, and
lock the other that's down the corridor to my room.

I can hear him breaking furniture, being sick.
At dawn I vomit and expect the high jump.

It never comes. Are they covering up
for their skiving? Or hasn't he snitched?

Anyway, the climate's curing my ringworm.

7. Dum-dam

Here in our high rank at the high table,
after thirteen starters and tumblers of white rum,
I face a vast brass tray of goat and rice.

My Urdu's doing well, with family smalltalk,
when drum and harmonium bring on the dancing girls.
They sidle round a curtain and peep from sari-folds.

Their bums and fingers dance and gesture expertly,
and now that all this rum's gone down so well,
it's impracticable not to barter ogles and grimaces,

though I know they're epicene sepoys with pretty faces.

8. Dashera

In the Autumn, black cross-eyed Kali
with her skull beads, long red tongue,
girdle of snakes and ten arms

is worshipped for nine days,
and then, on the tenth,
cast into the water of the Dasahara.

We sit at a raised trestle-table
with thirty nervous goats bleating below.
Havildars stand with sharpened kukris.

They grab a horn, whack the blade down,
and the heads roll clean.
The whole battalion watches religiously.

The goats panic, skittering
on slippery blood, the kukris go blunt,
and bad-luck second-whacks are raining down.

Tubby is hunched. He rolls
an anguished frog's eye at me,
bloodshot as a frightened horse's.

The goats are hung to drain in a smoky room.
We eat them raw, but luckily I don't
get eyeball in my rice.

Major Havildar Singh lost caste
by eating with Europeans. At home
his mother makes him take his meal outside.

KOHAT, SPRING 1946

   1. Holi

In springtime, togged in white,
we follow a tree tagged with red
from barrack to barrack.

The procession grows, and so does
the singing, till we plant the tree
ceremoniously and with dignity.

It's the start of a week-long booze-up.
Pails appear, and bamboo syringes,
and red water's spattering us piebald.

At night it's arms round shoulders,
swing left, swing right, swing left,
left foot over, right forward, and curried armpits –

Gadje Singh-a, Raneh Hatth-a ni janu:
We're singing about a man who
went into the mountains and came to no good.

2. Mrs. Eaton

Now there are women.
I dance with perfumed saris,

my breast to their breasts,
and enrage their husbands.

There are wives
flown out from England.

I sit by the swimming pool,
admiring Mrs. Eaton.

I'd like to commit adultery.
She's sunny and pretty

and perhaps she too
would like to commit adultery.

But we're loyal to Captain Eaton,
and we flirt about books.

Good dog! I tell her retriever.
You're so b-eau-tiful.

Just look at him, she says.
He believes every word you say!

LANSDOWNE, SUMMER 1946

1. The Regimental Centre, 9,000 Feet Up

Nowadays malaria's a court martial offence,
but a poisoned proboscis has poked me in Lahore.

Still with leave, I sweat it out,
and Moti brings me mepocrene.

Inside my cabin bed among the pine trees
I'm outside, on the needles, trembling.

Three white ghosts – Siamese triplets –
walk right through me, and I want to shriek.

Back on parade, malaria unreported,
I fall asleep on my feet.

In the Mess too I fall asleep
and miss the MO's funeral.

My new CO has noticed. I'm posted
nine thousand feet down, where

it's hot and we live in straw huts.

2. Straw Huts in Kumaon and Albert's There Again

It's sticky here, but Captain Gallup
and I swing Albert round our straw-roofed mess.

She goes to the women's quarters, smashes
their bathroom and eats their toothpaste.

I'm in for early demob, but this young
cold-eyed CO says it's not so.

He makes me Quartermaster. I have to sign
for each damned round and gun.

A week later, though, my papers are through.
I smile at him like toothpaste

and I pack and go.

DEMOBBED, SEPTEMBER 1946

Liverpool University

The university looks like a church
for the worship of muck and brass.

I climb a lavatory-tile staircase
to the Prof's eyrie and a queue of girlish smiles.

I chat with a little dark-haired one,
who, unfortunately, reminds me of my mother.

The Prof is silver, frail and
melting melodious notes to lutes of amber.

I stand erect like lead before
a Jacobean alchemist in search of gold.

In my utility trousers and new shoes
my heels are military, my shoulders bold.

The Prof is wincing. Three years
soldiering have made me gauche.

DEATH OF A HORSEWOMAN
i.m. Mary Lomas, 1940-1994

CORTEGE

Our little cortège walks the central aisle
behind the coffin. Your greater family,
friends and lovers, darken the pews –
the hundreds you made love you.

The limousines cloak the dirt road
to the hillock of leaning stones,
the Saxon tower, and the clay cavity
you'll lie in and I'll lie with you.

Scriptures are spoken to your box.
But what's this mouth – nostrils like eyes
nosing through the fence with steam,
sleek curiosity – and even compassion?

Oh horse, psychopomp, porter between
two fields, this November sacrifice –
is it the death of everything –
or is it what thinking can never think?

JE REVIENS

Eau de Toilette: Natural Spray.
So little in the bottle,
but enough to recover your fragrance.

Worth 75008 Paris.
Worth much more than that.
Worth a return from your Jerusalem.

Your photos smile at me from the wall.
Something's very funny.
What's the secret – laughter in heaven?

You always had one, a secret, secrets,
and you've taken them with you,
including the secret of your death.

All I'm left with is
the secret of your laughter
and a little fragrance in a bottle of *Je Reviens*.

SLEEPING

Sometimes you'd flake out even with people there,
on a couch at a dinner party or after riding.

Sleeping in the little chapel, body so beautiful,
in your immaculate gold and black hunting gear,

where were you? Colder than cold to the touch,
were you really not breathing on the undertaker's slab?

ANNIVERSARY

Today, and a year of your death, I put
this yellow lily on your grave, three red carnations,
and a spray of flowers like a snow cloud.

I listen for a horse neighing far off,
your usual sign, but nothing comes.
I leave the flowers without water to die.

The clouds have muzzles, hooves and wings.
Now you love me more than you
ever could, or not at all.

I love you in ways I couldn't show
and you couldn't recognise. You love me
knowing everything, everything, or nothing at all.

BROKEN CONTRACT

My publisher wants to break my contract,
but all I care about are
the marigolds I planted on your grave.

The only contract that bedevils me is ours,
which you have broken.
I'd like to share my strawberries with you,

but this is the only supper I can share.

SHADES

I sit here in your presence
and watch the evening failing,
everything turning grey: the sky, the sea,
waves rolling, pebbles, snow.
Grey has a glamour of its own.
Desolation is shifting and resting like the sea.

Whiteness. The combers take their time
even in the north wind. The snow
pocks the pebbles, freezes into flowers
on the windowpane. Did I dare to notice it
creeping into our lives, the whiteness
behind the north wind?

All I'm left with is this:
no clouds of irritation, no eager expectations,
just the knowledge of how I loved you,
love you and how, perhaps, you loved me,
perhaps more than you knew. Now, is it love
or yearning that invades the unknown?

A dark bird's navigating the north wind
and vanishing behind the Lookout –
careening out again – a sasm, a flutter.
Evening's setting, and all the shades –
slate, snow, wave-white and pebble-gold –
are failing from the grey flight of a single bird going northward.

DISTRACTED

In my dream I kiss you.
You accept my kiss without
returning it. Never a one
for much kissing and hugging,
you reject me by your death.

How could you hasten off
into the unknown without me?
Brave as you are, I'd want
to hold your hand. But you'd
want, I know, to explore your death alone.

Even dead and in dream
you accept my lovemaking. Your sex
is wet. We're almost one, when
something inside you, or from somewhere else,
calls you, with that *distrait* look, away.

VOICES

In a dream I've lost my helmet,
my gun, and my water bottle,
and no one, not even you,
can tell me where they are.

Yet you've so many voices.
*Till you can think of me
without pain*, I think you say,
you'll know I'm close.

You're bigger than the clouds, and yet
you choose a sentimental song:
... *at the end of a perfect day, the spectre
of a rose, you say you've found a friend*.

But is it you or I who claim no Mass,
no *De Profundis*, not even the paradise
of a kiss? You merely smile from a photograph,
enjoying the joke of your hidden death.

GHOST AT THE GATEWAY

It was always me at the airport
to meet you. Now at the same gateway
I meet your ghost.
Home again, I come
not home but to empty house.

Yet when the house is empty you reclaim me.
Not galloping now, or driving to friends,
you sit by the fireside
as you never did, in the evening,
by these flames.

Our daughter thinks you died
of happiness, and a friend thinks
you were needed for other work.
I can only ask you what you never wanted asked
alive and can't answer now.

BORED

The little girl you were
looks at me from my bedroom wall

in puffed white shoulder-sleeves,
pleased to be having her photograph.

Once you were so bored your mother was
stumped. *Oh well*, you finally said,

*I'll just go upstairs, I suppose,
and open a few band-aids.*

That was a child who was
really bored.

WAITING

A trifle too busy to be on time,
you turned surprisingly punctual

after I said the one waiting
tends to think of the late one's faults...

Yet now, waiting to find you again,
all I can remember are your good faults.

HEART

In the garden photograph your father
is a dappled *jeunesse doré*
in light filtering through pear blossom.

Somewhere unspoken in your systole
and diastole the adolescent row
before his heart failed lay unforgiven.

Only now, after your death, do I hear
that he changed his will, left you
out of his land, with a single cow.

And now, as you turned your horse from the jump,
slipped from the saddle, still holding the reins,
did you meet him, loving him, and dying of the same complaint?

DANCING

Dancing with me in Chelsea
in the small hours you flooded with tears
and couldn't tell me why.

I'd just won you and I
feared your love had faded
and you didn't know how to tell me.

Next morning we heard how
your little brother had been shot
dead at the precise moment.

Neither you nor your mother
ever spoke about this
in the years and years that followed.

DREAM DOG

Who was the little dream dog
that called for 'Mummy'
meaning you?

*Mummy doesn't
live with us
now, any more,* I said.

And the dog said
I know – grieving.

Was I always escaping from freedom
by making you
my mistress and my wife?

RED SHOES

Fast after the other dream car
I take the hairpin bend
and skid in a circle,
still pointing the new way
but out of petrol and blocking the road.

If only you'd talked more –
about the wounds you bandaged
with laughter and love.
When the mind doesn't speak
the body may say it instead.

Your red shoes were
horses' hooves
and motor-car wheels, the flight from
evenings by firelight,
weeping, or wasting time in bed!

After thirty years,
I never quite knew
if you loved me, or was it kindness?
Now all my questions
are still questions.

You left me for the Saxon tower.
In your new world
are you pleased? –
seeing my new choices, my house done-up,
the leap I'm taking?

GLASS DARKLY

I take the glass you had engraved
with HL and pour myself a whisky.
Since you went, I celebrate our
second marriage, and I'm becoming
newly acquainted with us all.

Today Elizabeth too came and sat with me.
Alive, hardly knowing each other,
she eighty, we shared Solomon's playing
of Beethoven's last and both heard, as now,
the dead musician trilling to heaven.

Old postcards are polysemous:
I see four kisses I might have
cared about; a girl rides by moonlight,
slightly ahead of the prince, leading him
to a palace built in the heart.

Sibelius is here, sharing my whisky.
In the years of the burning of the eighth

He'd sometimes ask his daughter about me –
seeing, perhaps, in my troubles his own?
And became my friend, though we never met.

Among the living I mourn alone,
but I walk through walls and share
your demesnes, your golden lake
and island temple that lie on
the blank pages between the stanzas of this poem.

MARY MOON

The moon silvers the sun's gold,
cools and purifies it,

but hides her dark
from her shining rationality.

Her light rises to the full,
to the instant of fading

and a dark as dark
as her hidden side.

The hare lives in the moon,
the three-legged hare,

pounding with its pestle
the mortar of immortality,

but the manface groans
at his load of logs.

SECRET AGENT

You've been seen
sitting by desks
talking to colleagues in your old domain.

My son dreams you're
working for the government,
cloak and dagger stuff, a secret agent.

Your agency in us
didn't finish with your death
and will it with ours?

DREAM CHOCOLATES

Waking from our life together
I find a record of an old dream.

The chocolates were poisoned,
and I miswrote children for chocolates.

And indeed one had mumps,
and the other glandular fever.

There are notes and photographs
and even memories to prove all this.

Yet everything lasted a moment
and so many moments are dreamt,

and now I wake to an old moment
and perhaps other poisoned chocolates.

PREMONITION

Just before John Ridgewell
went out in the little sailing boat
on the muscular Humber

and three months later
was found drowned,
eaten by fishes and water,

you saw his face as a
skull, picked clean,
which you only mentioned

once and never again.

AT SEA

Here I am, peering from the bridge again,
navigating the dark, lights
blurred by weeping, wind in my eyes.

All my false pilotage,
drifting with wrong charts,
is behind this crying.

And why were you always smiling?
Are you still smiling
in the land of your dying?

NOTE

Those little flirtations you
slipped in the books I lectured on:

I'd open the book and find your billet-doux
with a hundred student faces studying mine.

Now, thinking of each word again,
my only face is the face of the North Sea.

HORSES

I know she thinks I only think
you still love me because bereavement
dupes us with dreams.

Yesterday, driving from your graveside
to her house, not a whinny, not a backside,
except a horsetod on the road.

No, I said, and *No*
as I passed a pub sign with a rearing white.
Mary, I want a horse!

Then, at the car park, three great
Adnams dray-horses, two greys and a black,
who came to study our splendid *al fresco* lunch.

They pushed explorative noses over the rail,
like the nose of the dappled grey at your graveside,
and I spoilt them rotten with sugar and apples.

BURDENS

She was not sure of her motivation.
Jealousy even now when you were dead?

Her new man friend thinks you were
a bad influence: you taught her to lie.

But her chief need now was, I suppose,
to unburden herself, and I did want to know.

Some things you liked under wraps, yes –
and perhaps that's why you died so young?

I admit I wondered at my wife, but slept
on your misdemeanour, talked to you about it

and planted some winter pansies on your grave.
Seven horses you sent me! Five bays –

beautiful white tails at grass in a field –
a mounted girl as I turned by the lych-gate –

and a sweet white miniature pony on my way back.

DREAM SHOES

The slave went barefoot,
as I do in the summer.

A cobbler in dream accuses me:
these shoes are dirty.

The shoes are yours. Did I
give them too much space to dance?

I trace your footprints
and it's myself I understand better.

Prince Charming finds Cinderella
and himself through a red shoe.

But Death's a mosque: one's red shoes
too must be left at the door.

God's no cobbler: his work's
the kissing and washing of feet.

UNDER ANOTHER SKY

Often I was a floating spectator,
a cloud of air and water, sun behind me,

you chthonic, silver, huntress, priestess, queen,
among the thuddings and divots of earth and horses.

I gave myself and died and, with your
giving, rose in sun and fire.

After the fusion of sulphur and quicksilver
There's a new salt under another sky.

MARTHA

Mary, you were the Martha,
and I the Mary.

Now, even more, I'm the Mary,
pouring my ointment on your feet.

You inhabit my room in the evening,
as you didn't alive, and smile at me.

I can't see you, or your smile,
but you smile

from the sun on the wall, the wine in my glass,
a bird sitting quietly on a telephone wire.

PANSIES

The North Wind's killing my pansies,
some on your grave, some in my window box.

Death's a sort of classroom,
like life, but more studious.

Perhaps it's right to take
the coming as an academy?

At any rate the grave faces of the pansies
are Socrates with a hidden humour,

and the peripatetic North Wind
is a voice in a cave.

My thoughts are answered even when
I don't know what they are.

HOW TO DIE

I'd like to be riding,
preferably hunting,
and just go clunk.

The answer to your prayer,
which perhaps you didn't
count as a prayer,

led you to the tree
at Ilketshall St. Lawrence,
where you slipped out of the saddle,

still holding the reins,
sank to your knees, and,
asked if you were well, said

I don't think so,
and fainted
and were dead in minutes.

EVENING GOWN

I saw you in Verona
in a fashion window
in a black Armani dress
with shoulders bare.

It fell from straps
in a simple line from breast
to toe, half-veiled to the shoe
from a choker of black ivy at the neck.

It was you standing there
without a head
in a body of white plastic
by a giant spray of artificial lilies.

And I remembered how
elegant and brave you were,
how warm, how good, how loving,
how good in bed.

MANHATTAN

Barebreasted, a black man in kneelength jeans
roller-blades through the taxis on Fifth Avenue.

Bowling from Harlem to the Statue of Liberty
he's diverted by the Staten Island Ferry.

I sit by the beautiful energy of the Niagara
next to Burger Heaven in East 53rd Street.

A Japanese father's photographing his Virgin of the Waterfall
silhouetted with her child against the foam,

and I think of all the energy of all the cars,
a waste waterfall with a waterfall's extravagance.

Under a gold-coffered ceiling I consume
clams and oysters in a chandeliered rectangle.

I hear a voice like a dying fly discussing money: *Ordinarily
I'd not get involved in anything crazy as this...*

At the Harlem end of Central Park huge white goldfish
are too large to be able to afford the gold.

I sit before the stone reredos in St. Thomas's Church,
biggest in the world, no doubt, bigger than my doubts,

and think of the green boys, one reclining
and playing the flute, the other holding a dish so

peacefully even the sipping sparrows are well-behaved.
Nothing disturbs the peace but my paranoia.

And yet even the clouds are full of the one I love.
Perhaps all this is nothing becoming conscious of itself.

A VISIT FROM THE HILL
La belle dame sans merci...

BEACH

Nothing but pebbles, the beach doesn't
prettify itself, or pretend to be
kind to the feet, or not cold.
The wind's from the Urals, even in summer.

Like you. You take your clothes off
and lie there, your body still a girl's,
till you infiltrate the ocean, a seal, alien,
impossible, and unobtainable as the sea.

BEDROOM

This extra radiator in my bedroom
and the anglepoise on the other side of the bed
are new. I want to tempt you to live with me,
if only for a little.

So you can't live with a man? – can't write
with someone else in the house?
Can I tempt you into the attic? – Look,
a desk, a bed, perhaps soup outside the door?

I know you're a butterfly, and if I netted you,
even in my attic, say, you'd stop fluttering.
But can you really settle down
in the honeypot of your own self?

Even a self's a sticky prison.
Perhaps I've been sent to let you out?

CAT

Beautiful cat, you don't like
to be looked at in the eyes.
Your colours contemplate and
swallow me attentively, but while
I search them they slyly
shift sideways and you smile.

I need a diving bell, with a priest in,
not to desecrate your origin.
My torchlight drowns beyond the orange,
green and amethyst,
unable to light those many metres down
where neither you nor I exist.

COLD FEBRUARY

Now that you've gone
I take my usual walk.

The brook's rippling through
wrinkly mud and yellow reeds,

and my special oak, who's learnt
to recognise me, smiles as I come.

She feels my cheek on her bark.
I put my arms round her,

and the she I've wakened inside
looks out in her new surprise.

As I leave her, the wind puts cold
hands on my cheeks, the sun

tears through a cloud, looking at
my happiness because you're coming back.

WITCH GODDESS

I'm the pupil of a Witch Goddess.
Her breasts are stars, her navel the moon,
and her clitoris the planet Venus.

She's led me to the castle of the man,
whose skin strangely resembles my own,
and changed my three-leg dog for a mastiff.

I hide my hair under rags and rake the garden,
dreaming of night, stars, the moon,
the planet Venus, and a golden ball in the sky.

HANDS

My hand can speak,
love in its own way.

Hands eliminate sea and land:
I find invisible hands in my hands.

They stretch and take your shirt off.
Wherever you're touched, the hand is mine.

A burnt angel, reborn from ash,
I race through space with a blazing face.

BREATH

Though you've gone
you've left me your breath,
your eyes, and your body.

You have lashes like long grasses
nesting blue-green eyes
with hazel lights.

You lie beside me in my empty bed
at night and dawn, weighing nothing,
breathing and not breathing.

I'm forbidden to celebrate you:
it would loom a cage
round you, even if golden,

and a cage would make you
beat against the bars. I'm left bereft
of everything but your breath.

HYDROPHONE

I know I've touched you once
right at the centre, so
you'll never be free of me again.

I know you want to be.
You'd like to go on with
your nervous tedium,

your solitude, your
late nights writing,
your snow, familiar culture, familiar friends.

But life has other ideas for us.
Our angels are conferring,
and they won't let us sleep for ever.

MOON

The moon has two darks:
her own dark, turned away,
concealed, never changing till she
and her light drop from the sky.

Her other shadow's not her own:
thrown by brightness, darkening
her whole circumference:
darkness thrown by light that gives her light.

FIRE

Over my shoulder the cemetery's
strewn with the thighs
of long-gone selves.

Ashes are floating through
the airs of England, India, Greece
and Finland,

and people I've loved
who created me in their own image
mingle dead ashes with mine.

By a round Saxon tower
my actual flesh
lies six feet down,

but now I go to the ghats
to make the great conflagration
of myself for a new love.

ICE

I read you and ponder
you, longing for
those letters you're not sending.

From your distant Precambrian rock
your doubts drift over
the North Sea, on air waves and sea waves:

ice floes cut loose by global warming.

FURNACE

In the furnace I wasn't burnt.
In the pool I wasn't chilled.

If not chosen by the pool itself,
I'd have iced to a glacier.

Willing myself into the furnace,
I'd have been white ash.

TREE

She was a tree. I put a key in,
found milk in a dish.

Bent there by the tree to sleep,
I slept protected by the night.

Again I put the key in
and found a bed.

She quizzed me, no tree now but a woman,
though her arms were branches.

She sent me to the old woman's house,
to the room with the rings.

But the true ring was in the beak
inside the cage.

I ran with it and waited quietly
by the tree. It was night.

And suddenly her bark fell off.
She was soft and pliant.

HEAD

The skull contains a seed,
breeding the stalk of the future,
a head of corn at the end of life.

One of my brains is a woman,
the other a man. I sit between
in the *corpus callosum*.

My head wears a crown,
but ashes too, a fool's cap
and coals of fire.

If you could see through my brains
you'd see me, one eye up to God,
the other down to Hecate.

I've so many heads,
so many seeds,
though not the seed of Prudence.

HEART

When you tore out
my heart, it blossomed
in the afterlife.

But it's no diamond.
It's a lotus: the soft eye
at the centre is in your hand.

MURDERER

In anger there's always a little murder.

In anger there's always a little fear.

As a child fear fought the mother.

It feared to keep and lose her love.

In the dark hours the child speaks.

She cannot convert that child.

In anger there's always a little murder.

DISTANCE

A sad bald man is taking a solitary walk by the sea.

Daffodils push through the withered bracken.

A bird keeps hammering three notes on a tiny anvil.

Even at this late hour a child's out with his kite.

I've fallen in love with someone no one can live with.

LABYRINTH

There's a labyrinth inside her,
a womb of stone walls:

a place to lie with the Minotaur
half-awake in the maze.

She lies curled up there like a caterpillar
dreaming of butterflies,

stockpiling tongues,
ideas and other sexual weapons.

When someone begins to love her,
the Minotaur reaches for his phallus.

She sees the man who loves her,
no icon into heaven,

but a mirror of the horned beast
who whispers a lie to her heart.

And she bites her lover,
thinking to herself *Minotaur*,

as she licks him with her long red tongue.

BRIDGE

We make love on the shaky bridge
over the cold flow of our former lives
and the rumpus is bringing the bridge down

PILGRIM

Listening to her dreams
she trusts them more than her lover.

The staff and bowl, the flask and
scallop shell, are out of fashion,

but the trek goes on to the place
not to be stormed but found.

The new way lies between millstones,
in search of hell without hope of paradise.

ANGEL

Every angel throws a shadow.

In the cell of the flesh
her tongue is a lily

or a flute, a smoking
trumpet or a flaming sword.

The bearded woman
and the breasted man

listen to the angel
of the lurking shadow

with her question from Kali's tongue:
without death where is birth?

But every angel throws a shadow.

BLACK ONE

You've danced on my heart
and your feet are bloody.

Your red tongue grimaces
at the pain it's giving us both.

O thunder-goddess, I keep believing
you're the woman I fell in love with.

Can you prefer this triumph
to the rites of shared eyes and arms?

I entered your cauldron with terror.
In your arms I was reborn as myself.

I touched your veil but never lifted it.
You cannot be penetrated.

You're everything from the waters,
pearls, fish, dolphins and stones.

You're dove, swan, partridge and swallow,
but you bewitched the air into a cobra.

You struck me, paralysed my heart.
You're Friday, my death before rebirth.

KALI

Your veiled promise was hazel eyes
and the sex you filled the house with.

I lie here in these sheets,
thinking I knew who you were.

I wake in the night with nightmare.
I feel your body next to me,

but you're not there.
We'll never lie together again.

Your bite stunned me, my blood won't move,
I can't read, I'm deaf to music.

I suffer this bed of pain
with no resurrection but despair.

I thought those times in your arms
were times in your arms.

But now you show me your black face
and your red tongue and your necklace of skulls.

HARE

Along with the dog and the lizard
the hare's an intermediary from the moon –

white hare, master of the winds,
brother of the snow. In March he's madness.

Hero of the Dawn at Easter, he lays the Easter egg
of light in darkness, changing animal nature.

When the Buddha was hungry he offered himself
as sacrifice and jumped into the fire.

He's the guardian of the wild.
His defencelessness shows his trust in life.

He takes readily to water, where he swims well,
and he seldom breeds in confinement.

In the moon his pestle pounds the elixir
of immortality in the mortar of apparent life.

I'm glad you see the hare in me.

THE ACCUSER

Death's almost worse this time –
a kind of malediction on the living –
if I can be called living,
who only survive with a heart
like a hand grenade.

I'm amazed at the enemy I've made,
but I know your hatred is hatred
of dead lovers.
I merely take my place
in the ranks of the unforgiven.

I shoulder your enmity like a rifle.
But no, defence is warfare in another form.
And why must I accuse myself?
The court martial's already found me guilty.
I can only lay my case before a higher court.

PEARL

The pearl is the third eye,
crystallisation of light.

The moon's a pearl, an eye of pearl,
luring the lunatic and the lover.

Once the pearl was engendered
by lightning in the oyster's flesh

but its origin turned grit.

THE SIGN OF THE RAM

Your scent endures.
I try to remember you
quick-witted, risk-taking,
romping and flirting in bed.

Your sign's the Ram:
red chillies, capers, pepper
and honeysuckle. But oh,
your hawthorn and thistle!

Rosemary, too, but rosemary's
a funeral herb as well.
And bryony, black or white.
The black's leaves are heart-shaped.

But the berries of both
are poisonous.
Fifteen of the white's
can kill a child.

BLUE ROSE

So you were, after all,
the blue rose,
the unattainable,
the impossible.

Unfolding to fire,
you came from the void,
your radiation
was red and white,

till you turned sapphire
in the failing fire
and you were the blue rose,
the unattainable, the impossible.

THE VALE OF TODMORDEN
(1981 & 2003)

PENNINE WAY

   1.

We sailed from the North German Plain,
splashed down on East Anglia's coast,
plundered and murdered our way
north-west over England to the Pennines
and settled round the well in the little narrow cleft,
stealing our neighbours' sheep and horses
and listening to Beowulf in the evenings.
But after that, farmers, millworkers,
dyemasters, soldiers, survivors, sometimes
impregnated by randy gentry, we went
down in the world, and up, and down again,
till there were none of us in the valley,
though the valley was still in us.

   2.

This valley's beautiful not picturesque.
The folk who raised their heads to Stoodley Pike
had ears clubbed deaf by the ramming of looms.
The clog feet that clattered by the bedroom window
had squatted silently outside the peaceful mills
when humiliation threatened in the General Strike.
This is a cold country and a wet and the stones drizzle
on the moor sides and on the houses and on the tops.
The steep tilt of the valley drops the dark
fast in the evening: it's suddenly cold,
you're conscious of night. After the day's toil
toasted teacakes are buttered by the fire,
or water's hot in a tin bath with the flames on your skin.
The benighted streets are empty. The old houses
have black corners that seem occupied. Wind
buffets from Whirlaw to Stoodley, compelled by love
to the wisest and sometime cruellest thing
for the welfare of a people.

THE BLACK SWAN

Out of what black hole where my grandfather's standing
did I run as a boy? Behind whose parlour windows was I watching
the flies buzzing, tracing raindrop tracks, yearning?
Behind which bedroom window lay I in bed fearing
the damp-marks leering on the ceiling, hearing
the clogs of the millworkers in the morning,
imagining another track through buttercups, pollen and bees,
as I lay there with measles watched over by vampires?

It's a black swan that sailed past the black hole looking
towards my mother's and father's two windows
where they lay together suffering in their happier half-mad days.

And later came the demolitions and the rebuildings,
the end of the stained glass, the creaking landings,
the ruin of the eighteenth-century irrationality,
the night-kept rooms in the right tangle for the family,
bats sitting around in a circle waiting.

The demolitions first and then the breakdowns
in a house that still exists though not in stone.

WATER

I grip the mahogany
rim of the bath, try to
stand naked in the Pears-soap

lathering scent and the steam's
flat Pennine smell but need
my mother's hand to steady me.

At the paddling pool,
leaning down over the concrete
rim, I bend just too far,

tip over head down,
and I can't pull my head out
from under the water –

gulping, drowning, but Gladys
rushes over, pulls me out,
and it makes me dream

I'm smothering, being born.

BUCKLEY WOOD

Fingers trail and graze along a stone wall,
kissed by the scratch touch in the grit.

The soaking green-streaked beech trees
stretch their barks and grope for the sky.

Steep up, and puffing you out, Bluebell Wood
makes you wade knee-high through wet stalks.

You squeeze the stalks close to the bulb,
and they squeak and bleed stickily as they break.

A thick bunch is bouncing and rainy,
and their white stalks, glassed in a jar,

bring the hand-wetting drench and feel
of the long stems home to your house.

The sting of stone and bluebell skin
and the blue blur of the bells take your eyes

to the wet soil and another hot day too, when
a cloud of bees could set you running,

and they light up the bedroom where the dark's
full of holes going out and out and on and on forever.

GRANDFATHER GARNER

Grandfather Garner's dead, but he
and Granma still peep out of the sepia.

They're old twins but with completely
uncrinkly faces: little children

wrapped in yellowing flesh:
two faces with nothing to hide

and hiding nothing. His face is
my baby face at my christening

but wearing a beard and glasses.
But before his factory crashed

and he said to his Mason friends
Nay, Ah've lost me awn brass,

Ah'm noan losin nob'dy else's
did he sweat little kids like the others did?

GRANMA GARNER

Granma sits by the black-leaded fireplace
with its black kettle on the hob.

Her hair's split down the middle,
her glasses little golden ovals

with kind eyes watching her kitchen world.
Her memory's gone.

I'm eating mashed potatoes
and she says *Mind the bones*.

It makes me cross. I'm crawling
the kitchen carpet with a grumpy cat

who doesn't trust me,
and neither do I trust her.

We share the dark under the table
tipped by a bobble-fringed tablecloth.

I keep trying to stroke her fur
but have to keep pulling my hand back

from the sudden claws. Granma
smells old in her rustling satin,

but then I see her in her coffin
with the blond wood and silver handles,

where I've been told not to look.
Her nose is sharp and pointy above

white satin. It's the nose of Scott,
frozen, flat on his back in the ice,

and my nose tells me
there's another smell in the house.

MILLSTONE GRIT

Yes, there's the Pike, stiff black nipple
in the wind that strokes the sterile tops,
squeezing out stone for these cottages,
mills and churches, conducting blackness
into generations of sons that strut
the drystone walls with their teeth on edge.

Light can't nuzzle inside the cold cross
of Cross Stone Church but licks the four
black ears that tip the tower. The grit's
everywhere, in the cottage walls, in the bones
breaking out of the ruptured hillsides
with their crumble of afterbirth.

The hawthorns are prickly black,
the gravestones are black,

and as evening drops its cold
the moors go black, blackening the valleys.
Light breaks through the mourning,
the clouds crack and slant down light.

The wind jumps in your nostrils,
makes your lungs rear, and you know
you've got it, whatever it is, under your chest,
behind your brain and mind. The wind
is lice in your hair, saying what you
only hear on the moors and can't say.

IN THE OLD BLACK SWAN

Everything has always been
just like this: the bobbled tablecloth,

the prickly black chaise-longue,
the rain, the cotton mills,

the canal with its tadpoles,
sticklebacks and water-beetles,

the stone towpath, the black hawthorns,
and the early-morning clogs under my window.

They've always clacked by in the dark
at six o'clock every day. It's always been like this.

I'm on the sideboard, drumming dents
with my heels, then I crawl the floor

with my cattle and sheep, walk the lead dog
over the fields to my farm,

raise and lower the drawbridge on my fort.
I'm the besieger and the besieged.

SWAG

Among the pearls, brooches, and oval gold cameo
on my mother's dressing table gleam five gold discs.

Suddenly my mother notices her gold sovereigns
are gone. But I know where they are, and I'll show her.

I take her to my secret hiding-place, under
the newspaper, in the cupboard, in Gladys's house.

Together we smell the raw wood and the paper
and stare at the cache of gleaming golden treasure.

CARTER

He heaves a great clog on a moving spoke,
lobs upwards as the cart moves forward,
vaults on the platform with clicking tongue
and jerks on the reins and stands up bouncing
as the big-wheeled iron-tyred cart and its load
bone-rattle over cobbles and down the road.

Who's this huge man, cords corded at the knee,
mastering this straining and steaming and stamping
in bright brass? Invisibly he dekkoes round
at the dripping cottages, the running-down mills
and the drystone walls, as he pulls the reins
of his drayhorses, shaking shaggy fetlocks

like girls' hair above the mud. Look in his eye
for more than a moment, and you see
the conquistador, the desperado, the brigand,
the Cossack, the lover, rapist and killer,
and you look down, as you must,
from what you daren't understand.

MILES WEATHERILL AT THE VICARAGE

Miles's secret meetings with his sweetheart,
seventeen-year-old Sarah Bell,
had been snitched on by Jane Smith.

So the Vicar and his wife
dismissed Sarah from their service.
Miles stopped at the Black Swan for a stiffening whisky

and then he was at the vicarage,
with four pistols and an axe,
savaging the Vicar and his wife.

He shot the children's nurse, Jane Smith,
then quietly awaited his arrest
and was hanged at New Bailey Prison.

It was Manchester's last public execution,
with more than a thousand people watching
while Miles Weatherill met his ill weather.

MILES WEATHERILL AT THE BLACK SWAN

One Wednesday night in the 1970s glasses
explode in the bar of the new Black Swan.

Two customers watch as their gins and tonics
keel over and tip their contents on the floor.

A full pint glass shatters into fragments,
and a tray of 20 glasses fires off simultaneously.

Heavily-sprung fire doors open and close.
Beer barrel taps in the cellar suddenly turn off.

Footsteps plod about upstairs.
And in the old Black Swan in the 1920s

a huge winged figure over the roof
doesn't like me just lying there in bed.

FREEDOM

For me to cross the road, mother holds my hand,
then leaves me in the market place.

I go to school alone, but when I'm back
I stand in front of Jimmy butcher's window

and shout *Moother!* I'm ashamed. She hears me,
comes out, takes my hand, leads me across the road.

Before I cross the road, look both ways:
first to the right, and then to the left.

Rupert, my wire-haired fox terrier, can do it alone,
looks both ways though no one's taught him.

This Sunday morning, though, she's not looking,
and I don't look both ways, I just run

back and forth, back and forth, across the road
again and again in the way I'm not allowed to.

PERFORMING FOR GRANMA LOMAS

After neat thinly-sliced triangles of bread and butter,
brown and white, layered on a cake-plate,

tongue, tinned salmon, tinned pears and carnation milk,
home-made cake, jam and tea, with company,

she eggs me on to recite 'There are fairies at the bottom of
my garden'.
It's a command performance, but I know her blue-grey eyes

are laughing at me, and I feel daft, but I do it.
Tucked away for her own exclusive use, she has

a whisky bottle in a cupboard: a little golden treasure
for special sipping. Dad pinches some,

puts water in and waits till she knows. Then he
roars with laughter and pulls out another bottle

with a flourish. Dad's the best-looking of the brothers,
the maddest, the most dangerous, and when he flirts with her,

she's a queen and he's a courtier, and she knights him
with her laughing crinkly-cornered grey-blue royal eyes.

For years and years my grandmother is in bed
with arthritis. She loves a joke and flirting with her sons.

Her bed's a sort of throne, and she's a queen
giving her grace to her daily rising son.

GRANDFATHER LOMAS

The master-dyer sits straight up,
legs slightly apart, never crossed,

a quiet twinkly watcher in a fireside chair.
Everything's straight, his bowler, or cloth cap,

the pipe in his mouth, which he takes out,
stem between first and second fingers, like a cigar.

He wears a waistcoat and a narrow white
stiff collar above a striped flannel shirt.

His moustache goes slightly down at each corner,
as he reads the paper with gold-rimmed glasses.

He's set it all going and paid for it, and now
he watches it all going its own way by itself.

He's calm, just waiting. All he has to do
is wait, and what's coming will come.

THE TOWN HALL

The Town Hall's more of a Money Box
than a Greek Temple. The Corinthian columns
are Greek but no means of support.

It looks difficult to get in. The Elgin marbles
in the architrave allegorise the goodness,
beauty and home truths of cotton, wool and industry.

And the Fielden Monument, finger in waistcoat,
celebrates the Ten Hour Act of 1847 –
cutting down the hours of toil for the kiddies.

Others should have stood in the bays
above the entrance – the pedestals are there –
but no one came.

A hundred years ago a crowd of
straddle-legged, akimbo men with
no women are standing by the lamp-posts.

The pile they've built is bigger but not bossier than they.
They're straight-legged, straight-eyed, straight-hat
what-about-it hands-in-pockets kind of men.

PRINCES AND TOADS

I watch the shine on Grandad's spectacles,
and his moustache. He lives in his fireside chair
in a household full of comedians and jokers.

He watches and smiles, dipped in his silence,
a master-dyer. He's trained only one of his sons,
my Uncle Jim, the eldest, in his trade.

There probably wouldn't be room for more.
My father's always got a sense of grievance
about his lack of a trade or an education.

He's had to make up his own life
with what he had after leaving school at twelve
and his brilliant mind and sense of comedy.

He notices everything, but he's reckless,
gets sad when he sees something beautiful
and he bows to no one.

He believes in truth, practises it
and makes me afraid to tell a lie.
He doesn't believe in God. There is no God,

and if there is He is no friend of his.
Perhaps it's the war but he did survive the war.
I think my Dad's unbeatable.

My Uncle Jim told my father
we were really Derbys. My father
behaves like a prince disinherited and disguised as a toad.

CORNETS AND TRUMPETS

In the first war my Dad was a stretcher-bearer –
in the Divisional Band. When the Battalion Bands
were broken up, they picked him out for the Division
above several bandmasters. Tested, he decided to play
his own improvisations on 'Rule Britannia'.
He got straight in. When the Battalion was stamping the square
he liked to kick a football about where they could see.

When armistice came he was offered a Trumpet
in the Hallé Orchestra, but he turned it down.
I'd a sweet tone, he said, *but I wanted
the musical background.* When I was fourteen
I longed for a trumpet and got one through my Uncle Will.
We both used to play it – with the mute on –
till I slightly shifted a front tooth at rugby.

I'd learned to turn things down and once turned down
a fellowship. When my mother died my father
let the trumpet go with a pile of rubbish and my mother's
valuable clock: the lot for twenty pounds.
*You know, you could easily have mugged up any
music theory stuff you needed to know,* I said.
Aye – course I could, he said. *I know that now.*

Brass band music on the radio's hard to bear:
all those euphonious, sad, sweet, masculine sounds.

SOLDIERS

My Uncle Albert lied about his age,
joined up at sixteen, became a sergeant,

received a secret wound
and never had children.

Uncle Wilf was an infantry officer,
but didn't get picked off.

He still had his officer's pistol,
which weighed a ton when I played with Jack,

and the hammer would have
taken your thumb off.

My father was a stretcher-bearer.
Dad led the guffawing, the teasing,

leg-pulling his brothers and rivals
with lots to say and ways of saying it,

but though he met my Uncles Albert and Herbert,
by accident, near the Somme,

this was the only thing
they ever said about the war.

DAD

My Dad's a toff. He wears bespoke dark suits,
narrow stiff collars and sometimes knitted ties.

There's a clean white handkerchief
in his breast pocket, and his shoes

are shiny blackbirds. He tells me it's just as important
to polish the back as the front.

When he goes out with my mother he takes
a bowler out of a large wardrobe,

brushes it carefully with strong swipes
before covering his quiff.

He always looks people right in the eye
with king-of-the-beasts blue eyes,

knowing some joke they don't know,
smiling, but having them weighed up in a minute.

He'll have joined the mill at twelve, working
afternoons one week, mornings the next

at six-o'clock. In the back row at school
he'd feel sleepy, and the teacher'd kindly

let the half-timers sleep. At thirteen
he'll have gone full-time, ten hours a day.

Dad didn't learn much at school,
but he read Tolstoy, thought for himself,

and if he'd been a trumpeter in the Hallé
as he could have been, he mightn't have

married my mother, and I might still be
a ghost looking for a body to live in.

At night, other children wander above the clouds
wondering about the lives they never lived because of me.

ROCHDALE ROAD

Horsedung and snow on the Rochdale Road,
and the hens point their tails in the air
as they pick at the traffickless road.

The streetlamps are little taller than the folk
and modelled on giglamps
or lanterns on fluted columns.

We used to swing on the crossbar
for the lamplighter's ladder, and my dad was
once in love with the lamplighter's daughter.

White pots sit on the telegraph poles:
tall pines, wires and mind-forged
metal-contrived webs are sending along

news the boy doesn't know about
that will change his life. He walks
like someone going somewhere,

not just with two baskets to a shop.
Is it the feeling of coming from somewhere
that makes him lift his leg back so briskly?

And the other boy trotting down those
bulging cracked-pastry causeway-flags –
they have that walk from plodding the snow moors,

now cheek-cutting cold
with their starlings of dirt and white.
The houses are cosy.

They've comfy fires cut out of England
by bare-chested men
hacking and chopping long shifts.

The factory chimney's the pin
of a Catherine wheel, but so far there's still
fancifulness in the lamp-posts.

MR. HYDE

He measures my growth regularly
with scratches on the wall.

When he plays cricket with us kids
it's as if he were playing for England.

Once he makes me laugh and giggle so much,
I say *Mother, don't talk to him!*

He's a lunatic! He goes red,
disappears in the bar, and I hear

the knock of a whisky glass on the mahogany.
Dr. Jekyll's drinking his potion.

TRAM AND BERT

Dad was born weak and might die.
As a young man he was thin.

'Tram', short for Bertram, was a joke about 'tramlines'.
He built himself up with good butter.

Later he was 'Bert', a brawny name.
He admired Dr. Johnson, thought of him

as an accomplice, though Johnson was ugly,
and my father was handsome.

But Johnson had a 'constitutional melancholy'
and spoke his mind. He hated cant, like Dad,

and, like my Dad, married a woman
ten years older than himself.

Dad tuned into the best music
with his uncouth longing for love,

searching for some obscure beauty in himself,
and healing his moods of self-contempt

with whisky and the companionship
of his fellow melancholic, Dr. Johnson.

BRASS

The Lomases are a cut above
everyone else, including the Garners.

My mother's Beatrice, but
the other Garners come from brass.

My Uncle Dick's bald head and shining
successful smile are made out of brass.

His Mason's status comes from brass.
True, the brass comes from his own brain,

but that's brass too and he glows with it.
He has big cars and a big house

with a tennis court and clock golf
but there's no brass without muck.

Unbeatable in big battles,
Lomases need no Brasso.

REBUILDING

Men are pulling down the Old Black Swan.
Paradise is Going but Not Quite Lost.

We move to a poky little house
in Halifax Road, but there are new things,

new boys, and new girls, and
out in the streets at night new games.

We put on Fancy Dress Shows, turn
Uncle Remus into plays and act them out,

and in a long hot summer
we put on our swimming costumes,

and walk the hot pavements to Centre Vale Park,
and splash about in the Paddling Pool.

We get fat sunburn blisters, but
on the long walk home down Burnley Road

I feel naked. My body's out of place
among all this business and traffic.

THE ROCHDALE CANAL

Hillsides fold down from breast-top to treed slopes,
the cut of the canal, and the banks we used to walk
to the baths at Shade. We bought pies or parkin
with the bus fare, dawdling by dusty waters,
munching the gingery bread and fishing for frogspawn.
We came out of history too, redundant by the railway,
minutiae of the landscape, like a Roman road or an abbey –
we're glands and ducts of Dame Kind who remembers,
to walk along, look in, to fish in, or swim.

The Duke of Bridgewater, an Alberich licking the wounds
of unmasterable love, broke off his engagement
to cast out coal from his park at Worsley, where
Brindley accouched what Bridgewater conceived.
Aristocracy, art and economics engineered
generations of big-muscled bargees whose legs, clogging
the walls of quiet tunnels of stone-and-water echoes,
backs on barges, gently moved their watery homes
towards a sparkling exit, decorated with children and roses.

Eighteenth-century couplets of arches sent water bridges
gravitationally over Irwell on great viaducts,
deep into the Duke's earth, cutting the cost in half
of coal in Manchester. Big money, navvies
and stonemasons spaded, chiselled and styled
still more of the structures of childhood, the weeds
of the Rochdale Canal, the aboriginal railways
with grandiose branching lines, mills natural as trees,
and minds transmogrifying the earth with money.

Diving off the lock at Springside I pulled myself down
through bitty water to the mud at the bottom
and watched waving weed and brown sunlight
till water power pumped me up again into sparkling air.
A dytiscid beetle trapped in those waters
wolfed a half-moon steak out of the side of my stickleback
in the night, engraving me with quick-rowing legs,
digestive tracts, salivary glands and huge triangular
mandibles for competitive feeding.

FLY

We give our mice swimming races
in washing tubs, and I worry in case they're worried.

It's like the baths, so perhaps they like
paddling through the water, holding their whiskers up.

Once, though, I saw some boys pulling the wings off flies
and watching their funny walk.

I'm a mouse myself, looking back at me
out of the wet, and a fly waddling with no wings.

DARKNESS

The streets are dark, but with green gaslamps
and a bar to swing on.

And one night two girls show me what a girl's is like.
They squeeze the flesh round their elbow

into a little purse. It does look like that child's
hairless purse I saw one day by accident at the Paddling Pool.

It makes me go stiff. And bold. I pull mine out
and say *That's what a boy's is like*.

They shriek with delight and run off down the dark street,
and I know that's what they wanted and I did it.

GULLIVER

Gulliver was tied to the ground with strings,
and little men were swarming all over him.

He pulled a whole fleet with his teeth.
Then he was sitting in the lap of a huge woman

with warty breasts. Giant women
teased themselves by putting him under their skirts

into their smelly private places, like I'd done
with my white mice when my Auntie Jane Anne

saw me and called me a dirty little boy.
The Houyhnhnms were clean and kept

the smelly yahoos in their place. In Laputa
the wise were stupid. They had to have a boy

to hit them with a bladder
and shake me out of my daydreams.

CHEMISTRY

I scoop the copper-sulphate blue, the yellow of the sulphur,
hypnotised by the test tube's shine,

the blue and orange of the bunsen burner,
the chemical changes of the colours, the magic rituals.

I'm an alchemist making gunpowder –
saltpetre, sulphur, and iron filings.

I create bonfires in little tin-tops.
Put the powder in a corked test tube, heat it

and it'd make a big bang, and I want to.
But my steam engine's controlled power,

and it works, with its brass boiler,
inlet for water, and a safety valve on a spring.

The chimney's only for show, because
the boiler's heated with blue spirits.

I pour in the spirits, light the wick and wait.
The water begins to boil, and a pipe leads steam

down a piston like the pistons on train-wheels.
The piston moves, and it whirls a wheel round,

which drives machines I've made with my Meccano.
They start to revolve, and I'm alone with all this power.

I pour some blue burning spirit on the linoleum
of my bedroom, and it goes on burning there.

I watch it, and it doesn't set the house on fire!
I do it again and again, and it makes my dick go stiff.

SCIENCE

I've got *The Wonder Book of Science* for Christmas,
and there's a brilliant oval spectrum on the cover,

and inside photographs of artificial lightning-flashes,
though no one knows what electricity is.

At grammar school we're asked *Who knows
what science is?* I say, *Yes, I know:*

it's seeing how nature works. Then we do
nothing for a year but convert inches into centimetres

and back again. Science's been shown up:
just a boring way of making us do arithmetic.

And after that I'm no good at science, but
the teacher's eyebrows go straight across his nose

in a thick black bar, and when he talks he has to
keep licking his lips like a dog eating.

It's much more interesting than science.

LIFEBOAT DAY

There's something about a Lifeboat.
Todmorden's about as far away as you can get
from the sea in the British Isles, yet
the first Lifeboat Demonstration in 1895
commands not only a Boat towed through the land
but Officials, the Fire Brigade, and six bands.

After Fireworks at Home Fields,
cheers, high jinks and a Town Hall Concert at eight
the town will sponsor it every five years.

The procession's watched by belles and swells.
You can see how serious it is
from the men's and ladies' hats
and the way the men grip their lapels.

MAD MOUSE

One of my mice gave birth to babies:
tiny pink hairless creatures, like baby pigs.

I wanted to show them off, and anyone interested
had a peep in the smelly box.

There they were: mother and family
exposed to the light, and big faces

staring down at them. Girls got very excited.
Boys wanted to handle them.

The mother ate her little ones, went mad,
gnawed her way out of the wooden box

and escaped into the walls of the house.
Later, when my mother went mad

for a while, I remembered the mouse.

KEITH

Lying awake, we were both
a bit too excited to sleep,

and he said *Do you ever get stiff?*
How do you mean? I said

You know, between your legs.
Your dick. Yes, I think so, I said.

Does it make you stiff
just talking about it. Mm, I said.

His hand went slowly onto my dick
and found that it was stiff.

I could hardly breathe.
But then I put my hand onto his,

and of course it was stiff. *Do you ever
get a funny feeling?* he asked.

Mm, I said. Soon we were both
rubbing each other and having funny feelings.

His mother was divorced, a teacher,
and had asked me to sleep with him.

She thought, I suppose, I'd be
a kind of brother for her only son

and a good influence.

RABBIT

He keeps the rabbit I'm buying
in a remote attic. It's a large white animal,
the size of a hare, perhaps it is a hare,

with a powerful kick and a bad temper.
Put your hand in the hutch,
and the beast'll go for it and bite.

You slide its pot of food carefully
inside its hutch. When we're up there
the boy wants to suck my dick.

In spite of shame I let him,
and it gives me such a very powerful funny feeling
I have to ask him to stop.

Afterwards I'm scared, and ever after
the buck rabbit is guilt. I keep him in a hutch
nailed in the coal shed at the height of my head,

and his unnatural violence is a punishment
for my unnatural behaviour. One day,
when mother's feeding him,

he falls out of the hutch and
breaks his leg while I'm at school.
When I'm back from school

the accident and the execution are over.
The dead rabbit's been fed to Long Bob,
who sweeps up at the pub, is poor

and has a big family. They say it was delicious.
Long Bob and his family always seem
unnatural to me, like cannibals.

KISS

I kiss a girl in the dark coalshed
where I keep the rabbit.
I've never been so close to breath,

I hardly dare touch girls, and this
is more than touching,
this is tasting and smelling

and feeling a whole girl's body
next to mine. Then she tells me
how children are made,

and I'm unbelieving and burning
and believing
and somehow I don't hear her.

DOBROYD CASTLE

Turreted on the corners and with a tall keep
it's a full-size version of my toy fort
without the drawbridge. It's stood there for ever –
a place to climb to, natural as a nettle, unquestionable.

The men who imagined it wore hats like
mill-chimneys and rode light carriages.
Their intangible fantasies turned into mills
and castles and a whole county.

Swankier and more show-off than the stars,
it's the Fielden mind, castellated, battlemented,
neat nineteenth-century stone masonry,
each stone like a brick, with curved corners on sash windows.

Toil for the unemployed is a tax on the rich.
Hired men hew a waymark of surveillance,
making the surveyors surveyable.
Look down and eyes look up. A castle's like

wearing a diamond the size of a boulder.

DRINK

    1.

My Dad stands with Dr. Bailey,
holding his arms out at shoulder height.

Dr. Bailey likes a drink himself.
Both Dad and Dr. Bailey are joking

about the shaking. Dad is over
the hallucinations now,

not drinking, so becoming nice again.

    2.

The young Town Clerk from Cambridge,
Mr. Simmons, comes to our hotel

as a boarder. My mother admires him, so handsome,
courteous, and well-educated, a gentleman.

He seems to like and quite admire
my Dad, and one day they're off to the races

and have 'a drink or two'. Next morning
I hear Mr. Simmons retching in the lavatory.

Poor Mr. Simmons... Is he
Dr. Jekyll becoming Mr. Hyde?

   3.

One day my Dad's showing off by
running across a builder's plank

that sways up and down, bouncy,
going to a third storey window high above the yard,

and he falls. He keeps straight and lands on his feet,
breaks his ankle and his heels

and always has a slight limp after that.
He flourishes a knobbly ash walking stick

and makes his limp a swagger.
In a pub one day, when he's eighty,

a young man takes the stick outside,
and breaks it in two. He must have seen

something in my Dad that scares him.

LOVE

    1.

She likes to sing and play
a particular song. It's her song.

> *Gone are the days*
> *That to me were so dear,*
>   *Long, long ago,*
>   *Long, long ago…*

One day she's suddenly gone
and never comes back. I ask why.

Mother takes me on her knee
and says, *One night*

when I'd gone to bed before your father,
I woke up and realised he wasn't there.

I went downstairs and there he was
with this girl on his knee.

I feel old and don't know what to say or do.

    2.

I've set up my tent on the grassy patch
above our back yard. This girl

is a maid at David Greenwood's,
whose father runs a shop called The Emporium.

She's sitting inside my tent,
a queen in the glow of the canvas.

She points to some little dry spots
on her lips and says, *Do you know what those are?*

No, I say honestly. *Kisses*, she says,
smiling in a satisfied way.

BILLY HOLT

Billy Holt was put in prison in the Town Hall
for shouting communism in the market place.

At the mill, learning German,
he wrote the words in dust on his loom.

He travelled the world with a horse
and slept beside it and wrote books.

It's rather odd, he wrote, *that I,
a working man, should admire*

*true aristocracy. Some there are,
born natural aristocrats,*

*and can be recognised at once.
It has nothing to do with money.*

*When an aristocrat gets up to go out
the common people open doors for him.*

FATHERS, SONS AND DAUGHTERS

In very old age at last, and longing for death,
my Dad, with just the evidence of the big body

and gritty will, remembered me roly-polying
and how fast I did it in Todmorden park –

and he made me choke at the two of us young,
he thirty, running faster than me.

Once he could hardly run fast enough
to stop me roly-polying into a lake.

Pear trees in the wind, blossoms
confettiing off in the spring,

pears bumping the ground in autumn:
air in the tree, wind oxygenating off

the Pennines, or drenched from the Atlantic,
prevailing, knocking off pears and people.

If science could do it would you
resuscitate every human being who ever lived?

And somewhere I'm always climbing down a cliff
with a girl on my shoulders. The sun's

a blinder, and neither will ever grow old.
Picnic in hand, a bottle in the other,

we climb down to the sand. But where's the sea?
That must be it – a glint over there.

And later, hours later, we find the crack in the sea
the sun goes into and go back.

And somewhere I'm always
climbing the cliff with the girl on my shoulders.

The sands are behind. The hotel's gone.
The island's growing no older. The food's

for ever as good and always remembered,
the happiness, the wine, the big dinners, the talk.

WHERE ARE YOU NOW?

As I lie in bed, I hear you
playing and singing downstairs.

*Pale hands I loved beside the Shalimar,
where are you now, where a-are you now?*

You have the customers singing,
solo or together *Nelly Dean,*

*In the Shade of the Old Apple Tree,
Down at the old Bull and Bush.*

When I wander through the smoky
'back room' in the evening, given beery cuddles,

you play *Darling I am growing o-old,
Silver threads among the gold*,

specially to bring tears to my eyes,
relishing your power to make me weep.

*Grey Days are your grey eyes,
Grey skies your hair...*

And, after all, you were singing to yourself,
in your early forties, and still are,

and, hopelessly, grey skies and days still are
that dark hair of yours and your grey-blue eyes.

ROOMFIELD SCHOOL

The school builders must have
thought of it as a Chapel, without a spire,

Gothic but crouching. It's a stone lid
over the soil to culture this flat place

where we go through the Market
and down the narrow lane by the Calder

to the Infants' Class and are worried
by the smells of urinous trousers and individual bodies

and the hands raised to leave the room.
On the sills are the jam jars of sticky buds

and tadpoles, and at the break
there's the sickly milk or the Horlicks.

We sprain our brains with arithmetic and spelling
and if we're good Mrs. Graham will read us

The Wind in the Willows.
When she goes out of the class

the little girls stand up and show us their knickers,
and we write our reports on the books we've read: *I liked it.*

This is the slot we're posted through,
more or less carefully, and come out

the other end a different letter.
This is the millstone grit school

with the unmarried ladies in their beards
and long noses in *loco parentis.*

On the corrugations of the playground,
where the rusty-headed policeman's son

twice our size bumped his chest against ours
and twisted our arm, were we really,

like good poets, learning to erect
aspiring cathedrals out of our weakness?

Why do we need so much weight against us
to construct Charles Atlas muscles

or tumble to our weakness and give way?
Why, to slip through the slot of night,

must we be humped in a postbag all the day?

URINE

My first day at school girls
put up their hands up and say
Please may I leave the room.

They're openly admitting
they have wee-wee-outs
and want to wee-wee.

One boy sits in yellow corduroy
short trousers, always smelling of
wee. He does it in his trousers.

He sits in his urinal smell,
withdrawn and guilty,
a dog in disgrace.

I still remember the hot wee
flowing in my sleep
and the wee-wee shame.

BOOKS AT SCHOOL

I've already learned to read
from Rupert's balloons,

but here we learn to read and write
with our tongues.

We say capital 'A's and small 'a's
aloud together as a class.

Our Miss points to the letters
on the blackboard with a long stick.

Then, twisting our tongues,
we copy them between the two blue parallel lines.

We stand up in turn and read aloud from books
that show girls in old-fashioned frocks,

and we learn poetry by heart: *The fairy
nidding nodding in the garden,*

and *Old Mother Cherry blowing her nose.*
I'm huddled in the wigwam with Old Nokomis,

and up in the sky Gitchegoomi watches over
me and Minnehaha, Laughing Water.

The Indian corn grows from a grave,
and I know that death's not death

as I sail off in my canoe on my long
last journey into the sunset.

OUR HEADMISTRESS

Our headmistress stands at morning prayers
like a general. She's on parade.

She wears a dress of flowered cotton
down to her ankles: it's her uniform.

A fold rises crosswise across her chest
from her waist to her neck.

Then it becomes a sort of dog-collar
surrounding and hiding her neck.

My Dad says she tried to cut her throat,
and the collar hides a scar.

My eyes linger under her yellow face
on the collar. What is there underneath?

ALL THE ANIMALS OF EMPIRE

Britannia used to appear on every penny.
She seems to have gone, taking her
helmet and trident with her.

When Lord John Sanger came to town, with a carnival
of humping elephants, snarling tigers, white-horsed
equestrians, clowns and a military band,

nine horses hauled her coach. She was the top perch
of a quadruple-decker steam organ, carved with
staring Charons, bowed old men, scrolls

and field-marshal-faced red-and-gold
lions with bristly moustaches. A top-hatted coachman
gripped a clutch of reins,

backed by brass-helmeted soldier boys with pikes and shields.
Top peak of all, Britannia, in nurse's uniform and brass hat
sailed past the rooftops, a perilous girl.

The young men argued in emulous admiration
of her bonzer world-whacking beauty, till they got a close-up,
and the shock of her masculine sergeant-major face.

KNICKERS

In the top infant class,
as soon as she's out of the room,

some girl stands up, lifts
her skirt and shows her knickers.

If she's gone long, one boy,
sometimes two, will pull their

dicks out and show them, long and stiff.
Lenny has a surprisingly large one,

which curves slightly like a banana.
It makes him seem weird.

Is there ever an eye watching
through the little glass cabinet in the wall?

TEACHERS

Those with nice faces, like Auntie Madge,
marry and have to leave teaching.

Mrs. Graham sometimes comes
when teachers are sick,

and if we're good she reads us *The Wind in the Willows*,
but she's not the wife of Kenneth Graham.

She has black eyebrows and black eyes
like the stern commander of a sinking ship.

Bertha Longnose is greasy-skinned
and straggly-haired. Why does she have a nickname?

The other teachers are all 'Miss'.
Even my Auntie Madge knows her nickname

and smiles at it, which I feel is somehow wrong.
I don't remember any poetry

or exciting extras in her class, but once,
when I've taken a test and finished early,

she twinkles at me kindly, and she
almost seems beautiful, as if

an angel has come and stood over me.

AQUARIUMS

Our classroom has high windows,
so we can't see out, with blind,
ribbed glazing on the lower panes.

On the spring windowsills there are
jamjars with sticky-budded twigs
and sticklebacks in glass tanks.

In our aquarium we watch
caterpillars making little coffins on a leaf.
Then they come out wet and spindly-legged,

not the plump soft bags they've been.
I net frogspawn in the canal
and the little black spots in the jelly

turn oval, grow heads and eyes,
wriggle tails like blades,
push out legs, lose their tails

and finally turn tiny, squat,
throbbing frogs in striped skins.
I float in the water with them,

glassy-eyed, like on rainy Sundays,
when I sit among the Victorian furniture
and stare at the large window, where flies

crawl up the window, buzz
down again and toil up again,
as the raindrops hit the glass,

bulge and spill down the pane,
while the flies buzz dreamily
or fizz despairingly.

OLGA

Olga Wadsworth sits in a window desk,
with sunlight haloing her golden hair.

She's almost transparent, with eyes
like rainy bluebells in the wood.

I put my hand down to the bottom
of their cold squeaky white stems

and break them off just above
the bulb, dripping with raindrops.

But you could never touch
Olga Wadsworth, or even speak.

She's not a body, or even a flower.
She comes to my birthday party, but

all the glitter of cake and sparkle of lemonade
fade like the other children in her gold.

I don't speak. It's enough she's in the room.
She opens her eyes at my prince's kiss.

Then her family goes to America, and
I never see her again, except in films.

I see her in 'Our Gang', just for a moment,
and then she disappears behind another child.

MARJORIE GREEN

We know why we're going up
the hillside past Kenneth Marshall.

He's playing football in white shorts.
He smiles in a funny way,

as if he knows, and we climb up
among the trees and get under the mac.

We're both shy, and I can see her face
twitching like a deer.

We're just being close, very close,
touching and smelling each other,

feeling each other a bit, and it's
lovely hugging under the mac,

but afterwards we pass
Kenneth Marshall again

and he looks very healthy,
and next Saturday I'm there,

playing very hard, sliding about
a lot in the mud and coming back black.

MARY PRIESTLEY

Walking to school and back
across the market place
and down Roomfield Lane

I stare at the River Calder
through the iron gate in the stone wall.
Coming back at four

I climb the high black wall
in the playground, put my toes
in the footholds between the stones.

I'm climbing a mountain rock-face
to the higher street where Mary
lives in her house, and I might

get a glimpse of her
and she might stare and look away.
When I'm eight, in Bertha Longnose's class,

I'm moved up to Miss Lord's,
who has a beard. Everyone's older than me,
and they all know long division and fractions,

and Miss Lord, with her black beard
and red face, doesn't like me,
and soon I go deaf.

But Mary Priestley is there.
She passes a little folded note
from desk to desk,

whispering *Pass it on,*
and it says *I love you.*
At playtime I run up to the iron gate

like an aeroplane and hurl
my bomb across the bars:
I love you.

She picks it up and runs off with it,
and all the other girls shriek.
I wander the streets near her home

after dark, hoping she'll be there.
and we can play together,
hot with curiosity, never touching.

We'll swing on the green horizontal bars
on the gaslamps, play marbles
or skim cigarette cards,

but often she's not there.
The girls are constantly hopping,
skipping and jumping,

with ropes, crossing arms, dancing on one foot.
I roller skate everywhere,
swooping down the steep streets,

heading for each lamp post
and swinging round it
to check the rush.

THE RECHABITE CONCERT PARTY

    1.

I'm in a charabanc with a lot of
chattering smelly girls.

When we're there they powder
and perfume their bodies

with nothing on but knickers and vests
and then dance bare-legged on a chapel stage.

They link their arms, do high kicks
and dance in line like real chorus girls,

stamping the stage with their dancing shoes
to put the stress on the words:

> *Tinkle, tinkle, tinkle,*
> *What if the stars don't twinkle.*
> *Tie a little bell to your dancing shoes*
> *And the stars will shine.*

They begin to sweat, and then they change,
and I can smell them, and I try not to stare.

I'm shy and I'm the only boy,
but the girls aren't shy. They like me looking.

    2.

Dressed in my diplomat's uniform,
cocked hat, white stockings,

knee-breeches and eighteenth-century
tailed coat with gold tracery,

I march to centre stage, bow and speak:
The chorus will now perform "The Stars Will Shine".

I bow again and walk away with dignity.
When my own turn comes I announce:

The next item is a recitation:
"The Knight" by Geoffrey Chaucer.

I walk off and walk back on. I know
it's rather daft, but it gets a chuckle.

   3.

I always have stage fright.
Even the charabanc's sickening.

The Rechabites are a temperance society.
Someone on the platform says

landladies are loose women.
I've heard bad things about

'publicans and sinners' in church too,
but my mother explains that 'publicans'

in the Bible are really tax-collectors.
Once, on the way back, the respectable

white-haired Rechabite in charge,
obviously fond of me, sits me on his knee.

I know this isn't quite right somehow
and sit very stiff. Is anything what it seems?

SIN

Mary Priestley's in the chorus.
She's older than me.

I don't speak to her, but we look
and we both know and remember:

that day in our big bathroom
at the end of the creaking lobby.

One day when we were about two
we were all looking at each others' bottoms.

Kenneth Marshall was prizing the cheeks
of some girl's bottom slightly apart,

to see better, when my mother came in.
Though she was little she looked big

in the bathroom door and she bundled everybody out.
She wouldn't speak to me all day.

She whisked her skirts disgustedly away
as I tried to clutch at them in the kitchen,

and Mary Priestley had left
a black and guilty turd in a little tin potty.

STOODLEY PIKE

The portico of Stoodley Pike's the entrance
to a tomb of gold-masked kings, but who's

buried there, except perhaps the wind?
The big oblong hole of huge black stones

was built by flying lizards. No light-slits
lighten the stairwell. You spiral up the dark

to the big balcony and the stone balustrade
built to hold you back, an audience for the moors.

As you stand there, your stomach's flying down
the swerve of the opposite hillside, and your gob's

stopped by the strangling wind. Where are you going?
You're emptier than the black stairwell,

or the winds on the tops that stop you speaking.

LISTENING

The wind's listening, and the rain on Whirlaw,
and the valley's long shadows in the evening.

A late blackbird breaks in on the quiet
of moss and lichen, and I know I'm here.

The trees know I'm here, and someone else
knows I'm here, listening, as I'm listening.

It seems like myself, only older, stranger,
knowing I'm not really the little boy I am.

RUPERT

Rupert and I roam Whirlaw and Stoodley Pike
together, happy in high wind or heavy rain.

This is the life: he runs four times farther than I,
back and forth, happy in the freedom and friendship.

One day there are pools of what looks like spit.
Then on the hillside Rupert seems to be having trouble

breathing. He lies down tired. Then he coughs up
one of these pools of spit. I press gently on his chest

to help him breathe, but a cloud crosses his eyes,
and I know he's looking at death. We go slowly back,

and that week mother takes Rupert to Rochdale,
and he never comes back, and I know not to ask why.

DOG SHOW

I entered him for the dog event
at the Cattle Show in Centre Vale Park,

but after he'd been bathed
he rubbed himself back and forth

along a whitewashed wall
and was muckier than ever.

Moreover, he refused a lead.
He'd never had one.

A neighbour, though, lent me
his fox terrier, 'Crackers',

a well-groomed slave dog,
with a better beard,

and his back legs
thrusting out at the proper angle.

The ponce won the first prize,
and there I stood in *The Todmorden Advertiser*

in a smart suit and a Jimmy Coogan cap
with a clean dog that wasn't mine on a lead.

ALBION BARKER

Albion Barker, the organist, though small,
is enormous behind me.

He sends my back waves of hatred,
and he must hate 'The Harmonious Blacksmith'

even more than I do. All I want
is to play like my mother.

But as I sit here, seeing my fingers
mirrored in his grand piano's black shine,

so different from our own brown
upright fortepiano that plays 'Nelly Dean'

on beer-stained strings, I know my
real fingers are in the wrong place.

GRAMOPHONE

Under the mahogany lid
there's a smell of rubbed metal and static.

The baize turntable, the shiny
fold-back head and the tiny

tin box of bright needles
with a treble clef on the lid

make a boy sing 'O for the Wings
of a Dove' and 'Hear my Prayer'

from the black disc with
the whirling dog in the middle.

How nice, my mother sighs,
if you could sing like that.

And the next day I've asked to be
a 'probationer' in Christ Church choir

though I'm only six
because I'm that sort of boy.

CHRIST CHURCH

Christ Church stands with black pricked ears
and clocks among the dripping trees.

I take the back lane down the worn stone steps
between the church and the sooty black trees.

The church has blackening angels in its graveyard.
The vicarage is where the murders were.

But inside there are gold-speared wrought-iron gates,
a gold cross parked on the choirstalls,

lights, a reredos and music. I walk into an orchestra
of violins, trumpets, flutes and bassoons,

and out of a scratchy old record of
'Hear My Prayer' and 'Angels Ever Bright and Fair'.

THE CHOIRMASTER

Mr. Dennitt's fingers are white vermin,
with a life of their own, crawling the keyboard
of the groaning harmonium.

Their cold flesh and bloodless whiteness
come from the cuffs of a dark bank-clerk's suit.
He sways a little, backwards and forwards,

his ear cocked to you, and his eyes
like bats behind his large horn-rimmed glasses:
watching you even when they aren't.

He has ears and eyes all over his body
and in the back of his head.
He has Harold Lloyd's glasses,

though you'd never see him
hanging from a clock
in a crowded street.

His eyes belong to his bony white crabs that
creep up the scale, and he's an exalted being from an organ loft,
come down to our little vestry in disguise,

and it's weird, it's somehow wrong
when I watch those same fingers counting banknotes
across the shiny mahogany countertop of Lloyds' Bank.

CHOIRBOYS

Smelly behind their stiff white Eton collars,
black bow ties and starched surplices,

their hair's like marram grass.
I always noticed the whiff of one boy,

and the sweaty beads on his forehead.
He's dark, almost black, with shiny eyes,

and his brother says he sweats so much
because he's always fucking girls.

Smithy and I walk up the hillside
from the vestry to a cave,

to smoke woodbines or cinnamon bars,
and Smithy tells me 'fucking' is what

some dirty lads do: they put their dicks
inside girls' holes. That's how babies get bom.

And did our mothers really
let our dads do what that lad does?

SEEING STARS

They claim I scratch my head by
putting my arm over the top of it
and scratching behind the other ear.

There's a lad with a little perky nose,
oriental eyes and banana-shaped lips,
like a girl's. He's popular, a sort of mascot.

So one Sunday when they're all
getting at me, I go for him. He's my size,
and I'm hitting out at the lot of them,

and they know it, egging him on,
when his fist hits my eye, and I see
an astonishing star: amazing.

It's a flash I thought were only pointy shapes in cartoons.

FUNERAL MARCH

We stand by the black soil
as the box goes down on straps,

and we sing: *Yea, though I walk through
the valley of the shadow of death…*

So death's a place to go to. Back
in the choir stalls the organ booms and beats,

and Nick goes stiff, stands to attention
and breathes *The Dead March!*

The Dead rise. Invisible footsteps
tramp silently round the aisles

to the organ's hullabaloo. Nobody warned me
the dead were coming here too!

RIDGE-FOOT HOUSE

The dignified gate and driveway through the leafy garden
past the greenhouse to this moneyed stone house by the Mill
whose chimney fell when the Great War broke out

becomes a big white Olympia with marble floors
from Italy. Now faces of Frankenstein and Dracula
dream-play science, technology and capitalism,

while, behind all this, I kick my shoes
along the stone-kicking road to Christ Church
where the indissoluble ménage

of economics, suffering, necessity and force
was never christened, nor their divorce.

LEAVING THE CHOIR

The only words I can ever remember
him saying to me alone was when I said I was leaving.

He looked at me gravely. *I was leaving
just as I was beginning to be useful.*

It was a big surprise. I thought I'd been useful all along,
I didn't know I was only on a path to usefulness.

SLUMP

There's no one in the bar.
The taproom's deserted. The cards,
the piano, the dominoes are still.

Poverty hovers over the rooftops,
pours down with the rain, drenches
the roads and the streetlamps.

Depression seeps between the pavement stones,
dampens the bedclothes, sits on the windowsills,
watching the neighbours workless and waiting.

Dad's giving beer away to old customers.
That can't last long, but it's more cheerful,
and Dad's playing jovial with them.

Are we poor? I ask mother, seeing
a paleness on her face I know is poverty.
Poverty's an illness. Its symptoms are

worry and men in cloth caps sitting on cobblestones
outside the walls of closed-down mills,
and it may be catching and worse.

THE GOLDEN LION

In the photo the Fielden Memorial stands with
head cocked, waiting to welcome

the first-ever double-decker bus.
It comes rattling over the cobbles in mid-road,

fearing no on-coming traffic, with a bouquet of
bowler-hatted, wobbling joyriders on top

and an admiring procession trapesing
and gallivanting behind.

A single lonely man plods round-shouldered,
cobble-watching, past the Golden Lion,

with his back to it all. All this prosperity's
doom to the financially depressed.

DEPRESSION

I sleep in a top-floor bedroom
at the end of a long uncarpeted corridor
of creaking boards and empty rooms.

No one else but me sleeps or lives up here,
except an invisible black-winged bat
that hovers over the roof.

I lie in bed and look out onto
wastes of supernatural space
where malignant spirits materialise at will.

They prefer to be invisible,
but they hang about outside my bedroom door
and peer through the wallpaper

and watch from the black window.
I'm too scared even to take my
clothes off. I feel safer in clothes.

I get in bed with them on. Dare I put
the light out? It's scary, but I'm brave
and then I lie doggo in the inhabited dark.

In the photo my face is pale, overtired,
with dark rings round the eyes,
knowing the black-winged bat behind me

filling the pavements with the unemployed.

THE SENTENCE

Our sentence is exile from the Black Swan.
It's final, and there's no appeal.

I'm living in a story with a rotten plot.
It's too big for me, and I don't know how it'll end.

The foxes have holes, we have no home,
but it must be our fault.

I live with Auntie Edith, just
a short walk across the Rec to grammar school.

My father and mother come occasionally,
visitors, both putting a brave face on.

They're a penniless, rather handsome couple
who live at my grandad's.

But now I see very little of them,
and when I do they're people

I once thought would be there for ever
who are just passing through.

AUNTIE EDITH

She bakes wonderful cakes and lets me
scrape out and eat the sweet raw dough
from the sides of the mixing dishes.

The house is fragrant with the prospect of
dark brown bread or light lemony flavours,
spongy textures, or slab nut-and-fruit slices.

Sometimes I can eat them while they're warm.
The whole house smells good and wholesome.
She's beautiful, even though

the skin on her face has an angry chapped
reddishness, caused by frostbite in Canada,
where my Uncle Herbert once tried his luck.

She stands and walks as though she's
showing visitors into the drawing room
of her stately home. I stare at the inlay in the chairs.

Her beauty shows in her wallpaper
and the little tables with delicately-shaped
china ornaments, whose intricate designs

carry important indecipherable messages.

UNCLE HERBERT REXSTREW

I know the word 'Rex' from pennies,
and his name makes me think of a king.

He's a man of tall distinction, thin,
with thinning hair and thoughtful eyes,

but now he's always in his chair,
his pulse beats visibly in his neck.

He's a clever. He knows about books and politics,
can think and talk, though lacking schooling.

He listens carefully to what I say,
and once he applauds a remark I make

and asks my Auntie Edith to listen to it.
I'm pleased but feel shy, as if on stage.

TOMMY DODD THE DAISHER

> *This was the nickname given to Philip Ridgeway of Watty Hole ('daisher' being the local dialect for 'dashing young man')... Philip Ridgeway was postillion for Bill Barrett who rode out in a carriage drawn by twenty-four goats, Tommy Dodd running alongside. He also visited farms in the neighbourhood for the purpose of killing pigs for the farmers and was noted for the fact that all the pigs he killed appeared to have thrived without needing livers as part of their anatomies.*
> Roger Birch, *A Way of Life, Glimpses of Todmorden Past*, 1972

Even the dog's got an unswerving back
and a miss-nothing, metal-glint high IQ look,
his tail up between his legs like an erection.

Tommy Dodd's and the dog's lips
have the same despotic downcurve, though
the dog's are humourless and incapable of irony.

Dodd's a ramrod. Whatever policy his liver
and the livers are proposing, his vertebrae
prop him up like a tentpole.

His head has the horizontal slightly ruddled
policeman's eye-gaze of a
disproportionate carnival mask.

Left hand on glass, the other's been
thumping the arm-rest to hammer a point
about how people ought to go about things nowadays.

The dandy double-breasted waistcoat with double buttons,
huge flapped pockets, broad buttoned-down lapels
and a shackle of a watch-chain dangling like a security measure

has stood firm against the midriff and many winds.
The trousers would drop to the floor with their own weight
and no doubt he often did it with his boots on.

Behind, the photographer's screen's been prinked out
with some effeminate flowers,
a Matisse-like pillar and a balustrade.

It contrasts with the serviceable tablecloth
and Tommy's serviceable hard jaw. The hard words
from that mouth and the know-all regard from
                              the heavy-lidded eyes

will be the last word and eye-opinion on every topic,
biffed out with the manner of wit if not wit itself,
which there well might be in those days of creative talk.

There are no doubts in Tommy's mind on livers
or the cure for love. Out of the props Todmorden provided,
and a twenty-four goat carriage, a big waistcoat

and liverless pigs for slaughter,
he put together
a photographer's screen of a face.

GOODBYE TO THE VALE

As a child I was told 'Todmorden' meant
'The Valley of the Fox'. Later I learned
'Tod' was was German for 'Death'
and 'Morden' Swedish for 'Murder'.

Later still I read that 'Todmorden'
means 'Totta's Boundary Valley':
property names the animals
and all the boundaries.

Hlumhalghs – Anglo-Saxon for
'Lomas': it means 'The Well
in the Little Narrow Cleft',
a lost place somewhere in the North.

A Lomas lived at Blackshaw Hall,
the Vale of Todmorden, in the twelve hundreds,
and we were driven out of the Vale
in the depression of '35.

The night before we left I watched
fireworks burst and scamper
for the Jubilee of George V:
the inauguration of our end that started here.

WRITER'S WORKSHOP AT LUMB BANK

Not only a childhood but a century's infancy
is gone through a black hole in the galaxy.

These crumbling mills are the rubble of
clogged generations dispersed in the night.

The cotton-mill-man who built this house
and fixed the polite table where the poets

now sit with typewriters had nothing like this
in mind. Would he understand these words

and new well-soaped genetic arrangements
he's somehow given rise to? Child labour's

retreated to another part of the planet.
Oliver Twist sits in the clean lady's ideal home,

but not at the end of the novel, in the middle.
Life deals out its new unknowns, and its

trump of unpredictability. We sit here,
at other work, in our penultimate orphanage.

CROSS STONE CHURCH

When mothers die and they bury them
on snowy mountainsides in black and white
    Pennine mornings, after cold service
      in millstone grit unheated churches

sons will often bide at gravesides
feeling the ligaments of flesh –
    the other end of the cord
    now underground,

tense as a worm pulled from the earth,
tugged and tugging back in a beak,
    taught the quiet roadway
    under the hill with the cars.

But sons, so tugged by ghosts and
guests, must move to the banquet,
    guests of honour, but guests,
    past flowers to the cars.

It never ends: on ventilated summer days
coasting the sun-patched moors in cars
    their mothers bought
    with money left,

driving the hills with well-loved wives,
they'll know they're taking the same roads
    down the intersecting valleys
    with the telegraph poles,

beneath Black Stone Hill
where they used to walk with their dogs.

HAWORTH

From Liverpool we could return to a strange country
for half-a-crown: three busrides, two changes
and we were up the steep Haworth street to a private winter:
invisible weekends in the Bronte Guest House
with *The New Statesman* in the breakfast room and
arctic sheets after nightwalks in the graveyard.

In the Black Bull bar we sat by the fire where
Branwell drank himself into opium,

though we were outside on our minds, hair flying,
Cathy and Heathcliff, windshouldering the tops
in the landscape of Emily's head,
with the gale in our throats and eyes.

This was where they watched each other
spit blood and imagine. Looking into her great
cat's eyes, I watched my astonished exit
into greater uncertainty. We watched each other
as lovers and our way of loving and into our loving
we dredged our own and these other lives.

'ARTEMIDORUS FAREWELL'

The mummy case of Artemidorus; a young man of about twenty-one; with a painted portrait; from Hawara; Roman period; second century A.D; the British Museum.

Artemidorus, you were loved by the goddess,
called early by the one who sends plagues and death
among men and animals. Did she then
cure and alleviate you, as Isis perhaps,
on those lion altars of the other world,
protectress of the young? But Artemis
is a maiden deity, never conquered by love,
unlike your family, who bought you
such a beautiful coffin, preserving
the personality in your face till now.
She slew Orion with her arrows because
he'd made an attempt on her chastity.
She changed Actaeon into a stag simply
because he'd seen her bathing.
She slew the children of Niobe
who deemed herself superior to Leto.
She's represented as in love with
the fair youth Endymion, whom she kissed
in his sleep; but this legend properly relates
to Selene as the Moon; it's foreign to
the character of Artemis, who was,
as we observed, unmoved by love.

As a huntress her breast is covered
and the legs up to her knees are naked,
the rest being covered with the chlamys.
As the goddess of the moon a veil
covers her head.

                I'm looking at the red and the
black and gold of your beautiful mummy case
and thinking of the bundle inside, and a cold bit of earth
on a Pennine hillside, where two old people
were buried in winter and still haven't a stone.

NIGHTLIGHTS
(unpublished, 2007)

PASTORALS

ESSENCE OF LAVENDER

I'm filling my room with perfume:
a terracotta base for a nightlight
and, above, a little bowl
for water and drops of oil.

The fragrance occupies the air.
I lie in its odour,
taken up the tonic ladder
of Beethoven's last sonata.

I miss that other nightlight,
the flutter of her mouth,
her aphrodisiac odour,
half human, half flower,

the drops of essence
in the terracotta presence,
the water, the little bowl,
and the light she casts on the wall.

A YOUTH OF BEAUTY

And now, deep in the endless sleep
Endymion had beseeched the gods for,

prostrate, naked, deified
on the bare mountainside,

into his absence slips the Moon.
She folds him close and kisses him,

making slumberous love to his limbs.
She sips his hands, his scent, his lips,

his breath, his skin, his breast,
but before the silence of euphoria

she slips away satisfied, her cat's heart
aware that, some dark night,

he'll wake anyway, but not yet,
she doesn't want his regret yet.

LE PETIT PONT DE PIERRE

The little bridge's ochre stones
obliterate their weight with their own tensions.

Their ochre's the wild ochre of the bushes,
but they're more taught than the bushes,

as if self-aware of their rakish arc's
acrobatic airwalking precariousness.

With no handrail and the raving blue ravine below
none but the unvertiginous will dare the stones.

How lovely to die in that blueness,
if dying weren't such a large question mark.

WIDOWED ROSES

I bend to breathe them.
Their scent's inviting.

But no hairy bee
questing for bee-bread

will ever breathe them or
thrust a tongue in their bellies.

They'll bear no other flowers.
I bend closer to nose them,

their sweet scent only for me,
and for any future I may see.

MOTHER AND DAUGHTER

for Anne Beresford

*Little by little wean yourself
from an embryo nourished on blood
to a nursling drinking milk,
a child feeding on solid food,
to a quester after less visible game.*
                                        Rumi

    1.

She slept in the water
the beat was beating in
till a flood of blood and water
deluged her, she reached to reach
the ark of breathing, was
flying and crying

and settling on soft skin
and pink points where a sweet taste flowed.
So she sucked and swallowed
while the beating went on beating
and where was it coming from?
Things went dark.

    2.

On shore together,
mother lets daughter
  take all her clothes off.

  She lets them both
go swimming together,
  mother and daughter.

Mother dries daughter
and helps her balance,
   putting her clothes on.

As for mother,
   unlike her daughter,
she dresses in sea-green.
It's tricky for daughter,
   walking over pebbles
that make you fall over.

They go crunch under you!
   Mother and daughter
still smell of salt!

Daughter turns from mother
and waves at the water –
all this smelling

all this washing
   all this air
all this mother.

   3.

She'd eaten love
at the pink nipple, and there's
mother in the cooking.

The table's a breast.
She gags at the slime of egg,
the stench of cheese, tomatoes.

She grows with
mother's body, reinforced
with rabbit and Mrs. Beeton.

Her father says, *If you
eat cheese you don't want,
you'll become a mouse.*

She watches the play of mother's
cutlery as mother knocks her food about
before the next mouthful –

abstracted, thinking...
thinking about what?
Her life, and not relishing it?

   4.

And she grows older
and she wonders,
Why did I choose her?
Will she ever find her again.

Wherever she is, she's
someone somewhere else,
no womb, no ocean, no
pillar of salt, no passing cloud,

a permanent presence
always passing away,
with rights over her,
until she sits at

that final bedside
and watches mother fighting
for the ark of breathing
she no longer needs

as she swims out of the beating.

ECLIPSED BY THE MOON

Groping through ferns, we sense
the wizened faces of trees.

The moon's a cat over water,
watching our eyes.

Big boots have plodded across
her face on electric screens.

Now her disc of eclipse,
is widening our eyes within.

Australopithecus half-stood,
afraid of a great face in the sky,

and some poet saw Selene tending
the severest of her menstruations.

The clouds vanish, with the evening star
hanging below to the east.

And now the moon comes
to the full corona of her eclipse.

We're six: indigo, green,
moon-yellow, luminous,

but turning twelve as
her shadow crosses ours

in our further darkening
of reflected light.

DAYLIGHT COMES AND NIGHT GOES

Night. And the sea keeps whispering
the same thing in different words.

All the lights are out except
hers, even the street lights.

She gets up, changes the sheets,
vacuums the bed, fills the washing machine

and has a bath. Then she pours herself
a glass of hot milk and reads for an hour.

The rain rattles handfuls of drops
against the glass. The sound of her water

in the lavatory is like rain. She lies
in the dark, longing for the dark, though

dark's failing and her curtains glowing.
She draws them back, and the sun's

chroming the sea, and she wonders
who it is that's keeping her awake

and whispering the same thing
over and over in different words.

And then she draws back the waves.

THE FLY'S POEM ABOUT EMILY

Beelzebub sent me.
I ate their meat.
I was the fly on
the dead poet's feet.

I've a good tube
for the scents of food.
I love life
and find death good.

My little head
is as black as my tube,
but when she died
I buzzed and survived.

Later I ate her.
My buzz is no bell,
but I'm remembered on earth
as well as in hell,

and I was eating her sweat
when God received her.

THE EDGE OF EVERYTHING

   1.

Her little black poodle would love
to greet me. She calls and calls him.

Reluctantly he comes. She crunches
to the sea edge where a silver-gilt road

is paving the ocean from the sun to her feet.
She reaches down, scoops armfuls of air,

opens her palms and gives the air back
to the sun. Then folds her hands on her breasts

as a fishing boat, trawling the shoreline,
passes through the bullion and waves to her.

   2.

It's only half a rainbow,
ending in the sky,

its single foot in the ocean,
and firm – so firm

the horizon burns.
Who else but I can see it,

here and not here,
a covenant no more

solid than the bright light
of a dead star?

3.

A boy crunches up the empty pebbles,
toy windmill spinning,

grasping his father's hand,
who greets me, out of nothing:

Nice end of the day, this —
the sea claiming the land.

The sea's black this evening,
but tomorrow the stones'll be gold,

tomorrow, or the day after,
or the day after that.

THREE PRAYERS FOR CHILDREN

1.

Dear Nobody, I know
you write better plays
than Shakespeare,

you're cleverer than Einstein,
more musical than Bach,
Beethoven and Mozart,

wiser than the wisest psychiatrist,
funnier than Charlie
or the Marx brothers,

and you've seen everything:
nothing can shock you.
But do you exist?

Funny, whenever I wonder that,
it's as if
I didn't exist myself!

2.

Our Father, which aren't in heaven,
when it's very quiet

I feel you're there,
and when I'm crying,

I can sometimes feel
you coming to comfort me,

and when I'm happy
it's as if you're laughing,

but then I don't know
if it's you or I

who's being there,
laughing, and comforting me.

3.

Dear Darkness, it's so hard
to believe in you
because I can't see you.

It's so easy to believe in
trees and stars,
and dogs and cats,

because I can stroke them,
tickle their ears,
and listen to them mewing.

You don't bite, mew, bark,
but am I tickling you
when I'm tickling them?

BOY, APE AND FOOL

> El Greco: *an Allegory with a Boy lighting a candle in the company of an Ape and a Fool*

The boy's blowing on the ember,
lighting the candle,
and a lake of light's entering the dark.

The fool smiles, the ape
looks sage, and the light
whitens his white beard and the fool's teeth.

Everything's black and white
except the fool's yellow robe
and glow of scarlet cap,

especially the boy
whose bracketing hands
are cupping the light.

More there must be
in the black dark
but who's looking there?

CHRIST THE TIGER

Jesus pads the forest now,
fingernails glowing red
in the strange moonlight.

He's alone because
he's always alone
although he has so many friends.

He's eaten the lamb of God
and will be whipping the bankers
out of the temple.

His time has come
and no one's safe now.
We lie prostrate before the altar.

The tiger pads through the forest,
his fingernails glow red
in the new moonlight.

INTIMATIONS OF MORTALITY

I'm losing my language
forgetting where I'm

coming from but then
I see a pink light

full of strange sounds
not hurting like the

thing that sometimes
pokes into my side

here in this heartbeat
where it's warm

and out there waiting for me
there's some enormous darkness.

QUAKER MEETING

We sit here in the sauna of silence
wearing clothes, but souls naked
in the irradiance.

Occasionally we cast a scoop
of cool thought on the furnace
inflaming our skin.

It's *opus a hundred and eleven*:
written in silence
for the pianos of heaven and the future.

SAMADHI

Little yellow
chocolate-spotted frog,
what are you doing on the path?

With your face,
eyes, hands and fingers,
you sit there unbreathing.

But you're looking at me
from the top of your head
in a shifting yellow glow.

Even my favourite oak,
intent on her angel of gravity,
can sit no stiller.

Ten minutes later
I poke your stillness
to a safer place

with my stick from your sky.

GOSHAWK

Fluttering in wind a fledgling
isn't certain he can trust
feathers and a program to fly.

He teeters on a chimney pot,
not daring the air, though
finally he has no choice.

A lark struggles from the grass,
carols above the clouds
can't stop singing if he wants.

And wide-striped above his eye
the goshawk, quartering the wood,
is condemned to killing.

Yet a free man, living history,
watching a bird on a chimney,
can't choose a future.

New choices of himself
cringe in the claws of a goshawk.

ALL THAT'S TRANSITORY IS ONLY A TROPE

Alles Vergängliche / ist nur ein Gleichnis…
　　　　　　　　　　　Goethe, *Faust,* Part II

    1.

His wing purring like a little cat,
he picks a crumb in the sunlight

and sings *No, no, a bird's
not an egg's way of making an egg.*

And I ask *What is it, then, is it
death makes you want to generate?*

And the cat, a martial arts master,
concentrates like Zen in the sunlight.

    2.

Seagulls point their noses
into the wind. Is it emptiness makes them
huddle in their squadron of seven?

Even so they're not altogether
together: flung bread scatters them
in a vociferous competing space-walk.

They're very competent birds.
They can walk, swim, fly, all
elegantly, experienced economists

of every airborne gesture
and the navigation of thermals.
The only thing they can't do is sing.

    3.

Black jackdaw, you're a model of holy poverty.
You don't squirrel stuff away, or
build hexagonal galleries of sweetness
like furcoated bees among mallows.
You don't fatten for the winter like bears.
You're a pecker-up of unconsidered trifles
no one else can see, always perfectly dressed
for dinner, neat black, with grey earmuffs.

Your perky waddle is grown-up, unlike
the pettishness of dogs, cats and other infants.
At breakfast I hear you chak down the chimney,
and I chak back, though both of us know

you, in spite of your ability for
airborne acrobatics, always walk alone,
not missing any item, only needing
what you were given, and staying alive.

Oddly, I've never seen you dead.

    4.

Did you, Daddy Longlegs, with
your impractical double-jointed legs,
will to be born with elliptical wings

on fragile hinges? Giant mosquito,
clinging to my window, crucified by wind,
was this slim cigar of a body,

that bulge of abdomen, transom wings,
proboscis, and six hairs of legs
your image of adventure?

You never whinge, just
glue yourself with invisible toes
to a glass cliff and wait in the wuthering,

a cross of wings.
And when I look again
you're gone.

SWAN

A mullioned window
stands in a crumbling wall
where a swan tugs a green rope
to toll a bell

Time turns over
and a swan yearns for
something sweeter than green weeds
under dusty water

ELEGIES

THE MONTH OF HOLY SOULS

Tomorrow's your new birthday,
the day you were born into death.

Other things will happen, a visit
to the doctor, perhaps, a glass of wine,

and sometime, at nightfall, I'll pour
a glass of Bombay Gin on your grave.

Just now you fill the whole room
with your perfume. I sit by my fire

with the glass you had engraved,
and I see you by your dream-lake

with the goldfoil glittering under the water.
There's the little island with its

miniature Acropolis, and the bushes,
the trees you've somehow invited,

with otherworldly green fingers,
telling me, *Our father shows us how.*

And I wonder, *Will the garden
be there still, and will you?*

THE MATTER OF ETERNITY

   i.m. A.P

Your body was sphagnum moss
birch trees juniper a stained-glass lake

at white July midnight
boxing hares and an elk

suddenly met among the pines;
and after staring in those eyes

I fished in you for a lost sanity
an ecstasy I'd never known.

But we were twins too alike.
August moonlight silvers the forest

a nightjar whirrs an owl cries
a fish plashes and I feel you smile.

RESTAURANT ON THE SUMEDA RIVER

    i.m. Mary Lomas

This water passed by a century ago.
The five intricate women have passed by
like the pentatonic notes plucked on the long viol.

The woman cooking the delectable dish on a little tray
has turned to listen to the last note,
like myself, listening again

to the last postcard you sent me,
and all you meant,
which has passed by and is still passing like the river.

AT NIGHT OUTSIDE

Outside in the dark
there's another room
entirely made of light.

There are lampshades
and a statuette, ghostly furniture
and no wall at the end.

In my own dark Harry Seed
still cycles to school
with me on our bikes.

He's doing his
Harry Roy. The rain's
drenching, and we're drenched.

Rain creeps up the sleeves
of our yellow oilskins, under our sou'westers,
flies up our leggings from the road.

I go to the window and look through
a room of light into the dark,
where, bigger than the night,

essence of Harry
is cycling a roadway
entirely made of light.

BUT THE JEWEL YOU LOST WAS BLUE

> ... *and you were the blue rose*
> *the unattainable, the impossible*
> Ted Hughes, Birthday Letters

We both swam in the black canal, saw
the River Calder silvering its stones, stared at
Stoodley Pike, drank the wind on Whirlaugh
and watched the moorland sheep scampering
over windy grass and dropping pills.

I played by Calder's rapid stream with
the lasses, my dog, and white mice, while you
walked the confluence of river mouths
behind your brother's gun in the killing hills.
We both had fathers and uncles who never spoke

about Passchendaele or the Somme.
When I was playing with my Uncle Wilf's
World War One revolver and my Cousin Jack

in Mytholmroyd, you'd be toddling round
the little town somewhere, and I didn't know.

Whether from the steep walls of the valley
we got out of, though it didn't get out of us,
or from walks we don't remember
on the moors of sleep, our mouths
still wander the Pennine tops.

Then, only days before you died, I read how
you'd dreamed holding dead Sylvia's head
in the Underground, and I wrote that
life and death are not separate, and
relationships are never severed by death.

Now, I hold the letter you sent
three weeks before you died, and it tingles
with you still. And that both our books
should end, as they do, on that
particular poem is a bit uncanny, isn't it?

A CASUAL KNACK OF LIVING

Alan, you've gone
and taken your reticence with you,
your Indian smile,
and your capacity for easy boredom.

It was a great day when I woke up
to realise we were friends –
friendship we sealed in Finland with
saunas and laughter in the rain.

We shared a spiritual asylum, known only
to the sometime mad, with laughter
and dirty postcards. You never forgot that even the old sauna lady
scrubbed me into an erection.

You were tough. You interrogated Nazi submarine commanders
and swam with the dead bodies of gunners,

and after the war, with only one armed guard,
you escorted a whole German ship and its crew to the Russians.

You were sensitive. And when a peacetime submarine
sank where your own ship had sunk
with the loss of three hundred of your crewmates,
you went into your last depression.

Now your depressions have been torpedoed
like the Nazis, and what you most need
is your love of travel, your curiosity
about other horizons, and horizons,

as Bede said, are merely the limits
of our vision. At your grave I saw
two windmills on the skyline
and a grey dove flew out of a yew tree.

HAWTHORNDEN CASTLE

To be is to be perceived.
                George Berkeley

1.

The volcanic house on the rift
explodes at odd moments
with little earthquakes, like coal
unloaded deep down below.

They thud underneath the room
I'm chosen to work in,
the Brontë room, dark as
those millstone-grit tombstones.

Nights long gone in Haworth
I'd lie beneath the stars, smoking
on a wet gravestone, without
asking the ghosts' permission.

Now I lie in the pinks ochres
and blues of these other stones
in the room I'm given,
which is not for ever.

   2.

In a rosy castle with its own rules
who knows what we're standing on?

We might be standing on
what we're not standing on

reasoning unreasonably,
on stone like stained glass

over holes in a castle of stone.

   3.

One meets oneself and the dead
on street corners in foreign cities.

The world is my idea. Here
in the pink house my soul

lives in the well below. I know
because I am, an eye, skin that sees.

There was another house, a grey
lady, smoking, standing like a cloud

in the vestibule. On certain moors,
threading the ridges with her dog,

she was still walking. And who was
that other revenant in the graveyard

who pointed to an eggshell,
a pigeon and a leaping squirrel?

EPISTLES

AN DIE FERNE GELIEBTE
for. E.S.

Dear Fiction,
there you are, oceans away, not even
out of bed yet, of course.

You'll have been up writing into
the small hours of
the increasingly white nights.

And here I am,
2,000 feet up
in a converted monastery,

and out there on a sea green
as mountain pastures
little boats are fishing for clams.

The Apennines sneak out
their snowpeaks, but they're
present even when we can't see them.

You sometimes aren't, even when we can.
I sit among a scatter of chairs
that seem to be awaiting people,

perhaps you, though to love you,
I know, is to drown. Well, I can swim,
though some deeps go too deep.

Whom thunder hath joined together
let thunder keep asunder.

AEGIR

for Kevin Crossley-Holland

Grey slates, grey sea, grey sky,
three shades of adjacent grey,
white waves, and black telephone wires.

The head of Aegir,
president of the peaceful ocean,
watched from my wall till someone stole him.

His wife still spreads her net
to catch seafarers, steals them down
to her cave beneath the waves,

but treats them well, they say.
Now Aegir and his wife
are more than ever here.

A wily black jackdaw
sits with closed lids: behind
his eyes are wide open.

The praying mantis is my sister,
and the sparrow that falls.
The sea shaped our hands and wings.

Our mothers had sea inside their eggs.
We eat the wits of dead lovers
and forget our sisters and mothers.

EAU DE VIE

You put your perfume on your letter,
a dry thoughtful odour:

two registers of scent:
a musky cello, and a flute,

counterpointed with
organs of imagination.

Your scent's flowery,
vegetable, bodily even –

but a body nobody has:
not carnal, not celestial,

and, to be itself, it needs
the juices of the vagina.

The North Sea's seldom blue,
and often it's grey,

but sometimes it's silver,
or gold. Today it's

a huge bruise,
though the sky's salving the blue.

A VERY ODD ONE

    for A. P.

And suddenly I wanted you
to remember me. Imagine.
After such a time.

It shows there's always love
mixed with the sad reality.
Picasso has cleverly found you –

your eternal boy soul
behind the mask…

It's cold, about minus 14 C. *Snow,*
slippery, and all the faces
screwed up like old oranges…

Old postcards speak
so much more clearly
after twenty years –

turning up as a bookmark, say,
in Mozart's letters, or... And here's
a very odd one:

a hare sitting alone
in a railway carriage,
going God knows where

past houses that
through the carriage window
look like the little town where I live.

DEYÁ, MALLORCA

for Denys and Monica Sharrocks

I could live here, I think. Even the mountains
are decaying, though too slow to see.

I sit in a house carved from volcanic cliffs,
with the rich, and sip my drink.

The church where Graves lies buried
dongs six slow, mellow notes across the valley.

The palms, the pines, the yuccas, the large
sarcophagi of geraniums live with us

as if the whole thing were not run by money.
The grey cliffs are being colonised

by a Samson's hair of bushes and trees.
They'll breathe again and beckon to rain.

I finish my drink and think about
rich food. Every desert has an oasis,

if only the mirage of one. Now Graves
will know, or never know, how,

when everything decays away,
something remains that refuses to die.

THE WINK OF A FLY'S WING

for Freddie and Marie Lees

Twitter of little birds at another day
and the cuckoo, programmed

to meddle in other nests,
reiterates its romantic trochee.

Six deep dongs from the mountain church.
Soon, I'll rise and shave, he thinks,

*and assume the sacramental business of love
in a lifetime of conversion.*

The cuckoo lays an egg in his head
and the bells dong a hymn.

GRYPHON

for Wendy Mulford

The gryphon leads you
out of the churchyard,
out of the town,

up on the moorlands,
always upwards,
beyond the borders

of where you are.
Her face is forward,
you'll never see it,

and her wings outspread
are not for flight:
perhaps to shield you

from what you can't know.
Soon snow crunches
under unprotected feet

and you're higher now
than you'd ever go,
miles from the sights below.

The face and beak
are turned away,
but you know

the face has two faces.
You see the eagle feathers
at the head's back

the tawny lion body
the claws clutching the snow
and the wings guarding you

from all you can't know,
as over the moors
where no one ever goes you go.

LIGHT AND ANGELS

for Anne Beresford

Angels may be, like
radio waves, a light-form
invisible to the eye –

travelling in a second
300,000 kilometres.
Nothing faster here

so we won't need to wait
infinity when our yearnings get
too much for us. Recently no

feathers, those little visiting cards…
So often the gift of love or luck
turns out to be yet another gift

of the suffering that's so good for us
and we remember we're here
to study with a hard hornbook.

The whole planet over
we're learning the toil
of travelling to the emptiness

that's everything we long for but
can't conceive or faintly
imagine. Nor can we travel

faster than light; and for us too
infinity must adjust to that necessity.
I pick a feather from the street

knowing it's their lightness
enables angels to fly and I think how
light they are who can

destroy a city or navigate a star.

KENTUCKY

for Christopher and Wendy Matthew

Till the snow came
the landscape was in mourning
for its white fences
creosoted for economy.

Now five brood mares
stand tails to the wind,
heads hanging, and
waiting patiently

for the freezing to stop
and the first foal to fall.
The trees seem to be
listening to the cold,

but of course they're not,
nothing's listening
but I and these huge
aliens with no ears

whose thoughts would be
no colder than mine
if they had thoughts
and notions like subzero winds.

JOHN XXIII

for Father Murray Bodo

Angelo Roncalli, we kneel
by your glass coffin, hoping.

All around you prayer's happening
and they know you're listening.

Prayer's easy near your waxed remains,
by Peter's foot, worn with kisses.

And here is hope: to beg beside one
who holds more love than he can hold.

First fraught with your post as Pope,
you heard God say, *Angelo, Giovanni,*

don't take yourself so seriously.
Later you said, *If only you knew*

what God's about to do
through me, a peasant from Bergamo...

Angelo Roncalli, we kneel
by your glass coffin, hoping.

A FOUNTAIN IN HELSINKI

Saddest of all, Paula, are the little rocking-horses.
The classy new antique shops in Mariankatu

show their sad wares. People die and leave
their handsome decanters and happy brass corkscrews.

The new children play by the old fountain
that still blooms with a spume of water,

scattering drops over the stone basin,
disgorging through humanoid lion heads.

The iron pillars go on decaying,
and the chimaeras gag on what they vomit

into receptacles worn with centuries of water.
The children are playing too hard to look.

Near the queue of prams the nurses wipe noses,
natter, and keep alert for danger. The children

shout and play as if the monstrous stone were not,
though they don't know it, already theirs.

SEVENTH SEAL

for Susan Saint Sing

The almost-silence has made everything
bright as light. The chairs have an air

of being looked at. They might
get up and walk away.

The sunlight on the coffee machine,
the heavy breathing of the sleeping labrador,

the mosaic of shadow on the tiles, even
the creak of a chair, the voice phoning

in the next room, are saying something
that can't be said, about sunlight leaching

through Florida palm leaves, trembling on a pool,
alerting a room and claiming the silence

of half an hour. Even the dog crunching
his phoney bone outside in his cool morning

can't disturb the light from the trees,
greening so many greens.

The half-submerged yellow hosepipe
poses in the sun. But nothing's posing,

and nothing's here: only water vanishing
into absence and I liquefying in the cool pool.

But a brown tatter of palmleaf slips off
and down, slowly eases itself underwater

and floats, one tip raised like a drowning foot.
The palm trees are only grass.

GLASS

Susan, the glass with its ten fluted sides
has been easing in and out of lips

for years, just being useful,
and now, suddenly,

it's a collage of glittering quanta.
And here am I, sitting comfortably

if uneasily in this coolish morning,
with dreaming bees, while eel and salmon

career over oceans and up rivers,
driven by a genetic conviction

there's only one safe place for eggs.
And this is nowhere, simply sitting in

sunlight that chequers palm leaves.
Anything can begin to be weird, even oneself.

Am I just a passing phase of something
that once happened, or perhaps didn't?

SATIRES

NIGHT FISHING

They sit on the shoreline, under
a green umbrella, wielding quidsworth
of equipment and catching a few whiting.

At the eye clinic, behind me, a lady said,
She's so much older than him, you know.
She won't leave him alone. He's had to

take up night fishing. But no: they munch
a sandwich under the wind, share it
with their dog and stare at the silver

the moon's unrolling to their feet,
feeling how the world was before it was
so well-organised and understood,

and in the dawn a red ball rises
swiftly out of the sea
and disappears inside a cloud like a god.

SAPPHO AND HE

What, Sappho wondered, could she give
Aphrodite, who had everything?

*I'll burn the fat thigh-bones
of a white she-goat on her altar.*

He too would burn thigh-bones, the
thin hairy ones from a red he-goat,

though afraid of younger women.
But perhaps the ghost of Sappho

would meet his ghost by the ivory gate.
Of course I love you, she'd said,

*but if you love me, marry
a young woman. I couldn't stand*

living with a younger man. Now,
perhaps, their ghostly bodies,

young as they ever were, will fuse
like angels in the bedrooms of Persephone.

THE INSTITUTION OF THE FAMILY IN ANTARCTICA

I'm standing here in this blizzard
in this daylong night. Unfortunately

the females have waddled off
somewhere, swimming and fishing,

so I'm left nursing this egg on my toes,
warming it with the fat in my belly,

and in these months of night
nothing to eat but my own fat.

And with this egg I can only shuffle
to the others, try to huddle up for warmth.

Let the egg slip, and that's it: the ice'll
kill the thing inside bang off.

The blizzard's busting at us horizontally –
all thousands of us, all male,

all balancing an egg on our toes.
And some of us get shirty.

If you huddle too close, they'll
bump you with their shirt and make to beak you.

Try bumping shirts with an egg on your toes.
I stand here hunched, wondering:

*Are the others inside persons like me,
and do they remember what they've done*

to deserve this wind? I can't remember,
but I know it must be pretty vicious.

All I know is: I've got to protect this egg.
Then it comes to me: I hear the blizzard –

a sort of hysterical maths teacher. It tells me:
The sin you committed was evolution.

THE VEGETABLE WILL

The pretty little aconite, so
innocent in snowdrop-time,

is poisonous. Down it sidled
from the Alps into English gardens

and then escaped to the woods.
Aconitum ferox, ferocious aconite,

yields the Nepalese poison, bikh,
or nabee, the most virulent known.

Thriving, growing
peacefully beneath the trees,

their poison first sharpens then
paralyses the nerves, the touch

and the temperature. Burning
in the mouth and abdomen

they stop the heart in diastole,
their victims conscious to the last.

In the saintly mask of monk's hood,
or as wolf's bane, they cooked

their potion to poison eaters.
But how do beasts, though not the wolf,

learn not to nibble the little plant?
Will the aconite be feeding prettily

on my grave some day when my house
is undersea? Even now the wind's

wuthering and hooing,
as if with supernatural news.

SAM AGONISTES

Samson's jawbone of an ass
deprived the living of breath;
but that's only a trope. It means
he bored people to death.

Even dogs learn from experience,
but thrice diddled by Delilah

he did it again: risked his life.
Who else would trust that wife?

'Out of strength came forth sweetness'
doesn't justify strong-arm stunts.
What it means is that all soldiers,
are always hunting for cunts.

The Philistines were dottier than Samson:
knowing him a master of snuff,
they let him out with his hair on
to come and show off his stuff.

Which he did. But if the military were brainy
the whole war thing would flop.
And if politicians could govern
history would come to a stop.

STREAKY BACON

Suddenly I couldn't remember the name of
streaky bacon. Gammon, yes, back bacon, ham,

but at the point where streaky bacon
should be there was a black hole

like the centre of the galaxy, and my brain
was being sucked into its seductive gravity.

I decided to read a bit and come back
for the streaky bacon, but now

I was outside my brain, looking at its
irresponsible darkness. It was America's fault.

In the USA they only have one kind of bacon.
It's half an inch of fat with a cotton-thin red edge

and they don't call it streaky because it isn't.
I took down the *Encyclopaedia Britannica*.

'Bacon comes from German *bachen*, 'wild pig'.
It's a side of swine after removing the spare ribs,

pickling or smoking, has an extremely high
fat content and is not particularly nutritious –

American bacon by weight contains only 8.5 per cent
protein – but the article didn't mention streaky bacon.

I turned to my hostess, but she said, *We only have
one kind of bacon. Canadian bacon, though,*

is more lean. So I said, *In England we have lots –
back bacon, gammon, ham and – oh! – streaky...*

Suddenly the earth was flat, the sun was moving
left to right across the sky, our world was

the centre of a universe that has no centre,
the black hole had stopped swallowing the galaxy,

and death, though probably not far off,
probably wasn't coming to Florida today.

THE ARTIST SEEN AS A CAMEL

    for Christian Tyler

Only the wild camel of the Taklakan can drink
the bitter salt water of the Gobi, which no
domestic camel, let alone man, will touch.

Even the domestic camel lives a dicky life,
dashes swiftly over shifting sands and has
secret insight into springs and sources.

He'll stop and stomp the ground where
water lies and warn of impending dust-storms
by snarling and burying his muzzle.

He can carry tanks of live fish so that
others can dine in style. No jeep or lorry
can go where the camel goes.

Badly treated, though, he froths and bellows
and can kick the inflicter sprawling in the sand.
The hurt sometimes take an axe to him.

But his stamina's not unlimited.
When not properly fed and watered
he can die without warning.

Steady under fire, patient to a degree, stoical,
yet overtaxed too far, he'll drop where he stopped
and lie still till he dies, with an accusing look.

Kill one, and the ghost will pursue
the whole caravan with evil spirits.
Later, though, his bare skull and bones

will point the way to future travellers.

ANYWAY

    (Just a bash at Ashbery)

Otherwise. It's Sunday every day
except today. Lightness appals from the sky,
the pearls meet at infinity, and after all
there wasn't anything I could do:
the flies are flummoxed on the parquet,
while the daily papers stand
to attention.

I'm always about to go round the corner
when the train stops, going forward in time,
backwards in grime. I feel unsurprised.
Suddenly all heaven's let loose
for a short while, and outside the hotel
the suggestion of crime grows.
I'm not here.

It reminds me of the rabbits and the desks,
and all that laughing at the joke.
The stars were cluttered and uncomfortable
of course, and besides there were the teacups.
We'll never get over this, he said,
and we did, disregarding the smell of night
in the long daytime.

THE ALTERNATIVE WAR

In the alternative war the two presidents
hunt each other down in the mountains

with six-shooters. Tracked by satellite TV, they
bang it out at high noon in some foreign street.

The Generals are in the van, fielding stray bullets,
and the United Nations Officials have stopped

discussions and are hopping about
among the bazookas and megaton bombs.

The chairmen of the international companies
are black with mourning for their money.

There are no smoking oilwells, inflating prices,
just a Fast Buck at half mast on the screens.

The cormorants feed in clear waters,
and squadrons of geese gasp and squawk

as they creak eagerly in V-formation
towards the far reaches of some fertile shore.

RONDO ON THE TURD

A turd
        is neither obscene nor absurd.
A turd
        is a divine invention,
        like a bird.
A turd
        is essential to life,
        scaly, feathered
        or furred.
A turd
        looks simple, yet
        is complex as
        a Mass by Byrd.
A turd
        unlike bad noises
        emerges secretly, silently,
        unheard.
A turd
        communicates discreetly:
        it reveals its presence
        without a word.
A turd
        emerges
        as a model of the obstinate,
        the undeterred.
A turd
        comes kindly to us,
        not like stone
        but like curd.
A turd
        is a mild pleasure:
        after a first and a second,
        one longs for a third.
A turd
        forces even
        the most prudish
        to ungird.
A turd
        won't allow you
        to consider yourself
        not one of the herd.

A turd
        is one thing all mankind
        has in common, Muslim,
        Christian or Kurd.
You're
        unenlightened
        till you can see
        the Buddha in a turd.

THE SKIN IS GREATER THAN THE BANANA

I saw that he is everything that is good and comforting to us: he is our clothing – wrapping and enfolding us.
        Julian of Norwich, chapter five

For just as the body is clad in clothes and the flesh in skin and the bones in flesh with the heart in the breast, so are we, soul and body, clothed and wrapped around in the goodness of God.
        Julian of Norwich, chapter six

    1.

Knowing humanity not only will
but ought to be extinct as the cohippus,

that, a few million years, and cockroaches
will be building computers, banking,

and making the same mistakes, I
sink on my sofa and stare through the window.

But soon the failing light becomes
darkness, there are only the stars.

I am the stars, witnessing my own
glittering body. I sleep a while,

and then the morning light returns
the golden pebbles to the grey shore,

and with my window lightly misted over
I see my room becoming a home.

2.

In my kitchen window the geraniums
are struggling to get through the glass,

not realising how cold it is out there.
The longer I look through the window

the eerier it is, as if something were
answering our questions by not answering them.

3.

Henry Miller came to me this evening, said,

Don't give a fuck for the critics,
you're understood and appreciated here.

I was drinking a pernod. The dead
always seem huge, bigger than the clouds,

beyond the clouds. Henry was shining
like a saint. He often thought he was a saint.

Perhaps he was. Perhaps you only have
to believe you're a saint to be one.

Being's more important than doing.
As I sip my pernod, I wonder,

Shall I some day feel confidence that
I AM is breathing and playing

through the nine holes of my body?

4.

I lean on my palms on the beach, well-muffled,
waiting for the world to enact itself.

The seagulls too sit and wait,
fronting the wind like weathervanes.

Further out, round a little boat,
a flotilla of wings is waiting for nets

to flush up, hoping for the sea
and sailors to empty their fullness.

It's as if nothing but a great pile of shored-up
gold were keeping the ocean at bay.

   5.

I drift among the clouds, and the clouds
burst open, and I sail straight through,

winging up high beyond the gulls,
above the clouds, where it's still blue.

But I tell all the dazzle and solidity
they're only blinkers, as I spiral round

and study my soul for a black hole
to gravitate through to where I AM

is sitting on his throne, looking down
through a sea of glass at all the little I's

as they hare about their small affairs.
And back home again, as the sun

crimsonly picks its way through
my stained window, I know I Am

therefore I think, letting the Unknown
go on doing what He always did:

beaming through His glasses and
keeping His cards close to His chest.

NOTES / 421

PUBLIC FOOTPATH
p. 79 'Razmak'
Razmak is a military station in tribal territory, 6,000 feet up in Waziristan, on the North West Frontier of India.
p. 88 'Services 1. At the Maltings, 19 December 1976'
This was the date of the first performance of Benjamin Britten's Quartet No. 3, op. 94 and the first concert of his music at the Maltings after his death.

TROUBLE
p. 190 'Two-Hundred-Mile-An-Hour Winds'
I read in *The National Geographic Magazine* about two people and a donkey who were lifted thousands of feet in the air by a tornado, stripped and dropped, shocked but alive, miles away. This seemed to me too typical a human experience – at least at the psychological level – to be overlooked.
p. 192 'Unaccompanied Voices'
I tried to keep as close as possible to Montale (1896-1981) in 'Unaccompanied Voices' (1939) but occasionally had to rearrange syntax and guess or choose about obscure or ambiguous passages; so I called the work an 'imitation'. Any version of Horace is necessarily an 'imitation', but there is, of course, a long and healthy tradition of using the word for 'translation'. Why imitate? As someone said, all art is a collaboration.
p. 200 'The Wild Swans at Aldeburgh' and p. 187 'Remembering Adlestrop'
It's obvious there are many direct allusions in both these poems, but I suppose the point had better be explicit. There are, of course, other minor allusions in the book.
p. 210 'Keith Vaughan's Last Journal'
In this poem I've kept as close as I could to Vaughan's own words and images. The selection and arrangement are of course mine, and therefore partly interpretative. Suffering Vaughan's scarifying last words, I was most moved by God's efforts to reach Vaughan through what he loved, cared for and understood.
p. 226 'Notes on Lao Tzu '
Some time after I'd written the second 'note' of this poem, I came across this in Alan Ross's review of Brian Adams's *Such is life: A Biography of Sidney Nolan*: 'Such is life' were, reputedly, the last words to be uttered by Ned Kelly, the Australian bushranger, before he was hanged. I find such synchronicities intriguing, though probably meaningless? The same week I came down in the middle of the night, unable to sleep, went straight to Robert Graves's *Collected Poems* and opened it at a poem I didn't remem-

ber having read before, beginning 'Not to sleep all the nightlong, for pure joy...' Also, a couple of the poems in this book were proleptic.

Unpublished Poems from Selected Poems
p. 242 'Faustus Speaks 7. Earthly Paradise'
This poem acknowledges an endebtedness to *Animals of the Imagination and the Bestiary, the Prince of Hesse and the Rhine Memorial Lecture,* 1994, by Thetis Blacker and Jane Geddis.

Nightlights
p. 403 'But the Jewel You lost was Blue'
The title of this poem is the last line of Hughes's *Birthday Letters,* and the epigraph is the last line of my sequence 'A Visit from the Hill' in *A Useless Passion,* which Ted had seen and admired before he published *Birthday Letters.* The last sentence is from a letter he wrote me. In a book he sent me Ted wrote 'We got out of the valley, but it didn't get out of us'. The name Calder means 'rapid stream', and the 'black' Rochdale Canal runs along the Calder Valley. The name Mytholmroyd, Ted's birthplace, means 'confluence of river mouths'. Stoodley Pike and Whirlaugh are Pennine mountains.
p. 404 'A Casual Knack of Living'
The title refers to Alan's Ross's poem about shipwrecked sailors, 'Survivors': '... they won't forge / The confusion and the oily dead, / Nor yet the casual knack of living.'
p. 405 'Hawthornden Castle'
Hawthornden Castle is the home of William Drummond of Hawthornden (1585-1649), who was visited by Ben Jonson there. It is a writers' retreat near Edinburgh, where I was a guest. There are a couple of allusions to Schopenhauer in Part 3.
p. 426 'The Skin is Greater than the Bannana'
A clergyman dreamed he's been given the secret of life. Awake, he wrote it down: 'The skin is greater than the bannana!' To me this didn't seem meaningless.

BIOGRAPHICAL NOTE

HERBERT LOMAS was born in Todmorden in the Pennines, and *The Vale of Todmorden* is his poetic record of the town and his family in the twenties and thirties. He served with the infantry 1943-46, including two years with the Royal Garhwal Rifles on the North West Frontier of India, and his 'Called to the Colours' in *A Useless Passion* is a record of that. He graduated with first-class honours and an MA from Liverpool University and is a former Senior Lecturer at the University of Helsinki and Principal Lecturer at the University of London.

He was a regular critic for Alan Ross's *The London Magazine* and *Ambit* for thirty years, has contributed to *The Hudson Review*, *The Spectator* and other journals and is a regular translator for the quarterly *Books from Finland*. His *Letters in the Dark* was an *Observer* book of the year, and he has received Guinness, Arvon and Cholmondely awards. His *Contemporary Finnish Poetry* won the Poetry Society's 1991 biennial translation award.

He is a member of the Finnish Academy, and was made Knight First Class, Order of the White Rose of Finland, 'for his services to Finnish Literature'.

He lives in Aldeburgh, Suffolk, and has two children by his late wife Mary.

SUBSCRIBERS /425

The following people have subscribed to this volume which is published to celebrate Herbert Lomas's lifetime of writing poetry:

Fergus & Joan Allen
Mary Allen
Ann & Mike Bannister
Frank Barrie
Mary Barrie
Judith Bax
Martin Bax
Fiona Bell-Currie
Anne Beresford
Carol Bleiker
Colin Boswell
Sue Boswell
Penelope Bray
Rachel Hemming Bray
Lucy Bright
Mary Bright
Jim Burns
Katy Campbell
John Canter & Helen Napper
Fergus Capie
Lady Cave
Paul Cooke
Adam Crick
Kevin & Linda Crossley-Holland
Lord & Lady Cuncliffe
Geoffrey Darke
Jean Darke
Peter Davey
John F. Deane
Bridget Dickinson
Peter Dickinson
Anne Dobson
Dorothy Duncan
Janine Edge
Martin Elliott
Olga Rey Elliott
Barbara Erskine
John Forth
Annabel Franklin

Harriet Frazer
Simon Frazer
Joanathan Gathorne-Hardy
John & Jill Giles
Lamorna Good
Hilary & Pauline Graham
Sarah Greenwell
Jeremy Greenwood
Joyce & Robert Gregson
Ione Hammond
Penny Hemans
Joyce Hidden
Nicolas Hill
Daniel Hoffman
Simon Hoggart
Ursula Holden
David & Linda Holmes
Joan L. Hutchison
Canon Michael Jarratt
Frederick Lees
Soila Lehtonen, 'Books from Finland'
John Lucas
Tina & Christopher Lucas
Caroline Mackenzie
Michael Mackmin
Paul McLoughlin
Lady Marlesford
John Mason
Reggie & Jamila Massey
Wendy & Christopher Matthew
Madeleine Melling
Dolf Mootham
Wendy Mulford
Helena Nelson
Ruth O'Callaghan
Brian Ó Daimhín
Stephen Oliver
John & Finula Pepper
Edward Perks
Eleanor Perks
Neil Powell
Shena Power

Alexandra Quantrill
Malcolm & Esther Quantrill
Francesca Quantrill & Jason Siegel
Trevor Ray
Jill Richardson
Russell A. Robertson
Jane Ross
Mrs. Judy Ryland
Lawrence Sail
Ann & Bernard Saint
Fiona Sampson
Bruno Schrecker
Iris Schwanck, FILI
Denys & Monica Sharrocks
Michael & Marianne Shorrock
Ann-Helen Siirala
Hattie Slim
Joan Sheridan Smith
Tom Southern
Michael Stagg
Eira Stenberg
Sr Bernice Stenger, OSF
Dom Antony Sutch
Angela & Colin Sydenham
Ian & Janet Tate
Paul Templeton
W. J. & I. Thraveson-Lambert
Ann & Anthony Thwaite
Michael & Rosemary Tolkien
Lotte & Henry Troupp
Christian Tyler
Ciaran Tyler
Diana Webster
Mrs. R. Weekley
John Welch
Alan T. Wells
Susan Wells
Glenn Willson
Jean Willson
Marguerite Wood
Madeleine Wynn-Higgins